I0045567

Business Integrity
in Practice

Business Integrity in Practice

Insights from International Case Studies

Agata Stachowicz-Stanusch

Wolfgang Amann

business**expert**
Press

Business Integrity in Practice: Insights from International Case Studies
Copyright © Business Expert Press, 2012.

All rights reserved. No part of this publication may be reproduced, stored in a retrieval system, or transmitted in any form or by any means—electronic, mechanical, photocopy, recording, or any other except for brief quotations, not to exceed 400 words, without the prior permission of the publisher.

First published in 2012 by
Business Expert Press, LLC
222 East 46th Street, New York, NY 10017
www.businessexpertpress.com

ISBN-13: 978-1-60649-494-3 (paperback)

ISBN-13: 978-1-60649-495-0 (e-book)

DOI 10.4128/9781606494950

Business Expert Press Principles of Responsible
Management Education collection

Collection ISSN: Forthcoming (print)
Collection ISSN: Forthcoming (electronic)

Cover design by Jonathan Pennell
Interior design by Exeter Premedia Services Private Ltd.,
Chennai, India

First edition: 2012

10 9 8 7 6 5 4 3 2 1

Printed in the United States of America.

Abstract

The quest for integrity in business is not only a reaction against malfeasance in business and associated calls for reform, but also a result of changes and new demands in the global business environment as well as the latest economic crisis. Among the sources of these new demands are the expectations of stakeholders that corporations and their leaders will take more active roles as citizens within society and in the fight against some of the most pressing problems in the world, such as poverty, environmental degradation, defending human rights, corruption, and pandemic diseases.

This topical and much needed book constitutes an important part of the debate on the best practices for ensuring integrity in an organizational context.

This book offers essential insights not only to business leaders but also to management educators and administrators who understand the urgency and importance of developing further responsible global leaders. This volume offers and discusses case studies and examples from organizations from all over the world. The book distils practical advice and guidance, explaining in detail how leaders may build organizations with strong integrity foundations. It provides valuable research results as well as teaching tools, enabling course leaders at undergraduate, master's and MBA level in all business schools around the world.

Keywords

organizational integrity, crisis prevention, humanistic management, poverty alleviation, sustainability management, organizational values, culture of integrity, anticorruption actions, corporate social irresponsibility

Contents

Business Integrity in Practice

Insights from International Case Studies

List of Reviewers

Ainamo Antti, Aalto University

Wolfgang Bielefeld, Indiana University, Indianapolis

Manuel Emílio Mota Almeida Castelo Branco, Universidade do Porto

Federica Caboni, University of Cagliari

Andrew Chan, University of Nottingham

Maria José Charlo, University of Seville

Tom Cockburn, Henley Business School, Reading University,
    and Ulster University Business School, UK

Giovanni Battista Dagnino, University of Catania

Edoardo Della Torre, University of Bergamo

Dominic DePersis, SUNY-Broome

Cinzia Dessi, University of Cagliari

Michela Floris, University of Cagliari

Ernestina Giudici, University of Cagliari

Frederick D. Greene, Manhattan College, Riverdale, USA

Louise Kelly, Alliant International University, San Diego

Alfred Lewis, Hamline University

Francisco J. Lara, Universidad Católica de Valencia

Andrew Michael, Intercollege Larnaca

Anna Mina, University of Catania

Gavin Nicholson, Queensland University of Technology

Kohei Nishikawa, Konan University

Peter Odrakiewicz, Poznan University College of Business

Kemi Ogunyemi, Pan-African University

Joseph A. Petrick, Wright State University

Janet L. Rovenpor, Manhattan College, Riverdale, USA

Mercedes Sánchez-Apellániz, University of Seville

Helena Desivilya Syna, Max Stern Academic College of Emek Yezreel

Edgar Gray Wilson, Waikato Institute of Technology, New Zealand

About the Editors
and Authors

About the Editors

Agata Stachowicz-Stanusch, PhD, DSc, is an associate professor of management at the Silesian University of Technology in Poland. She is the head of the Management and Marketing Department. Professor Stachowicz-Stanusch has authored and edited 14 books, including co-authoring *Contemporary Management: Collaborating in a Networked World*, which will be published in 2012 by Palgrave Macmillan; *Organizational Immunity to Corruption: Building Theoretical and Research Foundations* (IAP 2010); and was co-author and co-editor, with Charles Wankel, of three books entitled *Education for Integrity: Ethically Educating Tomorrow's Business Leaders* (Emerald, 2011), *Effectively Integrating Ethical Dimensions into Business Education* (IAP, 2011), and *Handbook of Research on Teaching Ethics in Business and Management Education* (IGI Global, 2011). She is also the author of over 70 research papers in domestic and international journals and conference proceedings. She manages an international research team as part of the project "Sensitizing Future Business Leaders: Developing Anticorruption Guidelines for Curriculum Change" of the UN Global Compact and the Principles for Responsible Management Education (PRME) initiative, which is one of the projects of the Siemens Integrity Initiative. Pro bono she is a World Engagement Institute and International Fellow, Chief-of-Research of the International Higher Education Teaching and Learning Association, member of the Anti-Corruption Academic Initiative (ACAD), an academic project coordinated by Northeastern University and the United Nations Office on Drugs and Crime and member of Polish Academy of Sciences, the Committee on Organizational and Management Sciences, Katowice

Department. Other recent service includes Track Chair for Rome (2010) and Rotterdam (2012) EURAM conferences, PDW co-organizer and presenter for AOM Annual Meeting in San Antonio (2011). She is regularly reviewer of *AOM, EURAM*, the *Journal of Brand Management* (Palgrave MacMillan), *Journal of Organizational Change Management* (Emerald). She is also a cofounder and vice editor-in-chief of the *Organizational and Management Journal* edited by the Silesian University of Technology as well as a member of many journal Editorial Boards.

Wolfgang Amann graduated from the Harvard Institute for Management and Leadership in Education and from the University of St. Gallen's doctorate program in international management. After years in top management consulting, Wolfgang Amann has been marketing, designing, directing, and delivering executive education seminars for more than a decade. He previously directed, as strategy professor, the Henley Centre for Creative Destruction and was vice-director of the Executive School at the University of St. Gallen. He has also been a visiting professor in the field of international strategy and sustainability at Hosei University in Tokyo, Tsinghua in Beijing, the Indian Institute of Management in Bangalore, ISP St. Petersburg, Warwick Business School, Henley Business School in the United Kingdom, as well as Mzumbe University in Tanzania. He now serves as the executive academic director of executive education and faculty at the Goethe Business School of the University of Frankfurt. He has written more than a 100 case studies for his programs, along with a variety of books, such as *The Impact of Internationalization on Organizational Cultures* (2003); *Building Strategic Success Positions* (2005); *The Private Equity Investor as a Strategy Coach* (2005); *Humanism in Business* (2007); *Managing Complexity in Global Organizations* (2007); *Work-Life Balance* (2008); *Corporate Governance—How to Add Value* (2008); *Humanism in Business: Perspectives on the Development of a Responsible Business Society* (2009); *Complexity in Organization—Text and Cases* (2011); *Business Schools Under Fire—Humanistic Management Education as the Way Forward* (2011); and *Humanistic Management in Practice* (2011).

About the Authors

Helena Desivilya Syna, associate professor, PhD in Psychology, State University of New York at Buffalo, USA. She was a former chair of the Department of Sociology and Anthropology, currently is the chair of MA program in Organizational Development and Consulting at the Max Stern Academic College of Emek Yezreel. She conducts research on interpersonal and intergroup relations in organizations focusing on the role of gender and other parameters of diversity in intragroup dynamics, processes of cooperation vs. competition, team building, and development of partnerships. She is a member of the editorial board of *Conflict Resolution Quarterly*, *Negotiation and Conflict Management Research*, *International Journal of Conflict Management*, and *Global Management Journal*. She publishes her work in these as well as other organization-related journals, and recently published a co-authored e-book on the Paradox in Partnerships.

Michal Raz, MA in sociology and anthropology, University of Haifa, Israel. Areas of interest and specialization: organizational sociology, organizational behavior, diversity management in organizations, research methods and statistics for social sciences.

Amit Rottman, MA in anthropology, University of Haifa, Israel. Areas of interest and specialization: Educational Anthropology—Social Class and Schooling; Intergroup relations in the shadow of protracted national conflicts; qualitative research.

Kathryn Pavlovich is associate professor at the University of Waikato Management School in Hamilton, New Zealand. Her two research and teaching areas include "relational competencies" in strategic alliances, tourism destinations, networks, clusters, and partnerships from a collaborative perspective; and "inner technologies" that involve the development of spiritual consciousness for organizational flourishing.

William B. Mesa is associate professor of management and accounting, Colorado Christian University, Lakewood, Colorado. He holds a doctorate in management, from Colorado Technical University, Colorado Springs, Colorado. He is on the editorial board of *Journal of Applied Business Research* since 2010.

Yi-Hui Ho earned her PhD from the University of Minnesota, Twin Cities. She is now assistant professor at the Department of International Business in Chang Jung Christian University. Her research interests include cross-cultural management, issues in business ethics, and issues in accounting education. She has published articles in *Journal of Business Ethics, Journal of Human Resource and Adult Learning, Social Behavior and Personality: An International Journal, Annual Meeting of Academy of Management*, and others.

Chieh-Yu Lin earned his PhD from National Cheng Kung University in Taiwan. He is now professor at the Department of International Business in Chang Jung Christian University. His research interests include business ethics, environmental management, and supply chain management. He has published articles in *Journal of Business Ethics, Supply Chain Management: An International Journal, Social Behavior and Personality: An International Journal, Annual Meeting of Academy of Management*, and others.

Roberto Martin N. Galang teaches strategy at the John Gokongwei School of Management at Ateneo de Manila University. He recently completed his PhD in management from the IESE Business School in Barcelona, where he conducted his dissertation research on the impact of government regulation on organizational performance. He obtained his master's degree in development economics from Oxford University. Prior to becoming an academic, he has had close to 10 years of professional experience as an economic consultant in the United States and the Philippines, analyzing public policy issues for private corporations.

Manuel J. De Vera teaches negotiations and leadership at the Asian Institute of Management (AIM) across its degree and nondegree programs and is currently the director of the institute's masters in development management (MDM) degree program. He graduated from Harvard

University's Kennedy School of Government with a master's in public administration. He has also received training on the evaluation of social programs from the Abdul Latif Jameel Poverty Action Lab (J-PAL) of the Department of Economics of the Massachusetts Institute of Technology (MIT). He has extensive public service experience, having worked for the Philippine government in its executive and legislative branches.

Gustavo González Couture, Full Professor School of Management Universidad de los Andes (Bogotá, Colombia). Civil Engineer from that same University. Certificate in Mathematics (University of Maryland). MA Sociology (UC Berkely). PhD in Practical Philosophy (Universidad de Navarra—Pamplona, Spain). Actual areas of research and teaching: Business Ethics, Public Management, Public Policy, Management Foundations and Learning Communities.

Management Experience: Analyst National Planning Department, Assistant Manager National Institute for the Family, Director of the Engineering School Research Center, Provost of Universidad de los Andes.

Business and Consultancy: Representative for Colombia of the INVERESK GROUP LIMITED (St Cuthberts Mill security paper); MacFadden Cotton Merchants. Systems Approach applied to the Decentralization of the National Television Institute, and to the restructuring of a Credit Card Division of Banco de Occidente. Supplier and Employee's Ethical Perception Survey applied for SABMiller's six Latin American Subsidiaries (years 2008 and 2010). Transgenerational Potential for six Colombian entrepreneurial families within the STEP program of Babson.

Books: Asesores en Sistemas y Desarrollo: ¿los nuevos humanistas? (Systems and Development Consultants: the new humanists?). Gestión Pública: ¿asunto privado? Gestión Privada: ¿asunto público? (Public Management: a private issue? Private Management: a public issue?)

Verónica Durana Angel, psychologist (with a minor in philosophy) and MBA from the Universidad de los Andes. She is currently research and teaching assistant form the School of Management at Universidad de los Andes. Her research and teaching activities focus on business ethics, organizational behavior, and management competencies. She is coauthored of Organizaciones virtuosas y enseñanza de la ética *(Virtuous organizations and the teaching of ethics)*.

David Schnarch, bachelor in management from the Universidad de los Andes. He is currently research and teaching assistant form the School of Management at Universidad de los Andes. His research and teaching activities focus on organizational perdurability and management consulting. He is coauthored of "¿Lo social y lo económico: Dos caras de la misma moneda? La Fundación Social y sus empresas: 1984–2010" (The social and economic: Two sides of the same coin? The Fundación Social and its companies: 1984–2010).

Abiola Olukemi Ogunyemi holds a degree in law from the University of Ibadan, Nigeria, an LLM from the University of Strathclyde, United Kingdom, and an MBA from the Lagos Business School, Nigeria. She teaches business ethics and anthropology at the Lagos Business School, while doing her PhD in management at the school. Her consulting and research interests include personal ethos, work-life ethic, social responsibility, sustainability, and governance.

Tom Cockburn obtained his first degree with honors from Leicester University, England, both his MBA and doctorate (in management education) were gained at Cardiff University in Wales. Tom also has several professional teaching qualifications, including e-moderator certification and executive coaching qualifications from the UK Universities of Wolverhampton, Liverpool, and University of Ulster, the Waikato Institute of Technology, New Zealand, Hay Consulting (Australia), and the Edexcel Foundation in London. He is an associate fellow of the New Zealand Institute of Management and a member of the Cutting Edge Awards Committee of the US Academy of HRD. His leadership background includes 5 years' board experience on the executive of the Standing Conference of Welsh Management Education Centres and 8 years as head of a business school in the United Kingdom before a deputy head of school role in New Zealand. He has adjunct and visiting E-faculty member roles on Henley Business School (United Kingdom) and Ulster University Business Schools' MBA and MSc programs. Tom has been a member of a number of editorial boards of international academic journals including the editorial board for the *UK Journal of Further & Higher Education*, *Interface online journal* (United States) and of the editorial advisory board for the Emerald online Emerging Markets Case Studies repository.

Khosro S. Jahdi, MBA, MPhil, PhD is senior lecturer in marketing at Bradford College, Bradford, UK, has been teaching for over 25 years. He has published in the *Journal of Marketing Management*, *Social Responsibility Journal*, and the *Journal of Business Ethics* as well as some other academic journals. He submits papers to international conferences on CSR, ethical marketing, and corporate governance on a regular basis and is a member of the Social Responsibility Research Network as well as the editorial board of the *International Green Economics Journal*. He is a chartered marketer, a corporate member of the Chartered Institute of Marketing, and a fellow of the Academy of Marketing Science.

Edgar Gray Wilson has diplomas in both management studies and in teaching as well as an MA (Geography). He gained 28 years teaching experience in a range of secondary schools in New Zealand and the United Kingdom before subsequently being appointed regional manager (Waikato) for the Tertiary Education Commission for 6 years. He was then appointed head of the School of Education and Social Development at Waikato Institute of Technology, (Wintec) Hamilton, New Zealand. Currently, he is regional engagement manager—office of the chief executive at Wintec. His other roles include director and trustee of First Credit Union—one of the largest Credit Unions in New Zealand, elected member of the board of trustees representative of Waikato Diocesan School for Girls—an Anglican School of 670 students, a Government appointee as Trustee to Trust Waikato—a philanthropic Trust and Justice of the Peace for New Zealand

Peter Odrakiewicz, internationally renowned scholar, dean of managerial linguistics, Poznan PWSB/Poznan University College of Business, vice-rector (2007–2011), presently honorary vice-rector, visiting professor multiplex, HR Academy of Management Ambassador for Poland (2008–present), director of International Management Program at the Department of Economics and Management, in addition to his academic duties. He was appointed to the board of AMEX PPHU. He was previously with Daimler Chrysler Canada Inc. headquarters as representative, innovator, and leading teacher. He is author, co-author, and editor of more than eight scientific books, numerous academic research papers presented in Rotterdam School of Management, Erasmus University, EDINEB Vienna, Chicago and Montreal AOM conferences, and reviewer at the Academy of Management, USA.

Burcu Guneri Cangarli is assistant professor of organizational behavior. She received her PhD in 2009 in the field of business administration with management major from Izmir University of Economics. For her PhD thesis, "Bullying Behaviors as Organizational Politics," she worked at Hanken University for three months as a TUBITAK scholar. Her research area of interest includes healthcare management, innovation and entrepreneurship, and bullying and unethical events. On these issues, she published many book chapters and articles in reputable national and international journals. She has been teaching management, leadership, organizational behavior, human resources management, and organization theory courses at Izmir University of Economics since 2007.

R. Gulem Atabay is associate professor of organizational behavior. She received her PhD in the field of business administration with management major in 1998. She focuses on employee attitudes and emotions, and their effects on employee behaviors and performance. She conducts her research mainly in health care settings, especially with nurses. She published many book chapters and articles in reputable national and international journals. Since 2004, she has been teaching introduction to business, management, organizational behavior, organizational development, and current issues in management at Izmir University of Economics.

Adviye Ahenk Aktan is a PhD student in the management and organization area at Izmir University of Economics. She also worked as a research assistant at the same university between 2006 and 2008. Then, she worked in a government agency at the strategy development depart-ment, following which she worked as a recruitment specialist in an international recruitment firm. She has some published works in the field of organizational behavior. Her areas of interest include organiza-tional justice, ethical behaviors, strategic decision making, and entre-preneurship.

Throstur Olaf Sigurjonsson is assistant professor of strategic manage-ment at the School of Business of Reykjavik University in Iceland. He holds a PhD from Copenhagen Business School and his research interests include issues of corporate governance, strategic management, corpo-rate restructuring, and corporate social responsibility. Dr. Sigurjonsson is the director of the Research Institute of Public Private Partnership at Reykjavik University.

Auður Arna Arnardóttir is assistant professor of Organizational Behavior at the School of Business of Reykjavik University in Iceland. She holds a PhD from Virginia Commonwealth University in counseling psychology. Her research interests include issues of organizational behavior, HRM, and personal development, more specifically in matters of work–family balance, stress, job satisfaction, downsizing, motivation, and personal growth. Dr. Arnardóttir is also a licensed psychologist and conducts some work in a private practice.

Vlad Vaiman is professor of international management at the School of Business of Reykjavik University in Iceland and is a visiting professor in several top universities around the world. He holds a PhD from the University of St. Gallen in Switzerland, and his research interests include issues of both organizational behavior and international management, and more specifically, matters of cultural differences and their influences on leadership, motivation, and talent management in multinational com-panies. He is also a cofounder and an executive editor of the critically acclaimed ISI-indexed publication, *European Journal of International Management* (EJIM).

Business Integrity in Practice

Why the Journey Just Began

Agata Stachowicz-Stanusch
and Wolfgang Amann

A Reality Check

Economies around the globe continue to integrate at an amazing speed. Before the core European countries could perfect their own integration, negotiations on further expansion and even a cross-region free trade agreement continued and marched ahead, to name but just one example. The co-emerging problem lies in the fact that all coping mechanisms to ensure sound business conduct did not necessarily follow suit at the same pace. International regulation also lagged behind, let alone the establishment of effective international governance bodies. To top it all, there are not any normative frameworks for businesses around the world. The diversity of opinions and concepts on acceptable behavioral standards across cultures continues to thrive, as is expected. However, our societies as well as companies do need a discourse on the possibility of such a normative framework. Further discussions on business integrity can help create more value for society as well as minimize system shocks.

Granted, integrity inarguably represents a multifaceted construct. We identify at least the following three connotations. One focuses on overcoming inconsistencies—as integrity deals with consistency of actions, values, methods, measures, principles, expectations, and outcomes—integrity partially emphasizes more consistency and less contradiction whilst building more humanistic organizations. Mission statements and codes of conduct should be congruent with portrayed behaviors. In other words, companies ought to walk the talk. The second sheds light on over-coming insufficiencies—integrity emphasizes furthermore the obligation to close gaps between established societal norms and portrayed behavior. Companies and their constituents need to step up, create transparency about their moral compass, and follow set directions. A third connota-tion approaches the phenomenon with less emphasis on predefined value standards, but with the drive to overcoming incompatibilities. It is less focused on moral gaps but shows an interest in contradiction-free, "whole" organizations with aligned system elements. Thus, integrity shows a facet striving to address and overcome more or less open conflicts of interests and values in different organizational hierarchies, functions and mana-gerial roles, and proposing concrete solutions. These three different, yet complementary approaches need to be detailed and revisited in the light of building businesses with more integrity. Therefore, we compiled this book as a key resource to enhance our understanding of how to build better organizations from this normative standpoint. We faced two fun-damental options. We either argue our case based on theory and concepts, or alternatively illustrate with the help of critically discussed case studies on how to make progress. We have chosen the latter approach. To ensure a more realistic view, we selected case settings which vary as outlined in the following.

Structure of This Book and Our "Buffet of Ideas"

We have compiled our buffet of ideas in four main sections. Part I "Toward the bright side of organization" revisits the concept of ethical capital as well as integrity cultures. The chosen real world setting takes the reader to the United Kingdom and New Zealand. Tom Cockburn, Khosro S. Jahdi, and Edgar Gray Wilson jointly review three organizational case studies in how integrity and ethical capital is not only defined but enacted and accrued over time through the strategic and operational alignment of the core principles, policies, and practices of these organizations. The authors outline what the strategic values trajectory of each organization can and ought to be. As a point of orientation, they structure their thoughts with the help of 12 thematic areas. They add a thorough comparison as well as a critical evaluation in terms of three key dimensions of integrity vectors.

To reflect the strategic values trajectory of the organizations evaluating mission, operations and implementation, the authors adapted a three-dimensional framework derived from a strategic HRM model, enabling analysis and evaluation of the explicit alignment of organizations' integrity with their corporate philosophy, strategy, and operational practices.

Abiola Olukemi Ogunyemi continues our joint learning journey in Chapter 2 by deepening our analysis of individual ethical behavior and its key influences from organizational culture. While Nigeria serves as the learning ground for this link, there is room for generalization. Nigeria portrays a particularly difficult and under-regulated external environment. Nonenabling internal environments could entail a fatal blow to the good desires of employees who wish to do what is right. Besides, numerous problems arising from negative behavior can cost organizations heavily. A perception that management is self-interested could lead others to react by taking care of their own interests; policies and value statements that embody altruism but are not applied, or a reward system, may contradict the organization's intentions to promote other-regarding behavior. Ogunyemi warns that companies inadvertently allow elements of culture or climate that inhibit integrity, because they inhibit other-regarding behavior. Self-interest is outlined as one of the factors that affects the ethical climate of the organization and it is determined by testing how concerned the people in the company are about themselves or their own interests *vis-à-vis* their concern for others. By and large, this chapter illustrates these ideas with three caselets, emphasizing that workplace integrity requires fostering other-regarding behavior. It also offers insight into cultural traits that enable or inhibit such deeds.

Chapter 3 deals with the prominent topic of whistleblowing, with the author Agata Stachowicz-Stanusch choosing Poland as the location for empirical insights; "to blow or not to blow the whistle—that is the question" in her contribution. Detailing her thoughts and analysis, she addresses the significance of whistleblowing in the context of current conditions in Poland. The author presents definitions and classifications of whistleblowing as well as the recognized barriers for its implementation, including legal ramifications. These considerations are supplemented with cases of whistleblowers who have taken such actions in Poland. The chapter thereby includes references to the current state of research in this area.

Chapter 4 contributed by Peter Odrakiewicz provides an overview of anticorruption actions taken in an organizational context in order to enhance integrity. The chapter shows innovative methods of dealing with new challenges and by suggesting the most effective approaches in an organizational context. Integrity and anticorruption actions in management are core needs for success in a globalized, competitive, innovative enterprise. Integrity management in organization challenges us, as the author outlines, to face new experiences and enables us to develop a pro-integrity and anticorruption organizational philosophy. A pro-integrity, corruption prevention, and eradication managerial organizational position allows entire organizations to transcend the constraints of our past and present experiences and belief systems and to see the world in its organizational complexities, with the goal of building integrity-proof, corruption-resistant and rejecting corruption, while maintaining free organization, in the future. The process of discussing these emerging global integrity and anticorruption challenges is accomplished through the use of analytical review and synthesis of existing literature and definitions, and by describing briefly the historical context and the present integrity and anticorruption situation in international organizations and in social media in management, keeping in mind the role and constraints of organizational environments. Additionally, recent results of the research using video-interviews on integrity and anticorruption situations in an organizational context conducted under the author's supervision will be presented, with suggestions for possible improvements. The key role of values and norms in organizational culture are closely related to integrity, moral and ethical and corruption prevention concerns, and should be given the highest priority in managerial actions in all areas of human resources, marketing, organizational behavior strategies, and strategic and corporate management, including transparency in all communication in organization challenges. Building an integrity-proof, corruption-free organization of the future should be an aim for all organizations, in order for them to succeed in a complex, intertwined, intercultural, globalized marketplace. The organizations that successfully implement pro-integrity and anticorruption management will gain competitive advantages benefiting their owners, shareholders, and all stakeholders including local communities where they operate and function.

Part II of our book continues by including elements of a more humanistic management system and thus strengthens the foundation for building organizational integrity. Kathryn Pavlovich links integrity and poverty alleviation through enterprise in Chapter 5 on "Faith, hope and care." Her thoughts inductively examine the role of integrity in enterprise development through focusing on three qualities of moral principles, consistency, and wholeness. It studied three entrepreneurs who have developed enterprises solely for alleviating poverty. This combination of commercial and social purpose provided a rich context to explore how their "calling" to such work involved an integrity of care for others to develop a more humane and just society. The research themes that emerged from the qualitative inquiry for discussion include the discovery of purpose, the creation of social wealth, and integrity for social justice. The theoretical contributions from this study demonstrate that the first quality, moral principles, is a central condition for integrity. The second quality, consistency, emerged as a practice for the development and refinement of integrity. The last quality, wholeness, is an outcome of ongoing consistency of action embedded in moral principles.

Chapter 6 contributed by William B. Mesa enhances our analysis of the role of integrity in building better and more humanistic organizations. The author presents and discusses a consulting model clarifying core values and promoting greater organizational integrity. The kinds of meaning that are most important to an entity are ultimately acted upon by the entity—whether the actions are beyond goals of profit or focused on profitability shaped by values. This chapter explores how three organizations (a business, a performance arts organization, and a winery) act beyond a goal of profitability and have a vision that generates clarity during times of turbulence or flourishing. Core values acted out by the entity represent expressions of integrity which in turn make up the kinds of meaning that are most significant to the entity. In summary, humanistic organizations are concerned with the kinds of meaning that will sustain it for the long term, as outlined by the author.

In Part III of our book on "Values and virtues as milestones for integrity in organization" two more chapters add substance to our analysis and learning journey toward more integrity in business. Yi-Hui Ho and Chieh-Yu Lin share how integrity can be managed in Chinese organizations. This chapter analyzes the dimensions and meanings of Confucian integrity, the importance of interpersonal relationships, and integrity leaderships in Chinese culture, and provides the perspectives of how integrity is managed in Chinese organizations. Moreover, the chapter attempts to provide some clues to the answer by analyzing the integrity value of TSMC, a Taiwanese semiconductor company with excellent corporate social performance and integrity culture. In addition, the chapter critically discusses possible challenges in developing integrity, and addresses issues of managing integrity that are rather unique in the Chinese context—such as saving face. This chapter emphasizes the international flavors that integrity can adopt. Insights on the western Judeo-Christian outlook show not only the natural geographic boundaries, but also that they are just one piece of a much larger patchwork of cognitive patterns. The book thus offers the reader a pathway for understanding the dimensions of integrity in Chinese cultures and the integrity managing in Chinese organizations.

Roberto Martin N. Galang and Manuel J. De Vera continue this train of thought in Chapter 8 by shedding light on how to build integrity amongst organizations in Southeast Asia. More specifically, the authors raise the question, "how do you build organizational integrity in societies where corruption is rife?" This chapter looks specifically at two programs designed to change social norms that could potentially lead to an improvement of integrity across firms, despite limited improvements in the quality of the national legal systems. The first case study revolves around improving integrity in the Filipino private sector. The Integrity Initiative is a private sector-led campaign that aims to promote higher ethical standards among companies through the creation of integrity validation systems, and recognize companies for exemplary performance in a set of awards. The second case study is based on the Integrity Education Network and the development of integrity-based university courses in Indonesia. The aim of the Indonesian program is to generate and teach courses to university freshmen that explain the differences between corrupt versus ethical behavior, in hopes of battling the cultural embeddedness of corruption. Through this comparative case study, the chapter seeks to document the factors that lead to the successful achievement of improved integrity and accountability among Filipino and Indonesian organizations.

Chapter 9 compiled by Gustavo González-Couture, Verónica Durana-Angel and David Schnarch-Gonz Couture focuses on how an Executive MBA ethics course can contribute to humanistic management. We thus progress in our storyline beyond just issuing a normative call for more integrity, and move on toward clarifying how to make progress. We increase our geographic scope as well—to Latin America. As the authors argue, Latin American organizations share some universal management principles of efficiency and efficacy in order to endure. However, its complex context challenges managers in unusual ways. With the analysis of these challenges in mind, this chapter describes the experience of an ethics Executive MBA course developed in the Universidad de los Andes (Bogotá, Colombia) that contributes to the moral awareness of its participants. The course shows that neither the rules (e.g., corporate ethics codes) nor the goods (e.g., favorable organizational goals) are sufficient to ensure an ethical behavior. It takes a joint effort by three ethical dimensions: goods, rules, and virtues. The experience clarifies how, through constant self-observation and self-reflection framed within the mentioned ethical dimensions, students at the end of the course register a change in their perceptions about their ideal behavior and their commitment; they became less naïve and more critical.

Part IV on "Integrity priorities during and after the crisis" strengthens our point of view that integrity management may have a substantial situational nature. Burcu Guneri Cangarli, R. Gulem Atabay, and Adviye Ahenk Aktan take the reader to Turkey in Chapter 10, one of the fastest growing and most promising economies on the planet. Organizational integrity has gained a great deal of attention in recent years. Since 2003, Turkish healthcare industry has witnessed radical changes, and it's argued that these changes seriously damaged the trustworthiness of healthcare organizations and made their reputation questionable in the eyes of public. In that regard, the case explains the main dynamics of Turkish Healthcare System with the effects of recent changes based on the opinions of physicians. Hence, five physicians with different backgrounds explained the main dynamics of healthcare system and its effects on integrity. They also offer suggestions to create a healthcare system that stimulates behaving with integrity for physicians, healthcare clinics, and organizations.

Throstur Olaf Sigurjonsson, Auður Arna Arnardóttir, and Vlad Vaiman enrich our discussion on integrity in business in Chapter 11 by outlining what happens to business ethics and integrity after the financial crisis. Their emphasis is on Icelandic businesses, in light of the financial collapse of 2008. The authors argue that the Icelandic financial collapse was caused, to a large extent, by the lack of good ethical practices in the Icelandic business culture. Using new data as an empirical foundation of this paper, the authors draw conclusions on relevant measures for businesses everywhere. The authors argue that in order to learn from the devastating experience of the financial collapse in Iceland, the societal business culture needs to be changed. Recent research reveals that, unfortunately, little has changed in terms of the unethical behavior displayed by Icelandic business people since the financial crisis.

Finally, Helena Desivilya Syna, Michal Raz, and Amit Rottman outline their thoughts in Chapter 12 on how to improve organizational integrity through humanistic diversity management. The authors present the case of minority–majority relations in academic institutions and healthcare organizations. Humanistic diversity management is explored in divided societies, engulfed by protracted national conflict. The authors' conceptual framework integrates two bodies of knowledge: the characteristics of diversity and its management in organizations and the effects of protracted conflict on relations among adversarial and diverse groups in organizations. Two Israeli cases demonstrate the impact of mixed nurses' teams and the consequence of Jewish and Arab students in an academic college. The cases indicate that both medical staff as well as students in demographically diverse institutions face intergroup biases and tensions due to the salience of social categorization and the faultline phenomenon. They also experience difficulty in dealing with diversity issues related to the national conflict, which therefore remains hidden. The chapter presents an action model aimed at improving humanistic management practices, thereby potentially enhancing organizational integrity—organizational justice, sense of inclusion, and the capacity to express an authentic voice by individuals and diverse social groups. This action framework focuses on the relations between minority and majority, emphasizes the role of subjective perceptions, and the need to move them from the hidden sphere to the overt level. It assigns a central role to interpersonal and intergroup negotiation, places the intervention in the specific organizational context and emphasizes the need to interface and coordinate diversity management at the micro (group) level and the macro (national policy) level.

How to Best Enjoy This "Buffet of Ideas"

This book's editors encourage the reader to read selectively, contingent upon the individual interests when it comes to regions, industries, and topics presented in this book. Not all of the chapters are likely to be of equal priority. Reflection is furthermore dear to us editors. We therefore added suggestions for further reading as well as questions to review the content of each chapter.

We also invite you, as the reader, to critically reflect on the very complexity drivers characterizing the integrity field and its very debate. There are four main complexity drivers worth mentioning. First of all, there is diversity. Integrity portrays multiple connotations as such. For some, it first and foremost deals with the need to close unacceptable gaps with societal norms. Organizational leaders and managers must step up and eradicate whatever inefficiency persists when linked to the larger societal expectations and demands. For others, integrity represents an intracompany challenge. The board or top management issues codes of conducts, mission or value statements, and somewhere, someone in the organization defects. Others in turn see in integrity less a compass to follow, but a clear risk issue. The threat of fines and reputational damage even up to what has been labeled less elegantly in the new media world as "shitstorm" need to be avoided at all cost. For an additional group, integrity represents a core management tasks. Some parts of the organizations simply do not fit together, causing conflicts of interest and friction where it adds zero value to the customer as well as the company and its stakeholders. Diversity also materializes when we reflect on the industries we present in this book. Each one of them, at times even each player in them seems to have unique challenges, rendering general one-size-fits-all recipes misplaced.

Interdependency is the second complexity driver. It affects the integrity discussion, for example, when we add the international dimensions.

Politics, philosophical underpinnings, local business culture and economic development status can have severe impact. At times, a lack of integrity in the form of corruption emerges only when economies are underdeveloped Integrity competencies and respective training—as we outline in this book—can thus mediate the relationship between the actors in the system and their business challenges. Demanding more integrity without allocating the resources for training represents a recipe for disaster. Ignoring the interdependencies with local elements in one's business context merely equals an oversimplification of the analysis. This leads us to the next complexity driver—ambiguity. Which leaders and managers can actually know of all these local shades of integrity? When it comes to the value expectations of societies, there is ambiguity. Would society want jobs, innovations, environmental, and social safety? What are priorities? Same considerations hold true for top managers which set the tone in firms. They may not know what really happens in different parts of the organizations. They may also deem consequences uncertain. Any solution to integrity challenges therefore must reduce the harmful ambiguity in the system. Eventually flux emerges as the fourth driver of complexity. It alludes to the speed of change as well as the number of directions in which change can happen. After all, values and norms change. They may be temporarily suspended in times of crises. With further economic wealth, other dimensions of a high quality of life transpire. The same holds true when economic conditions change. Standards are lowered, although we remain purely descriptive, not evaluative. Our chapters on integrity in a crisis situation shed more light on this phenomenon.

Next to encouraging you to serve yourself selectively from our compiled buffet of ideas and to consider the inherent complexity, we want to stress the need to implement situational solutions based on individual cases as our third main message. As there are probably as many integrity challenges and preconditions as there are companies, so would the option space for solutions reflect this richness. Each leader and manager must therefore not only understand this contingent nature of integrity solutions, but also ensure the skills to build at times highly temporary solutions in their own, unique setting. They may, but at times may not find all the answers from elsewhere. They have to construct these answers which often cannot be merely found, but have to be developed, experimented with, rolled out, constantly improved, and in due time retired to make space for new solutions. Successfully doing so requires focus, heart, energy, and courage as the "new book" on integrity then has to written. If the book at hand at least partly serves as a source of activation, inspiration, encouragement, and learning, we have achieved our goal.

INTRODUCTION TO PART I

Toward the Bright Side of Organization

The first contribution in this section provides, on a strong empirical foundation, ample and critical reviews on how integrity is defined and enacted through principles, policies, and practices of three organizations. Interestingly enough, all organizations emphasize integrity and rely on it as an integral part of their strategic positioning. This interplay between conceptual clarity and empirical application covers three different local and legal contexts, clarifying the contingency view we apply on integrity. Practical steps taken rely on organizational culture through the establishment of a "giving voice to all" in the system, a proactive stakeholder engagement, a compelling vision, a reasonable resource allocation, the finalization of a realistic action plan with feasible milestones, openness to reality checks, accompanying staff development initiatives, technical support, gaining scale and ensuring consistency in the process, and revisiting the master plan on a continuing basis. This approach thus excels through its comprehensiveness and degree of professionalism.

This section continues by emphasizing the softer elements of integrity management, not primarily viewing it as a legal or compliance challenge only, a mistake frequently done. We explore the link between individual behavior and the influences of organizational culture. Empirically, we move from an Anglo-Saxon region to Africa, more precisely Nigeria in this inductive chapter. Building on three cases, the authors clarify how individual behavior is shaped and in turn determines elements of organizational culture when it comes to lowering or enhancing integrity standards and norms. The authors distil critical enablers and inhibitors when trying to generalize beyond the empirical setup. The good news for leaders emerges that through setting the right tone through caring, empathy, and assistance, they can increase their impact. Through biases, hostility, indifference, and disregard, they have an opposite effect. Leaders thus can and should no longer reject responsibilities and blame others when it comes to explaining defection of subordinates. They lead by example, which is critically discussed in the light of the case studies.

The next contribution dives deep into one of the key challenges when it comes to ensuring organizational integrity. It sheds light on what to do if there are problems. It explores what companies can proactively ensure for future eventualities. "Whistleblowing" represents such a crucial means to overcome issues. Poland is the chosen country set up to provide a strong empirical foundation. This chapter thus focuses on whistleblowing as a tool to fight with irregularities. The author discusses the value of courage as well as the cost of silence in this context. Based on the presented analysis, as well as empirical evidence, the implementation of whistleblowing mechanisms in organizations represents a small step, but one which ought to be taken when creating a formal ethical infrastructure. Organizations actually adopting such an infrastructure should also be open to recommendations on effective mechanisms for a more effective abuse detection mechanism. It becomes obvious though that formal guidelines and a corresponding infrastructure do not jumpstart integrity alone. Only holistic approaches will work, which in turn must be built on understood and optimized individual parts.

A fourth chapter rounds up this first section. It shows how integrity leading and anticorruption actions awareness in management in organizational contexts are core needs for success in a globalized, competitive, and innovative enterprise. Integrity management in organizations challenges us to face new experiences and enables us to develop a pro-integrity and anticorruption organizational philosophy. A pro-integrity, corruption prevention, and eradication managerial organizational position allows entire organizations to transcend the constraints of our past and present experiences and belief systems and to see the world in its organizational complexities, with the goal of building integrity-proof, corruption-resistant, and rejecting corruption, while maintaining free organization, in the future. The organizations that successfully implement pro-integrity and anticorruption management will gain competitive advantages benefiting their owners, shareholders, and all stakeholders including local communities where they operate and function. As such, all four chapters thus contribute essentials parts to our better understanding of what integrity is, how it works, how it can be enhanced as well as why.

CHAPTER 1

Ethical Capital and the Culture of Integrity

Three Cases in the United Kingdom and New Zealand

Tom Cockburn

Khosro S. Jahdi

Edgar Gray Wilson

Introduction

This chapter reviews three case studies on how integrity is defined and enacted through principles, policies, and practices of three organizations that regard integrity as a core value and Unique Selling Point (USP) in marketing their products and services. Integrity has been variously defined, and we will seek to address this central aspect of building sustainable ethical capital in organizations in our introduction and outline of this chapter in terms of paradigms, practices, and perspectives of the foundational ideals intended and applied.

In 2012, the International Year of Cooperatives, it is fitting that the three case organizations are based on the principles of cooperation. Each organization is, however, embedded in different local and national contexts, so legal constraints vary although they share some common philosophical foundations and historical bases. Two of the organizations are in the United Kingdom, arguably the birthplace of capitalism and the industrial revolution; in the United Kingdom, 2011 has been a year of resilience and growth of the cooperative sector. Currently "... the co-operative economy is driving a value of £33bn in the UK and engaging 800 million members and providing over 100 million jobs around the world."[1] The other case study organization is in New Zealand; a country known for its "clean, green" image and whose largest business is Fonterra, a farmers' cooperative.

These three case organizations are from different sectors in the economy and range in size from an established Small and Medium Enterprise (SME) to a major retail bank. The three organizations will be compared and contrasted in terms of how they have not only interpreted but also enacted their ethical missions. Have they operated with integrity? How is this demonstrated in their policies and practices? What are the elements they share and are there any areas in which they differ in absolute or relative terms? What can we learn? We will focus on the organizational level rather than individual level and will assess the responses using a three-dimensional model to visually illustrate the organizations' relative positions on each axis.

Defining Operational Integrity as Ethical Capital

The central problem with any social science research is that it deals with reflexive subjects (i.e., people). People think about what they do and how they present this to others in order to convey what they regard as an acceptable impression.[2] It is fundamental to a research activity that distinctions are made between concepts, theories, and issues, at the different levels of analysis relevant to the domains under consideration. We propose to provide the reader with a brief overview of how integrity has been conceived or defined within the wider research literature.

The original usage is drawn from old French and Latin and has a connotation referring to wholeness in the sense of the word, "integer," but we are less concerned with that meaning except insofar as it relates to the "wholeness" of organizational integrity as understood and routinely practiced in workplaces.[3] Collins Concise Dictionary and Thesaurus proposes three slightly more modern definitions (with examples in italics): "**integrity** n **1** honesty **2** the quality of being whole or united: *respect for* *a state's territorial integrity.* **3** the quality of being unharmed or sound: *the integrity of the cell membrane.*" On the same page, under the thesaurus section they elaborate as follows: "integrity **1** candour, goodness, honesty, honour, incorruptibility, principle, probity, rectitude, righteousness, uprightness, virtue, **2** coherence, cohesion, completeness, soundness, unity, wholeness."[4]

For everyday purposes in organizations there are simpler definitions, though these all inevitably involve a continuum representing varying degrees of "fudging" or compromises with practical reality of leaders' or others' agency, company cultures, and emotional and cognitive understanding of the collective implications in their implementation of their boundaries and benchmarks,[5] derived from the terms. In order to operationalize the concept we simply define organizational integrity as follows: The proactive structures, principles, and systems for accruing "ethical capital" by promoting, monitoring, and developing shared norms designed to identify and avoid potential conflicts of interest, abuse of office in any function, role, or location in the business. Issues such as the managers' personalities, skills in managing others, managing relationships with peers and bosses, managing self and coping with setbacks and disappointments are thus accounted for in the definition.

Ethical capital might be described as the accrued differences between the goodwill "assets" and perceived moral liabilities of an organization as expressed in the coevolving relationship of customer loyalty and manifest employee integrity. Thus, assuming that the competitiveness of the product or service is comparable to rivals, then *ceteris paribus*, as integrity rises customer loyalty is also likely to increase as a part of the differentiating "unique selling point." In line with that there is a need for an interactive and empowered set of relationships in the specific community using the cooperative services and products. However, as Kulik[6] suggests, irresponsibility or lack of integrity in dealings with others is just as likely where "empowered" and "innovative" cultures exist but where certain conditions such as individualist incentives are also in place, hence the concerns expressed by our respondents about checks and balances in various places so that, in a period of economic crisis, the corporate integrity has to be perceived as above reproach.

The Three Case Study Organizations

The first organization from the United Kingdom, Suma Wholefoods, is essentially a retail workers' cooperative specializing in health foods. Suma is also the youngest organization in the trio. Suma Wholefoods has an egalitarian culture and is a voluntary, open-membership, workers' cooperative owned by its members as well as an SME and was initiated in 1975 by a group of friends. Members may be employees but employees do not have to be members. Members have extra duties and responsibilities but in order to avoid discriminating against those lacking formal qualifications, the only "qualification" required is ability. Suma has created a member job description outlining the duties of members over and above those of employees. Members are rigorously selected and have to undergo a compulsory 3–6 month probationary work trial period before they become eligible to apply for a "trial membership" in the first instance. Suma hires nonmembers as contract staff and as casual workers for peak business periods though many such workers then go on to become permanent members. As membership is voluntary, staff may opt to remain as nonmembers without any adverse impact on their employment although recurrent regeneration of member numbers is a requirement to keep the cooperative alive and some cooperatives have ceased due to declining membership or unevenly distributed workloads.[7]

It is also credited with being the very first organization to introduce fair trade products in the 1980s long before all the major UK supermarkets "jumped on the bandwagon" some decades later. Suma has an annual turnover in the excess of £25 million and supplies approximately 6,000 product lines to over 2,500 UK and overseas customers and employs 150 people. Their customers range from small independent wholefood retail stores to restaurants, hotels, bakeries, and food manufacturers. They also have grown their frozen food and export trade with countries such as Norway, South Africa, Lithuania, and countries further afield such as the Middle East. "Suma is the UK's largest independent wholefood wholesaler/distributor, specializing in vegetarian, fairly traded, organic, ethical and natural products. We are a workers' co-operative committed to ethical business" is how they describe themselves on their official 2012 website.[8]

Although they have an elected management committee, the Suma website proclaims the cooperative is not bound by "the conventional notions of hierarchy." In practice that means that everyone gets the same pay, an equal say in major decisions, and is ready and willing to help out with any and all necessary tasks regardless of professional status or position. The Suma cooperative encourages multiskilling, enabling staff members to engage in many different facets of the business, and claims that this also improves job satisfaction, decision making, and performance overall. Business decisions and plans are made at regular general meetings with the consent of every cooperative member. ".... there's no chief executive, no managing director, and no company chairman. In practice, this means that our day-to-day work is carried out by self-managing teams of employees who are all paid the same wage, and who all enjoy an equal voice and an equal stake in the success of the business."[9] Cooperative teams are delegated and self-managing with coordinators rather than captains, so consultation and communication skills are the key to their success.

The Credit Union

The second organization, First Credit Union (FCU), is the second oldest organization of the three studied here. FCU operates in New Zealand and is largely, though not completely, focused on the indigenous Maori and Pacific Islander populations in New Zealand as well as ethnic minority populations of more recent immigrant groups such as Indians and Africans. Credit unions are simply described as not-for-profit financial institutions owned by and democratically operated for the benefit of those using their services. FCU is one of the 20 members of the New Zealand Credit Union Association and has four branches in the North Island. It was originally formed as an initiative of some members of the Catholic Church and targeted at other members of the Church; St Mary's Credit Union, as it was known, paid out its first loan of £100 in August 1955. Although it has since evolved to enable members of all faiths and no faith to become members, FCU retains the same philosophy and mission to support members to handle their finances with dignity.

Credit unions are registered under the Friendly Societies and Credit Unions Act 1982 and are not registered banks. It is a matter of pride that staff will readily tell you that they are *not* a bank, that they are locally owned by their customers, and are not-for-profit thus they are a trusted alternative to banks. The FCU, like others, is 100% New Zealand-owned and operated. They do not have the pressure to maximize profits for external shareholders, as banks do, so profits are redistributed back as a combination of better rates, fairer fees, responsible lending, and community support as well as improved customer service. The members' funds are retained in New Zealand and are not used to fund any offshore investments.

The FCU's lending criteria are "… humanitarian… FCU evaluates loans through a values-based approach placing character of the applicants above capacity and collateral; reversing the usual order of the '3Cs' of loan applications procedures used in banking, in effect. All three factors are taken into account but… If the person/family's character and local 'groundedness' or familial 'centre of gravity' are sound, then FCU adopts a constructive perspective of 'How can we make this work?' The respondent gave examples such as one case where a Pacific Islander family in the area had been refused credit elsewhere and was subject to a threatened mortgagee sale, the FCU arranged a loan to save the family from eviction."

The FCU is also a member of the New Zealand Association of Credit Unions (NZACU)—the key New Zealand credit union association. FCU is also a member of the World Council of Credit Unions (WOCCU)—the leading international trade association and development agency for credit unions, again signifying their global engagement and alignment with international principles of credit unions as well as their parochial viewpoint.

The Co-operative Bank

The third organization is the Co-operative Bank from the United Kingdom. The bank is a major financial institution which has evolved from a retail cooperative started over 150 years ago. The largest consumer cooperative in the world is the Co-operative group in the United Kingdom. The group has an annual turnover of more than £9 billion, over 4,500 stores and branches, 87,000 employees, 4.5 million members, and plans to increase its membership to 20 million whilst doubling its support for green energy to £1 billion in future. The Co-operative group now also provides financial and banking services as well as retailing goods.

The original 1844 retail cooperative founding principles were as follows:

1. Membership was open to all.
2. Governance was democratic, that is, one person, one vote.
3. Profits were distributed amongst members and customers in proportion to purchases made from the cooperative as a member's "dividend."
4. Limited interest paid on capital.
5. Political and religious neutrality.
6. Cash trading only.
7. Education and personal "betterment" was encouraged.

The pioneers collaborated with other cooperatives and diversified into other businesses. The original set of principles were also extended and updated in the twentieth century to cover wider social concerns such as antiracism and antisexism. However, they still retain their aim to educate and advocate for their principles whilst operating responsibly and ethically.

In 1872 the Co-operative Wholesale Society opened a Loan and Deposit Department, which became the CWS Bank 4 years later. Almost 100 years after that, in 1971, the bank was registered under the UK Companies' Act as Co-operative Bank Limited. The mission statement was drawn up in 1988 to reflect cooperative principles. The bank has over 340 branches since its 2009 merger with Britannia Building Society. The CWS group also currently has exclusive negotiating rights with Lloyd's bank over the potential sale of 632 Lloyd's bank branch offices. Although large by many typical cooperative and credit union standards, the Co-operative Bank is still not a mainstream, "high street" bank. The majority of the UK population do not put their money into the Co-operative Bank rather than the so-called Big four global banks. Furthermore, it is amongst the small minority of UK banks that has *not* been rescued by public funds from the brink of financial annihilation.

In relation to integrity and values, the Co-operative Bank's website highlights its "Ethical Policy" as covering six major sections:

- Human Rights—endorsed by Amnesty International
- International Development—supported by Amnesty International *vis-a-vis* child labor and so forth and The Fair Trade Foundation

- Social Enterprise—in the shape of support for credit unions, community finance initiatives, and so forth
- Customer Consultation
- Ecological Impact—supported by Forum for the Future. The Co-operative Bank views itself as a "green advocate" and complies with ISO 14001
- Animal Welfare—endorsed by BUAV (antivivisection pressure group); as a matter of principle rejects customers involved in "blood sports."

As recorded on the bank's webpage, the Co-operative Insurance arm became the world's first insurance company to launch a customer-led ethical policy to guide the social, ethical, and environmental aspects of its investments in 2005. The topics in the bulleted list above can be seen in the 2011 launch of an ethical operating plan across the entire Co-operative group's retail as well as banking businesses. It will establish a benchmark for Corporate Social Responsibility (CSR) on CO_2 reduction, fair trade, and community involvement.

Furthermore, the Co-operative Bank will increase its involvement with schools in the United Kingdom and create 2,000 apprenticeships in the next few years, as well as invest £5 million annually to tackle poverty around its stores and branches. The most ambitious target of the group is the reduction of its carbon emissions by 35% by 2017, which the Co-operative Bank asserts is the most progressive policy of any major business in the United Kingdom. It has plans to ensure that by 2020 90% of its developing world primary commodities will be certified as fair trade.[10]

Research Methods

All the authors were familiar with one or more of the three organizations in a research or governance capacity. Nevertheless, we also conducted interviews with senior members of the organizations using the questions below to interrogate the organization as to their culture, processes, and formal systems for reinforcing behavioral integrity. We also examined webpages and documents produced in each of the organizations.

We sought to qualitatively analyze, compare, and evaluate answers under the following 12-key thematic areas.

1. **Vision and Goals**—considers what the organization identifies and defines core ethical values, principles, and how these are to be integrated and embedded in everyday business conduct as well as strategy.
2. **Leadership**—assesses the "tone from the top," that is, at senior executive and board governance levels.
3. **Ethics Infrastructure**—explores how the organization structures and organizes its ethics and integrity function, roles, or unit to ensure effectiveness.
4. **Legal Compliance, Policies, and Rules**—includes key legislation and the internal framework which supports ethical behavior and practice, for example, codes of conduct, recruitment policies, and guidance for staff.
5. **Organizational Culture**—addresses how ethical behavior is promoted or reinforced in the corporate culture and through the mission, vision, structure, and strategy processes.
6. **Disciplinary and Reward Measures**—considers how the organization sets and enforces its standards of ethical conduct, including by means of its performance appraisal process. Is ethical conduct linked to compensation?
7. **Whistleblowing**—explores how the organization treats individuals (both internal and external to the entity) who speak up and report questionable conduct. Do they encourage and support them or discourage them? Are they enabled to make confidential and anonymous reports and protected from retaliation or retribution and harassment by others?
8. **Measurement, Research, and Assessment**—seeks to determine the organization's level of commitment to continuous improvement, based on their benchmarks and evaluation technologies and methods such as research into ethics strategies.
9. **Ethics Training, Education, or Confidential Advice and Support**—basically refers to what specific forms of provision are made to train staff in ethics, providing which skills, knowledge, and attitudes, and how far such training is integrated with other organization-wide training and support structures currently in place or planned.

10. **Ethics Communications**—summarized as how ethics and integrity initiatives including green issues are articulated and promoted, both internally and externally, and what the target audiences are.

11. **Green Issue Policies and Awareness**—summarized as concerning the organization's awareness of "green" issues and how it deals with environmental sustainability concerns.

12. **CSR**—summarized as a broader theme describing relevant government relations, environmental consciousness, sustainability, and community impact sought by the organization.

In the 24 questions in the interview schedule there are a number of areas which overlap and are interrelated. This not only enabled some cross-referring and confirmation but also allowed for some extra probes to elucidate and clarify or extend the discussion of each of the 12 thematic areas. There are areas where the three case organizations overlap and a few where they differ in terms of normative expectations of staff and members and practical means to ensure good risk management without compromising core values and strategic performance objectives.

Illustrative Quotations for Each of the 12 Thematic Areas

Vision and Goals (Question 1)

The Suma mission statement is:

> "... To provide a high quality service to customers and a rewarding working environment for the members, within a sustainable, ethical, co-operative business structure. To strive to promote a healthier lifestyle by supplying ethical, eco-friendly, vegetarian products."[11]

The 56th Annual report of the FCU for 2010–2011, states:

> "First Credit Union is a financial co-operative and our purpose is to provide financial services that enable our members to handle their financial affairs with dignity."[12]

Paul Flowers, current chairman of the Co-operative Bank states:

> "The compelling co-operative alternative is built on the same values that inspired the Rochdale Pioneers to create the first Co-operative business 168 years ago—voluntary and open membership; democratic control; economic participation; autonomy and independence; education and development; and concern for our community. It is the resonance of those values with customers and investors alike that underpins our ambition to become a real force in UK financial services."[13]

Leadership (Question 2)

Suma as both an SME and advocate of worker participation is keen to ensure that it has a form of direct democracy, "Company officers who act as executive managers of Suma participate in the Management Committee, but have no vote. The nonexecutive (elected) directors have the authority and power and not the executives. This prevents the executive running the organization for its own self- interest."

For FCU, "... the FCU leadership are expected to be exemplars of best practice not only in technical savings and loan administration but in maintaining a high ethical standard towards colleagues and members."

Ethics Infrastructure (Question 3)

FCU has a code of ethics and an ethics committee charged with overseeing and judgment of relevant actions with respect to sanctions applied for ethical infringements at any levels in the organization.

Their code encompasses respect and fair and confidential treatment of staff and members irrespective of age, gender, disability, ethnic origin as well as ensuring legal compliance. FCU sees the trustees as a key part of the ethics infrastructure: "... The trustees act as the asset and liability Committee and are responsible for overseeing the treasury framework including approval of rates for loans and deposits. There is a complete trial balance each day and exception reports.... The Ethics Code also encompasses maintaining the FCU reputation, dress standards as well as indicating communication and behavior standards regarded as indicative of respectful behavior between people and in discussing *others* privacy and confidentiality is maintained rigorously...."

The Co-operative Bank's "Ethical Policy" covers six major sections as listed earlier. The Co-operative Bank consults with members and staff to determine ethical policy and practice and has demonstrated that it is prepared to accept the costs of maintaining ethical behavior such that ".... The Co-operative Bank has withheld more than £1 billion of funding from business activities that its customers say are unethical."

They further state "... Our asset management business introduced the world's first customer-led Ethical Engagement Policy, and is committed to use its influence to push for improvements in the social and environmental performance of its investee companies."[14] Suma believes that their democratic structure and decision-making apparatus serve the same purpose as the Co-operative bank's customer-led Ethical Engagement policy.

Legal Compliance, Policies, and Rules (Question 4)

Each organization fully complies with domestic and, where relevant, international legislation regarding employment law, licensing requirements as financial institutions, and reporting requirements. Each asserts that they go beyond the minimum requirements. FCU respondent states, "There is a legal regulatory compliance environment that relates the governance and capital requirements, loans issue and debt provisioning. The Credit Union is registered under the Friendly Societies and Credit Unions act 1982 and its operations are monitored for compliance by the Trustees Executor Ltd.... There are internal financial audits and financial reports are independently audited."

Culture (Question 5)

In Suma, "The General Meeting [GM] of the members agrees strategies, business plans, and majority policy decisions. Such meetings take place 6 times a year. The General Meeting decisions are mandatory on all members. Six of the GM members are selected to form the Management

Committee (MC) during whose weekly meetings the implementation of the agreed business plan and other GM decisions are initiated. MC members act as Suma's elected directors, appointing company officers, personnel, operations, finance, and function area coordinators."

In FCU "... Members, staff and the community are active stakeholders.... Members and staff shape the culture in a mutually interactive manner e.g., in custom and practice such as 'no talking out of school' about business, in reference to the community initiatives and to other areas such as perceived worries of staff and members about security."

Of course Suma and FCU are smaller organizations although the staff members in FCU are more geographically dispersed of the two with branches across the North Island of New Zealand. Thus, some differences in scale and scope of operational and organizing arrangements might reasonably be expected to impinge on processes for stakeholder involvement, especially in routine matters.

The scale of operations is much bigger in the Co-operative Bank, although they maintain a democratic approach involving consultation by the management team with staff and members "...Asking cooperative members (including employees) to feed into the policies by way of open consultation" and getting "... staff buy in at all levels." The respondent at the bank further indicated most effort in the organization was directed towards gaining staff input and support for policies, although they are also influenced by the efforts of environmental pressure groups.

The extent of the norms of equality, mutuality, and reciprocation of obligations between staff and customers and within the staff cohort varies across the three organizations. Broadly, the Co-operative Bank is on the conservative end of the continuum and Suma is closer to the radical end with FCU somewhere between the two. So for Suma, "All Suma staff, member, employee or casual, receive the same daily net wage plus allowances and overtime. Job variety is emphasized within the firm, drivers will drive for a maximum of 3 days and then be employed in the warehouse or office. Office workers are required to perform manual tasks for a minimum of one day a week." As members of a workers' cooperative, this way of organizing staff employment is not unexpected, however, it does possess unique elements which are not seen in the majority of customer owned cooperatives. However, for the FCU "... some 'rules' were developed regarding members wearing 'hoodies' and 'shades' in the premises—a common robber's 'uniform'—and use of profanities when speaking to staff or others. Members have also taken this on board and begun spontaneously to exercise additional 'respect' by removing gum-boots before entry as is customarily done on entering houses in the New Zealand community."

Disciplinary and Reward Measures (Question 6)

Many organizations now tie ethical behavior to employees' performance reviews or career goals—though this alignment and respective action depends on reliability of data gathering.[15] "FCU has had only had to dis-miss two staff for serious violations in 30-odd years in the Credit Union." As regards rewards, "FCU has no KPIs pushing loans or performance management."

Suma has indicated that their democratic scrutiny processes ensure transparency and prevent or reduce opportunities for staff or members to engage in unethical behaviors and "… the co-operative structure of the organization ensures that any policies are followed by consensus. Additionally many members of the co-operative are involved, both in the course of their work and on a voluntary basis, in environmental and social initiatives." The Co-operative Bank "… is the only UK bank with an Ethi-cal Policy that is voted on by its customers and their Ethical Engagement Policy was launched after consultation with their insurance and invest-ments customers."

Whistleblowing (Question 7)

Suma considers that their democratic systems, as discussed above, negate the need for a specific whistleblowing policy or structure.

FCU currently has no formally assigned whistleblower support struc-ture but suggested that the trustees as independent, community repre-sentatives, scrutineers, and auditors perform that role by default.

The Co-operative Bank has a committee meeting at least four times a year dealing with risk review arrangements whereby staff may raise concerns, in confidence, about possible wrong doing in financial reporting or other matters (i.e., whistleblowing).

Research and Assessment (Question 8)

The Co-op bank has a continuous structured review process involving CSR accounting and financial audits and a series of public reports covering current or projected issues relating to measurement, research and assessment. First Credit Union is closer to the Co-op approach and includes reports from external agencies, trustees and consultants such as S&P. On the other hand, Suma relies on plenary meetings to agree on current and future research assessment and metrics.

Ethics Training or Confidential Support (Question 9)

Suma's ethical policy seeks to ensure they "... source goods at the best possible quality and price within acceptable ethical parameters" and such goods must fulfill Suma's criteria such as promoting fair trade, "green," GM (genetically modified)-free, cruelty-free and healthy, vegetarian, eating. Further they aim to avoid or boycott products containing harmful food additives, with minimal environmental impact, and will actively boycott goods from countries or companies with proven poor human rights records.

Suma regard their proclaimed principles, transparent procedures, multitasking, and volunteering arrangements as largely fulfilling this training role; they also enable staff to attend or present at ethics and environmental workshops and seminars as part of their development.

The FCU interviewee commented that it was also a part of their culture to train staff well. He noted "there is extensive and continuous staff training and development in house and external professional education and training related to staff development or promotion e.g., for professional accreditation or university degrees. Staff get an initial training of 2 weeks including, where relevant, subsidized external courses, accommodation and transport, etc. Leaders and managers also attend WOCCU (World Council of Credit Unions) events, Strategic Planning, and training. This ensures a 'pipeline' of trained staff for succession planning and talent management purposes and builds commitment."

Ethics Communication (Question 10)

Suma says that in addition to a structure promoting workers' rights "Co-operative teams are delegated and self-managing with co-ordinators rather than captains, so consultation and communication skills are the key to their success." They are well-known in the industry and it is very clear amongst staff and members that, for example, they will only sell "fair trade" and have a "zero tolerance" policy for sale of any nonvegetarian products.

Green Issues, Policies, and Awareness (Question 11)

We asked the respondents to rate their organization using the ladder of "green-ness" (Table 1.1).

Suma advocates vociferously and frequently for Green issues and is very aware and committed, regarding itself as occupying level A, top of the ladder, but noting that issues "... tend to revolve around balancing the need to get the job done in good time with getting things done as 'greenly' as possible. For instance, waste segregation (keeping cardboard and plastic packaging separate) sometimes suffers when the warehouse is being cleaned up in a big hurry before the day's order picking starts. Additionally, there are members of the co-operative who need constant reminders to switch off office equipment when they leave, rather than leaving things on stand-by."

Table 1.1. Ladder of Organizational "Green-ness"

Ladder of "green-ness"	Summary description
A. Militant Green	"Activist" for Green cause
B. Green partner	Collaborates with activists
C. Green Advocate	Openly supports Green issues/cause
D. Green Client	Accepts advice by Greens on issues
E. Neutral/passive	Not interested, uninvolved, or unsure
F. Green Consumer	Use of Green products/services
G. Suspect Green	Ambivalent about Green issues
H. Anti-Green	Against Green causes

At FCU, they regard themselves as occupying level C on the ladder of Green-ness, see Table 1.1. The respondent provided documentation and reports to sustain the comment that "First Credit Union also has a sustainability report and several initiatives including sustainable offices, recycling, tree planting, university/polytechnic/schools' based activities and awards for sustainable endeavours."

Co-operative Bank's website highlights its "Ethical Policy" covering Ecological Impact, supported by Forum for the Future. The Co-operative Bank views itself as a "green advocate," complying fully with international benchmarks such as ISO 14001 and as noted above as having plans in place for 35% more reduction in its carbon emissions by 2017.

CSR (Question 12)

Some observers perceive an instrumentalist orientation of many CSR and ethical projects and regard that element as tainting the beneficial outcomes. Thus, the Suma representative interviewed replied that "vendors of management consultancy solutions who… assert that there are greater profits to be had by adopting such measures. Pursuing objectives that favor ethical and environmental standards, becomes rather suspect when such pursuit is profit motivated." It was also stated that when using Google to check CSR, one would find Kellogg's on top of the list and yet a "Which?" survey in 2006 called "Cereal Offenders," which analyzed 275 major breakfast cereals from leading manufacturers on sale in the UK supermarkets indicated that 75% had high levels of sugar and around 20% had high levels of salt[16] although some have since been reformulated to reduce salt and sugar content.

Nevertheless, the latter comment does have to be tempered by pragmatism and business realities that necessarily intrude into moral calculation for Suma too. The cooperative is an SME and business survival means it does have to take account of costs as the respondent indicated, "…the cost has to be carefully assessed and the operating period over which any such cost can be amortized can be taken into account. Our business works on very small margins so operating costs feature heavily in such decisions."

Like Suma, the business practicalities of the FCU have also to be taken account of and "Staff meetings are rotated—sometime staff members are accommodated when living away from home in their role as temporary cover! The IT software used allows staff also seconded temporarily to other offices to meet work role requirements at their own office as well as getting to know branch colleagues and form an understanding of local areas. There is also communication through the staff newsletter."

David Anderson, the Co-operative financial services chief executive, is quoted as saying, "... those things that started out in the Ethical Policy have become Public Policy and we want to lead that Public Policy forward... with the revisions to the Ethical Policy that are being made now. The fact that 80,000 of our customers have participated in updating it just shows how important it is to them and we think... a third of the Bank's profits come from customers who've joined it just because of the Ethical Policy. So, it's been a real differentiating factor for the Bank. It's been part of our heritage and we see it as central to what the Bank stands for going forward."[17]

It is not only employees whose actions may tarnish an organization's reputation and diminish its ethical capital. For example, it has been argued that the perceived reputation and integrity or publicly accepted legitimacy of Finnish Forestry companies became questionable due to the unethical tactics and actions of their Brazilian business partners, and thus their integrity was called into question when they did nothing to challenge the Brazilian partner with respect to CSR.[18] The Co-operative Bank also "seeks to change companies from the inside, by engaging with them on social, ethical and environmental issues" according to its website. The Co-operative Bank interviewee suggested that they are "not unique in having some of the policies e.g., Food ethics in the grocery business but several are bespoke to the Co-operative and to the bank."

Analysis: Integrity Vectors

We decided to opt for a more "rounded" view by adopting the idea of three-dimensionality from the Gratton and Truss[19] model for analyzing strategic HR alignment in organizations. Regarding levels of impact on business, values may be regarded as a strategic vector (vertical alignment), tactical vector (horizontal/process alignment), or operational vector (action/implementation alignment). We plotted the various responses to the interview questions against each of the vectors in Table 1.2 and

Table 1.2. Ethics and Integrity Themes Comparative Overview

Integrity theme	Suma	Co-operative bank	FCU
1. Vision and Goals (Vertical–Strategic)	Stresses democratic values and practices of staff/member empowerment in General Meetings (GM) to decide strategic development	Stresses Co-operative Bank's principles of customer consultation on strategy and legal accountability of the organization executive	Stresses strategic community values, of founding ("people helping people") philosophy
2. Leadership (Vertical)	Direct participation of all staff in strategic decision making in MC	Hierarchical decision making but with some staff consultation on decisions on strategy	Chairman = "head coach," Board of trustees ensures community input on strategic decisions and scrutiny of leadership and operations
3. Ethics Infrastructure (Horizontal–Processes/tactics)	Well-developed policies and practices on membership and employment	Well-developed policies and practices	Well-developed policies and practices
4. Legal Compliance, Policies, and Rules (Vertical–Horizontal)	Goes beyond legal compliance- extending actions to fair trading in sourcing supplies	Compliant and refused major deals to ensure principled business and CSR	Systematic adherence to compliance and to founding philosophy
5. Organizational Culture (Horizontal + Action/depth—In Operations)	Somewhat Kibbutz-like everyone helping out in work tasks without status distinctions, democratic vote on decisions at GMs	Corporation structure and roles related to position description and member consultation on key changes or strategic direction and initiatives	Corporation structure and roles related to position description and member-directed AGM.
6. Disciplinary and Reward Measures (Horizontal + Action/depth)	Collectively determined and administered sanctions and flat rate salaries dependent on collective agreement	Standard formal ethical and disciplinary codes and some bonuses based on targets	Following 3Cs for loans; rewards closely related to values and serving client needs

(Continued)

Table 1.2. Ethics and Integrity Themes Comparative Overview (Continued)

Integrity theme	Suma	Co-operative bank	FCU
7. Whistleblowing (Horizontal + Action/depth)	Not formally but issues may be raised at meetings and put to a vote	Yes—formal structure in place	None in place formally but see trustees as a channel enabling whistleblowing
8. Measurement, Research, and Assessment (Action + Horizontal)	Transparent measures agreed and reviewed at meetings	Public Reports/CSR accounting/ Financial audits	Legal/CSR reports/S&P audits, Trustees' reports
9. Ethics training, Education or Confidential Advice and Support (Horizontal + Action)	Cooperative system and democratic voting, on-the-job training infrastructure, otherwise Ad hoc training systems	Some formal training related to levels of job and role	Some training for all (e.g., on induction and orientation on operations plus Trustee role)
10. Ethics Communications (Horizontal + Action)	Centrally Embedded in systems and corporate literature	Centrally Embedded in systems and corporate literature	Centrally Embedded in systems and corporate literature
11. Green Issue Policies and Awareness (Vertical)	Very explicit green-ness (Militant Green as per Table 1.1)	Green partner (see Table 1.1)	Green advocate—passive (see Table 1.1)
12. Corporate Social Responsibility (Vertical + Action)	CSR = core component of strategy, processes and impacts on operations	CSR = core component of strategy, processes and impacts on operations	CSR = core component of strategy, processes and impacts on operations

this allows us to later present a visual representation of the three axes of the alignment, their relative strength, and overall trajectory of corporate integrity. This will enable executives to review corporate integrity and make needed changes in specific areas to build a coherent, balanced, and integrated ethical strategy.

Each of the three organizations regards these values as realistic as well as central to their "brand" marketing and thus as more than mere rhetoric. However, each applied these differentially across these vectors, for instance, in terms of how explicit, systematic, or well-actioned their policies, codes, and procedures are. We have illustrated some of the differences with brief quotations and comments on each of the case organizations. The strength of each of the three dimensions is represented in Figure 1.1 as height, width, and depth (i.e., vertically, horizontally, and from front to rear of the figure).

The Co-operative Bank has a "clean" image despite some recent concerns by some commentators.[20] There are suggested downsides insofar as the responsiveness of the bigger cooperatives to change and the level of bureaucracy required, disseminating and canvassing opinion,[21] though the Co-operative Bank is amongst the very few UK banks that survived the global financial upheaval without a government bailout which they attribute to their philosophy and not seeking quick profits. In line with other management concepts, growth in size for the Suma collective may yet pose more of the kinds of conflicts they already see between espoused

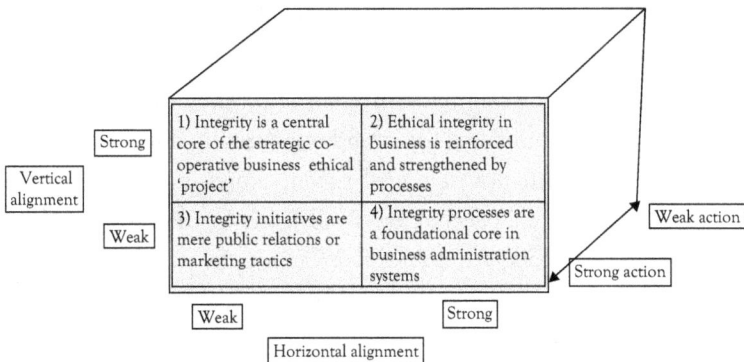

Figure 1.1. *The action/implementation of policies are shown from front to back in the three-dimensional model.*

ideology and practicality though these need not prevent them from growing the business with integrity as the Co-operative Bank has attempted to do. Growth for cooperative enterprises is an under-researched area and thus there is plenty of scope for further research in each of the three cases.

Conclusion, Recommendations, and Future Research

These three organizations are neither typical of modern capitalism nor for-profit corporations (in terms of their cooperative missions and structures). Further, they are each at different stages of their organizational "lifecycles." Nevertheless, the three organizations clearly see themselves as being part of a wider social change and riding the crest of a wave of ethical consumerism. According to the interviewees, there are bottom-line benefits accruing as a result of ethical capital growth from their integrity. In implementing their values they perceive themselves to be at the leading edge in their respective sectors as we shall see below. In the postglobal financial crisis and upsurge of interest in co-operatives of various kinds, now is a good time to study their development paths.

Practical steps taken by cooperatives accommodate well the following 10-step process—a variant of one outlined elsewhere by one of the authors:[22]

1. Champion and commit to transparent, organization-wide emotional literacy using a "no blame" approach and surfacing the "undiscussables" to give voice to all workers and members of the cooperative.
2. Engage proactively with key stakeholders and the wider community through a steering committee invested with genuine authority, influence at all organizational levels, and responsibility for the work.
3. Develop and articulate a shared vision, expressing the high hopes and dreams of all stakeholders at all levels in the organization in order to bring energy and a positive focus to the work systems.
4. Conduct a needs and resources assessment including emotional impact and resilience across the organization. Identify specific issues to address; build from what's already in place and working well wherever possible.

5. Develop an action plan and timeline with sufficient flexibility to cope with emerging complexity in the business environment. Include the shared stakeholder goals and objectives as well as a plan for attaining, measuring, and evaluating their ongoing strategic alignment and using technology such as social networking tools to ease administrative and bureaucratic burdens whilst attempting to maintain active communication and participation of the whole community with enhanced accessibility.

6. Select evidence-based programs and strategies; begin building a shared vocabulary and framework of understanding. This creates consistency and coherence for the stakeholders when reviewing strategic identity branding, operational projects, codes of practice, or implementation concerns.

7. Conduct initial staff development for "onboarding" new staff to ensure that they fully understand and can apply with integrity and consistency the relevant principles as a practical frame of reference alongside technical best practice models embodied in behavioral guides or codes. This will be increasingly relevant in a period of growth.

8. Provide a technical support infrastructure as well as a values-based communication network and help staff or members become familiar with and experienced in the required skill set.

9. Expand instruction and integrate organization-wide, to build a consistent cultural environment and experiences for all involved.

10. Revisit activities—adjust for continuous improvement and emergent challenges. Check on progress to resolve problems early.

Key Terms

Integrity—defined as the proactive structures, principles, and systems for accruing "ethical capital" by promoting, monitoring, and developing shared norms designed to identify and avoid potential conflicts of interest, abuse of office in any function, role, or location in the business.

Co-operative—defined as a member-based form of organization structure based on open membership giving access to all. Governance is democratic (i.e., one person, one vote) and members regularly consulted on strategic decisions. Limited interest is paid on capital.

Credit union—defined as a cooperative form of not-for-profit financial and lending institutions owned by and democratically operated for the benefit of those using their services.

Ethical capital—defined in the chapter as the accrued differences between the goodwill "assets" and perceived moral liabilities of an organization as expressed in the coevolving relationship of customer loyalty and manifest employee integrity.

Three integrity vectors—the strategic direction of an organization, the organizational systems including its policy frameworks and the implementation or operational actions.

Strategic values trajectory—the direction, strength, and alignment of the overall patterns of interrelationships between the three integrity vectors on the emergent strategy of the organization. That is the direction and strength of the intersecting dimensions of strategy, systems and processes and actions taken to implement policies, goals, and mission across the organization and thus enabling "gap" analysis and corrective action by leaders.

Unique selling point (USP)—a marketing term which simply indicates what the organizational leaders believe, based on perceptions of customer preferences or key values the organization aims to project, are core "brand" values which "sell" the organization and its products or services in their market.

Study Questions

1. Using the themes as in Table 1.2, analyze an organization you are involved with as an employee, or volunteer, or as a member.
2. Critically reflect on any perceived gaps between leaders' rhetoric and customer/employee reality.
3. Why are there such gaps?
4. How have these gaps arisen?
5. How might the gap be closed in future?
6. What sorts of visible measures, rewards, or auditing of ethical capital is required for best effect in the organization you are studying?

Further Reading

Allan, J., Fuller, D., & Luckett, M. (1998). Academic integrity: Behaviors, rates, and attitudes of business students toward cheating. *Journal of Marketing Education 20*(1), 41–52.

Benjamin, B., & O'Reilly, C. (2011). Becoming a leader: Early career challenges faced by MBA graduates. *Academy of Management Learning & Education 10*(3), 452–472.

Brown, M. T. (2006). Corporate integrity and public interest: A relational approach to business ethics and leadership. *Journal of Business Ethics 66*, 11–18.

BITC/Radley Yeldar. (2007). *Taking shape—The future of corporate responsibility communications.* Retrieved on March 6, 2007 from http://www.bitc.org.uk/resources/publications/future_of_cr_comms.html

Carson, T. L. (2003). Self-interest and business ethics: Some lessons of the recent corporate scandals. *Journal of Business Ethics 43*(4), 389–394. DOI: 10.1023/A:1023013128621

Devinney, T. M., Auger, P., Eckhardt, G., & Birtchnell, T. (2006, Fall). The other CSR. *Stanford Social Innovation Review.* Retrieved on January 6, 2007 from http://www.ssireview.org/articles/entry/the_other_csr/

Entine, J. (2010). Eco marketing: What price green consumerism? Retrieved 16 February, 2012 from http://www.ethicalcorp.com/environment/eco-marketing-what-price-green-consumerism

Kasper-Fuehrer, E. C., & Ashkanasy, N. M. (2001). Communicating trustworthiness and building trust in interorganizational virtual organizations. *Journal of Management 27*(3), 235–254.

Kisamore, J. L., Stone, T. H., & Jawahar, I. M. (2007). Academic integrity: The relationship between individual and situational factors on misconduct contemplations. *Journal of Business Ethics 75*, 381–394.

Kizirian, T. G., Mayhew, B. W., & Sneathen, L. D. Jr. (2005). The impact of management integrity on audit planning and evidence. *Auditing: A Journal of Practice & Theory 24*(2), 49–67.

Lorsch, J. W., Berlowitz, L., & Zelleke, A. (2005). *Restoring trust in American business.* Cambridge, MA: MIT Press.

CHAPTER 2

Individual Ethical Behavior and the Influences of Organizational Culture

Kemi Ogunyemi

Introduction

Individual ethical or unethical behavior has been found to often reflect the culture, the ethical climate, or both,[1] of the organization in some way.[2] This is because although individuals may have their own tendencies to put self-interest above the common good, or may have deficiencies of the moral judgment required for ethical decision making, the company's culture may still inspire, promote, discourage, or totally inhibit personal ethical action.[3] As Gellerman observes, even good managers, at times, act without integrity.[4] The reverse is also true—individuals' unethical actions contribute to shaping the culture of companies and can therefore create an unethical climate over time.[5]

In countries where corruption is rife, such as Nigeria, it is particularly important to watch out for this, as the individual already has to contend with a difficult external environment and therefore nonenabling internal environs could deal a fatal blow even to the good desires of those employees who wish to do what is right. This is also important because unethical behavior, or negative behavior, can result in heavy costs to the organization[6] since organizational performance depends to a large extent on employee behavior.[7] Such problems could arise in numerous ways. For example, a perception that management—comprising those in formal leadership positions—is self-interested could lead others in the organization to react by taking care of their own interests;[8] or there could be policies, value statements, or both, that embody altruism but are not applied;[9] or sometimes a reward system may contradict the intention of the organization to promote other-regarding behavior as well as ethical behavior.[10] In all three examples mentioned here, the organization would have set the stage in such a way that employees would find it easier to take unethical decisions than they would otherwise have done.

The organizational factors that influence ethical behavior could be a reflection of the extent to which a company's culture promotes considerateness and altruism. Sometimes, companies can inadvertently allow elements of culture or climate to thrive that inhibit ethical behavior because they inhibit other-regarding behavior. According to Treviño et al., self-interest is one of the factors that affect the ethical climate of the organization and it is determined by testing how concerned the people in the company are about themselves or their own interests *vis-à-vis* their concern for others.[11] Thus one of the ways in which to promote ethical behavior could be to promote and reward selfless action.

This chapter talks about how unethical behavior could be a result of organizational culture more than individual decadence. It uses findings from case study methodology—three caselets and seven narratives of experiences of some young Nigerian professionals—to illustrate this and to discuss what facilitates or inhibits ethical behavior, especially emphasizing that best practices for improving workplace integrity include fostering an atmosphere that encourages other-regarding behavior and therefore inhibits unethical behavior. The use of case studies gives depth and detail to the study that might have been otherwise missing and that enhances understanding of how the integrity of individuals in organizations is influenced by what they experience within the organization.[12] As unethical behavior inevitably harms the firm and its stakeholders, as well as society in general, this chapter also advocates that fostering selflessness and the virtuousness that accompanies it as an organizational value works for long-run business success.[13]

The basic principle here is that many, if not all, human beings are influenced by the people around them. If a person can be influenced by a single person, that person can be even more easily influenced if there are many people within the organization who have similar values.

This could be called a "bad barrel approach" to explaining unethical behavior[14] and it is compatible with the other approaches since it deals with only one aspect of the phenomenon.[15] The newcomer can be persuaded, consciously or unconsciously, to change his values in order to fit in with the rest of the group. We begin by looking at three real life examples of employee experiences in Nigerian businesses: the first showing a perception of self-interestedness in one's reporting line, the second showing the impact of dead policy, and the third showing the benefits of an aligned reward system. The protagonists are Kole, Yakoub, and Abata, respectively.

Kole: Adapting to One's Boss

Kole narrates his experience working with Mr. Obike, the then-head of operations of a Sarfa Bank branch:

> "Let me give a brief profile of Mr. Obike. He was 36 years old. He had a beautiful wife and two children—a boy and a girl. He graduated with a first class in civil engineering from the university. He had no additional qualifications except an ICAN* certificate.
>
> Mr. Obike had worked only in Sarfa Bank from his youth service till date—for 12 years. He has totally lost his individual will and functioned like a robot. He was efficient. He was not a very sociable person; he worked strictly by the book which was to an extent convenient for the industry he was in (banking), but at the same time alienated him from colleagues and created an unsympathetic and cold work environment among all the people who reported to him. No one cared about the others—each person did their own work and moved on. There were often minor but hurtful disagreements due to inflexibility on the part of one person or the other. Sometimes, this would impact customer service negatively, but no one cared.

---

*   Institute of Chartered Accountants of Nigeria (this certificate is obtained after a series of rigorous professional exams).

During my first week in that branch, I reported directly to him and so we worked in the same office. He often told me sentences like 'you do not have a choice'; 'you have to harden yourself and work this way'; 'there is no room for emotions here'; 'you just have to cover your back'; 'this is the only way to survive in this system.' This started affecting my thinking pattern and I too started coming to work every day thinking I did not have a choice but to live and work that way. This mentality did not just end there; it spread to every other aspect of my life. I did not treat people well any longer; there was no point.

Mr. Obike was always the last to leave the office and most times the first to be in the office. During one of his late nights in the office (I had also started staying behind in the office because I really did not feel like going back to my empty house), something happened and we had our first and only ever real conversation. I discovered that it was not that he did not love his wife or his kids and did not want to spend more time with them, he just did not know how to. He was like an empty shell—like a madman that had lost his way. This discovery shook me. I saw clearly that I did not want to become a person like him, who I had also begun to realize derived pleasure from breaking his subordinates emotionally. I realized I was already changed and acting that way. I decided to get out of the system of Sarfa Bank."

Kole was lucky. The others in the system had not realized the danger and had not reacted. According to Kole, "I am grateful to him because he unconsciously gave me my power of choice and I chose to improve myself and try to be of value to not only myself but to others around me. I chose not to end up like him. I got out of that system and I am a different person now."

Kole was gradually changing to become like the people he found around him. However, he got a wake-up call and snapped out of it by leaving the system. Not every employee has that opportunity. They, like Obike, gradually become part of the system and pass on the values they have imbibed to those coming in after them. They exhibit antisocial behavior and end up harming themselves, others, and the company without even realizing the damage they have done. If the management realized what was happening and, through a few of them, deliberately pushed the growth of a counterculture of integrity in the organization,[16] the strength of reciprocity might be able to turn the scales and eventually raise the level of altruism and integrity in the system.[17]

Akpabio, Yakoub, and Ulomma: Living with Dead Policies

Yakoub was the bank's branch manager and Ulomma his operations manager. Akpabio was a marketing officer. These three were the only remaining experienced staff in the branch in 2007. According to the bank's corporate statements, initiative and team spirit were valued aspects of its culture and way of doing business.

> "Yakoub was well educated and smart. He was good at his job as he had more than fifteen years of banking experience. However, he was manipulative. Banking is a business that involves much risk taking. Yakoub did not like signing off on documents but preferred giving verbal instructions. He wanted to preserve himself from any possible trouble by making sure others would take the blame if something went wrong. The branch staff did not like this. They reacted by scrutinizing every instruction Yakoub gave to make sure that there was no underlying problem he was trying to push to them. This slowed down the processes and we lost prospective clients at times. Many of our customers were unhappy. Some left for other banks.

> Yakoub was also very autocratic; he believed that as the branch manager he should always make the decisions. He was not the type of person who worked toward developing personal relationship with people except for the high profile customers. He picked on Ulomma a lot.

> Ulomma was a new operations manager, having been promoted from being a customer service officer. She was target-driven and

understood the importance of making her unit perform at all cost because she faced the risk of fraud constantly. The job was very demanding. She did not like the fact that the branch manager was always trying to overrun her work with her team. He would neglect the marketing staff and nag her all the time.

Akpabio was a good marketing staff. He was always ready to assist anyone in need and sometimes acted act as an intermediary between the branch manager and the operations manager. He was cool-headed and organized."

It seemed that the conflicts between Yakoub and Ulomma started to affect other people, including Akpabio. Yakoub constantly tried to manipulate and force Ulomma into doing what he wanted. This usually backfired and led to arguments and after a while it created a rift between the operations and marketing staff. The operations staff felt that the branch manager gave preferential treatment to the marketing staff since he let them do whatever they liked while he persecuted the operations staff. They reacted by dropping their productivity level and refusing to do anything extra. They would always only just meet their operational target. There was little or no team spirit. The discord increased when Yakoub gave Ulomma very bad appraisals despite her hard work. Some of the traits identified by Schmincke as outcomes of selfishness in organizations can be seen here in the behavior that became the norm among Yakoub's staff: blame shifting, avoidance of accountability, power struggles, and so forth.[18]

Akpabio was left alone often without the support of Yakoub who was after all his boss. He did his work and Yakoub's excellently without complaining. He ended up being the one who knew most of the customers. Akpabio kept on with this for a long time until one morning he just walked in and submitted his resignation. He had not hinted to anyone of his intention to leave even though he had been planning it for months. He was the only experienced marketing officer and the branch had no backup for him. He refused to stay on to work out his notice but rather prefer to give the required salary amount in lieu. He apparently felt he had no reason to be considerate when that was not part of the organization norms in practice.

On his exit, the branch lost a lot of its customers and the balance sheet figures reduced. Yakoub could not manage the situation because unfortunately the discord between operation and marketing had been created and could not be easily wiped out. Many staff were not ready to help each other out in order to serve customers. Many more customers left. All attempts to get the staff to work together were futile. Reminding them of the bank's corporate values of initiative and team spirit made no impact, especially coming from Yakoub. As at the time of writing this case, Yakoub was still heading the branch and the balance sheet had continued on a downward trend.

Yakoub had fostered a culture in which animosity was high and no one was ready to think about the others. Since there was no coherence between what was proclaimed through the company's statements and what was actually practiced, there was lack of integrity in the organization and this affected the people within it. People tend to look outside themselves for guidance as to how the organization expects integrity to be lived and when they get contradictory signals, they change their behavior.[19] For a long time things continued that way. No one noticed when Akpabio changed so much that he who ordinarily started out as a considerate person who had team spirit ended up leaving abruptly, without being interested in what would happen to those he left behind, or to the customers, or to the firm. This was the outcome of "systems that encourage or support flawed behavior."[20] Policies have little or no effect unless they are implemented and lived in the organization.

Mr. Abata: Rewarding the Walk

Mr. Abata had an Information Technology company in Nigeria. The company had succeeded in acquiring a fair share of the Nigerian market and he began attempting to make it a multinational. It was tough. He frequently traveled to other countries to give lectures on the competence of his company and submitted proposals here and there, but he failed to penetrate the global market.

He gave up and decided that it was better to concentrate on the Nigerian market. At this point, he reflected that he had made a lot of profit from the business and decided to compensate his staff that had worked hard to move the company forward. He started giving scholarships, salary increase, holiday packages, and housing loans to them. He organized training programs for his staff periodically and when they became better in their various fields he gave them more freedom to bring ideas and suggestions. He made it clear that he was rewarding their diligence and commitment to the organization. After one and a half years, the company's profit margin increased significantly.

One day, one of his staff who had gone for a three-month training program in England called with news that he had finished as the second best in his class and had got a job offer from a company in England. He had declined the offer and now told Mr. Abata that he would rather open a branch of Mr. Abata's company there. The new branch was set up and within four months it had made double the returns from the Nigerian market.

Mr. Abata's magnanimity with his employees had succeeded in establishing a culture of integrity in the organization within which other-regarding activity was acknowledged and rewarded. He had shown them he appreciated their committed contribution to the organization's progress by investing in their personal progress. That was why his employee was able to act selflessly as he did in resisting the more financially attractive offer and instead further the interest of his employer who had trained him.

Walking the talk is not enough; the organization also should reward those who do the walk.[21] If the organization rewards things other than the walk, then it will be difficult for others to walk the talk even if they see management doing it. Abata chose to reward the values he wanted his staff to practice and he got positive results for the climate of integrity within his organization and also for the financial performance of the business in line with the findings of Caza, Barker, and Cameron that organizational virtuousness impacts performance.[22]

Organizational Integrity and Attention to Enablers and Inhibitors

The three caselets above clearly show that employees react to what they perceive or experience in the organizations in which they work.[23] They are influenced by the culture and climate of the organization and tend to act the way the others around them act. If they experience self-interest, they are more likely to take selfish decisions too. If they, on the other hand, are treated in an other-regarding manner, then they may commit themselves more to the good of the organization and their fellow workers and this gives them more reason to act in upright and ethical ways.

In trying to ensure that the barrel is not bad,[24] it could be useful to look for what makes it better and what makes it worse. Hence, further discussion of some cultural factors which can affect integrity in the organization by inhibiting or enabling ethical action and organizational commitment follows.

Cultural Enablers of Individual Ethical Action and Commitment to the Organization

When asked what they have found encouraging or discouraging in their effort to do things right and perform selfless actions in an organization, a number of young Nigerian professionals gave the following experiences. Each experience reflects the individual's perception of the integrity in the organization and his or her reaction to it. Enablers comprise real experiences which make it easier for the employees to act well because they themselves have been treated well, while inhibitors are those real experiences which showed a lack of integrity in the organization in regard to the way employees were treated and therefore, in return, provoked those employees to act contrary to the common good.

Caring

A's manager noticed that the young man was not looking happy so she took him out to lunch and asked what the matter was. He said he was tired of the marketing department and wanted a change. She immediately asked if he wanted to go back to his previous unit—the cash and teller department. He said yes. She advised him that he seemed to have the skills to do well in customer service and should try that unit if he was leaving marketing rather than go to the cash and teller. She did not mind that losing one staff from marketing might affect productivity; she took to heart A's interests in a way that made him feel cared for and ready to care in turn for the organization and his colleagues.

Empathy

B had a boss who always noticed that something was wrong even before the person concerned spoke up. Once, B had lost a loved one the previous weekend and so was not able to submit her call reports for the previous week. She was expecting a query and instead the manager walked up and asked her what was wrong.

Assistance

B's manager then helped with her tasks for the day and also counseled her through the problem. Before the end of that day, she was more cheerful and by the next day she was more than ready to take up her responsibilities with even more commitment.

In sum, experiences of caring, empathy,[25] and assistance reaffirm the level of altruism in the organization and thereby create a supporting environment for employees to also act ethically and other-interestedly toward their colleagues and toward the organization. This automatically reinforces the capacity for integrity in the organization.

Cultural Inhibitors of Individual Ethical Action and Commitment to the Organization

Biases

C's boss seemed to operate on the assumption that some people had nothing to offer and he treated them thus. In reaction to this differential treatment, cliques formed within the company. Those who felt marginalized never saw the point of trying to give their best since they felt it would not be appreciated anyway. Team spirit was affected and eventually business was also.

Hostility

D spent 6 months in an industrial training program at a real-estate firm in Lagos. One of his key responsibilities was to supervise maintenance and repairs carried out on the facilities at CBN marina branch. He worked with a team of seven in-house technicians and with some contractors. His major challenge was to get some of the in-house technicians to be focused and stay committed to their jobs. Most of them had personal jobs outside the office because salary payments were usually delayed and could even be outstanding for months.

D's supervisor, the facilities manager, was perceived by other staff to be arrogant and wicked because he hardly smiled and they felt that, for him, everything was all about work. No matter what happened, the job had to be done. The management felt that this was the only way to gain employees' respect and make them do their jobs. This approach led to a communication gap between staff and management. Because D felt bad about this treatment they were getting, he could not bring himself to report to the management that the technicians had other jobs, contrary to their employment contracts. The culture was one of not caring about others and it eventually affected even the young man who had come to stay only six months in the company.

Indifference and Disregard

A technician at the power house of the company deliberately left the generator running on a little amount of diesel until it stopped working. As a result, the client, an important one, had no power for about 45 minutes and this really caused a problem in the facilities department. The technician, who was known to be very dedicated to his job, later confessed to D that it was a deliberate act. He said that he had often made sacrifices to make sure that there was always power. He would leave the office late just to make sure everything was in order for the next day but he got nothing in return. Rather, he got complaints and was once accused of stealing diesel. So he decided that he was not going to order as usual for reserve diesel since people did not respect him. His reaction to the disrespectful culture was to treat people the way he felt he was being treated.

Disrespect

E worked in a school that was reputed to be the best and oldest school in a local government in northern Nigeria. The owner was Madame F.

The school was preparing for its 25th anniversary but the owner found it difficult to mobilize her staff to take ownership of the event. The school was characterized by meetings where superiors shouted at subordinates and, though ideas were solicited, they were often dismissed as "dumb" and never adopted. Therefore, a lack of enthusiasm for the job was common to staff. This affected the outcome of the event. The next days were filled with more recrimination, tongue lashing, and finger pointing. E got the distinct impression that there was an urgent need for a change in the school's culture to one that communicates to staff their worth, in order to get the kind of initiative that could move the business forward, and he understood that manifestations of disrespect and aggressiveness would have to be totally eliminated for this to happen. He himself could not wait to get a new job. He had realized he had also begun to raise his voice unnecessarily from time to time, especially at the students.

Biases, outright hostility, disrespect, indifference, and disregard are examples of experiences on inconsiderate treatment that make employees unhappy with the workplace and because they reflect a high level of egoism and provoke employees to look out primarily or solely for their own self interest, they are likely to undermine the integrity in the organization.

Conclusion

In two of the three caselets discussed, different employees were influenced by circumstances within the organization to behave in ways that were unethical or at the very least counterproductive[26] and therefore unhelpful to the organization and damaging to its integrity.[27] The third caselet drives home the insight that in each of the three situations, an experience of other-regarding behavior as the norm in the organization would have led the employee to imitate it and be considerate of the organization and fellow workers in taking personal and professional decisions. It is important that those in leadership positions display integrity[28] and act ethically toward other employees,[29] that the policies and codes reflect these values, and that the reward system is aligned with them.[30] This is how the signal is sent to employees as to the organization's expectations of corresponding integrity and ethical action, both of which ordinarily entail considerateness.

Thus, any organization that wishes to improve the practice of integrity and ethics among its employees would do well to look closely at the experience the employees get from the way they are treated themselves in the workplace. The more they experience selfless treatment, the more they themselves will be inclined to be selfless in their service to the company and to other stakeholders.[31] Examples of what employees consider considerate treatment include the enablers above—assistance, care, and empathy. The opposite treatment is also exemplified above—bias, disregard, disrespect, hostility, and indifference. The first three fit within a selfless culture that can be the solid foundation for organizational integrity while the other five fit within a culture that promotes self-interest.

It is clear in all three caselets that having an other-regarding culture is also the way that better promotes the profitability of the organization, both, because it reduces unethical or deviant behavior and its possible costs to the organization[32] and also because it promotes altruism and therefore a more successful organization[33] which in turn would then have a more positive impact on society. And, in the final analysis, for an organization to be said to have integrity, it should be that kind of organization that promotes and fosters ethical and other-regarding behavior by the people who work in it.

Key Terms

Integrity—unwavering adherence to moral or ethical values; honesty.

Considerateness—a habitual disposition to thoughtfulness and active attention to others' feelings and needs.

Organizational culture—the underlying and intangible ethos of an organization, comprising values, beliefs, principles, and so forth, and reflected in the way its people judge situations, take decisions, and act. It is passed on almost unconsciously to every newcomer to the organization.

Organizational climate—the observable and tangible characteristics of an organization—its structures, policies, procedures, and practices; for example, reward systems, which influence the way its employees act. It is to an extent easily perceived by the employees or by parties interested though more external to the organization.

Ethical culture—the extent to which the organizational culture supports behavior that is in line with moral or ethical values.

Ethical climate—the extent to which the organization's climate facilitates or obstructs ethical behavior.

Study Questions

1. What would you describe as a nonenabling environment? How could an organization communicate to its people in a practical way that integrity is a core value in the organization?
2. Is there a relationship between selflessness and virtuousness; other-regarding behavior and ethical behavior; considerateness and integrity? Please give reasons for your answer and illustrate it with practical examples.
3. Identify and discuss the inhibitors and enablers of ethical behavior in any organization to which you currently belong.
4. In your experience, what kind of behaviors would an employee expect to observe around him when working in an organization which states that integrity is one of its core values?

Further Reading

Elegido, J. M. (1996, Reprinted 2002–2004). *Fundamentals of business ethics: A developing country perspective*. LBS Management Series.

Elegido, J. M. (2003). *Business ethics in the Christian tradition*. LBS Management Series.

Melé, D. (2003). Organizational humanizing cultures: Do they generate social capital? *Journal of Business Ethics 45*(1), 3–14.

Melé, D. (2009) *Business ethics in action: Seeking excellence in organizations*. London, UK: Palgrave Macmillan.

Melé, D. (2012). *Management ethics*. London, UK: Palgrave Macmillan.

Ogunyemi, K. (2011). The importance of a culture of considerateness for business performance. *Business & Management Journal 1*(2), 72–82.

CHAPTER 3

Whistleblowing in Poland

To Blow or Not to Blow the Whistle, That Is the Question

Agata Stachowicz-Stanusch

Introduction

Although the term *whistleblowing* has been known since the Middle Ages, recent economic crises and corruption scandals that resulted in the collapse of such giants as Enron, WorldCom, and Tyco have caused a reexamination of this concept in both scientific research and managerial practice.

Despite the fact that in the 1980s extensive research was conducted on this phenomenon,[1] recent years are replete with research from across the world that focuses on the essence and effectiveness of this mechanism. The ACFE's *2012 Report to the Nations on Occupational Fraud and Abuse* states that 43.3% of abuses are revealed through tips—information from employees (50.9%), customers (22.1%), and anonymous persons (12.4%). Much more effective tools of abuse detection include the managerial supervision/review (14.6%) and internal audit (14.4%).[2] Thus, whistleblowing is a tool for abuse detection regardless of the region or organization's size. In organizations that use hotline solutions, abuses are detected by tips even more often in 50.9% of cases. Moreover, their implementation results in the increase of abuse detection effectiveness by the internal audit function (16.3% vs. 12.8%).[3] In total, whistleblowers helped to detect nearly one-fourth of analyzed cases of abuse.

In North America, 96% of companies using whistleblowing systems recognize them as effective. In Europe, it is 78% of companies, in Africa 74%, and the global result is that 81% companies perceive this mechanism as the effective one. What seems to be especially important is the fact that, according to the research conducted in the United States, corporations that use whistleblowing systems receive sevenfold return on capital invested in these systems.[4] Lawsuits involving whistleblowers are also effective, and the costs of investigations bring of the thirteen times higher return.[5] The research also confirms that the most popular anticorruption practice among the companies from Global Fortune 500 (2008 Index) is whistleblowing,[6] which in fact can benefit a company in terms of productivity and corporate growth by inhibiting internal corruption.[7] Unfortunately in Poland, those statistics are not so optimistic, as revealed through comparison results for Poland presented by Piotr Hans in his blog.[8]

But what is whistleblowing, and what are its characteristics?

1. Definition and Types of Whistleblowing

The whistleblowing phenomenon is being discussed and considered in research of both legal and social sciences representatives. One of the most popular definitions that is often used in research[9] describes whistleblowing as "the disclosure by organization members (former or current) of illegal, immoral, or illegitimate practices under the control of their employers, to persons or organizations that may be able to effect action."[10] On the other hand, on the websites of Transparency International (TI) we can find the following definition: "The disclosure of information about a perceived wrongdoing in an organization, or the risk thereof, to individuals or entities believed to be able to effect action."[11]

In the literature of the subject we can find whistleblowing classified into *autonomous whistleblowing* and *legally backed whistleblowing*. The first one refers to the human nature and is treated as an autogenous and independent social phenomenon. It is a spontaneous disclosure of irregularities, not only when they affect the safety of the employee but also when they threaten the wider social environment.[12]

Practical experiences confirm the thesis that early disclosure of irregularities enables a business to identify and eliminate the problem, prevent harm or minimize damages that have already occurred, and diagnose not only abuses but also other problems occurring in a company.[13] Those findings became an inspiration for the concept of enhancing whistleblowers' attitudes in companies by[14]

- application of the appropriate law;
- application of stimulus such as rewards for whistleblowers—at least balancing the negative effects (like retaliation, infamy, etc.) of such a decision;
- creation of infrastructure that enables someone to inform about irregularities to corporate governance entities in an efficient and unambiguous way.

Legally backed whistleblowing exists if an infrastructure enables a person to inform about irregularities in an efficient way and verify this information while supporting that person in a possible lawsuit.[15] As in the case of some managerial practices, we should be aware of the fact that existing legal provisions, as well as certain social instruments, are not perfect, and people who act in good faith and care for common goodness by revealing the irregularities or unethical behaviors can be exposed to mob mentality, loss of employment, or professional exclusions.[16]

Another criterion for whistleblowing classification was inspired by the United Kingdom within the Public Interest Disclosure Act. Based on this document, we may categorize whistleblowing into *internal disclosure*, *external disclosure*, and *public disclosure*. If irregularities are revealed inside an organization and discussed only within it, that is an internal whistleblowing. When suspicious irregularities are reported by an organization's member outside the organization (to the appropriate entities) while omitting the appropriate persons or units of his or her own organization, that is an external whistleblowing. Public whistleblowing occurs when both the employer and the appropriate entities of supervision have been deliberately omitted and the problem of observed irregularities is presented to the mass media, for example, in order to disseminate this information broadly and to attract public attention.[17]

2. Whistleblowing as the Tool of Fight with Irregularities (Unethical Behaviors) in Poland

In Poland, the phenomenon of whistleblowing is not as well known, and is applied less frequently than in other countries. It is not connected with a lower rate of abuses occurring in Poland. It is quite the opposite. Similar to other countries, representatives of executive managers and employees of Polish companies are perpetrators of numerous frauds.[18] The most common frauds are employee embezzlement (theft) (35%), unwarranted purchases (33%), private purchases with company's money (20%), unwarranted use of computers (18%), bribery (18%), conflict of interest (18%), information theft (16%), invoice falsification (15%), and nepotism occurring during the recruitment process.[19] In public opinion, the most popular crimes against companies committed by managers are use of companies' assets (cars, phones, etc.) for private purposes (38%), falsifying private travel as business trips (30%), making payments for unnecessary or fictitious services (29%), bribery (28%), and nepotism (25%).[20] The above findings prove that there are many aspects that should be controlled and reported.

The limited application of whistleblowing in Poland can be seen throughout history. There is a particular mentality in Poland of tolerance for known irregularities. Despite the fact that anonymous reports are commonplace acts, they are primarily associated with malice or a willingness to hurt somebody. Actions defined as whistleblowing are automatically referred to as condemned practices of collaboration with the secret services of occupiers, SB (Security Service of the Ministry of Internal Affairs), and the political apparatus of the PRL (People's Republic of Poland).[21] The term *whistleblower* is disparaged as "ratfink, eavesdropper, sneak, or secret service collaborator." With this negative association of a person and the activity connected with whistleblowing that is rooted in the history of Poland, they are not an isolated case. In fact, history is replete with the selfsame bias against whistleblowing throughout the world:[22]

- In China, whistleblowing through such means as corporate hotlines can have ominous overtones of the worst of the Cultural Revolution, when children were encouraged to report "illegal activities" their parents might be conducting, students were encouraged to report on their teachers, and neighbors were to report other neighbors, forming a web of suspicion throughout the country.

- In Germany, anonymous whistleblowing most obviously brings to mind brutal Gestapo tactics used during WWII and the infiltration techniques and execution tactics of the Stasi in the former East Germany.
- In South Africa, whistleblowers called *impimpis,* apartheid-era informants, could be put to death in public.

It should be noticed that in other countries with more grounded democracy and with different social attitudes, a whistleblower is treated with greater respect, sometimes even like a hero.[23] For instance, *Time* magazine selected three whistleblowers in 2002 as their "Persons of the Year": Cynthia Cooper of WorldCom, Coleen Rowley of the FBI, and Sherron Watkins of Enron.[24] Despite results presented in a report by the PwC, "Global Economic Crime Survey 2011,"[25] that there has been a decrease of whistleblowing effectiveness as a tool for abuse detection, there is an undeniable fact that whistleblowers have helped in detecting nearly one-fourth of the cases of analyzed abuses. Unfortunately, statistics for Poland are much worse than what is confirmed by comparative results with other countries. According to the "Global Economic Crime Survey 2011," organizations may use the following methods to find out if a fraud has been committed:[26]

- "Corporate controls" including internal auditing, fraud risk management, electronic and automated suspicious transaction monitoring, corporate security, and transferring people
- "Corporate culture" including internal tip-offs, external tip-offs, and whistleblowing
- "Beyond the influence of management"—finding out by accident or through the media, for example.

Figure 3.1 presents the popularity of those methods among companies participating in research conducted by PwC in 2011 and among Polish companies.

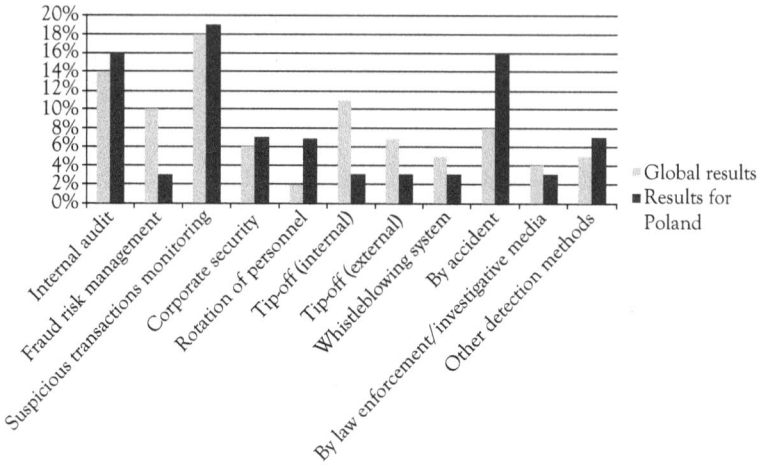

Figure 3.1. *Detection methods in 2011—comparison.*[27]

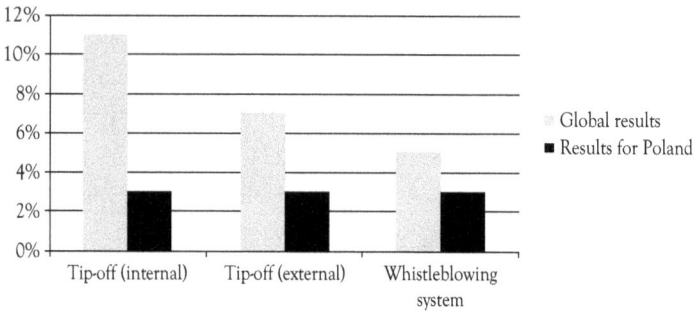

Figure 3.2. *Popularity of corporate culture in detecting economic crime in 2011—comparison.*[28]

When we focus on the popularity of particular elements constituting the segment of "corporate culture," namely internal tip-offs, external tips-offs, and whistleblowing, the difference between their use by Polish companies and by organizations analyzed by PwC is highly significant. Figure 3.2 illustrates the difference.

As noted by Piotr Hans, the comments of PwC representatives for the Onet.pl portal as well as on websites of PwC Polska leave no illusions about the Polish specificity. Dariusz Cypner emphasizes that, according to the report, there is a lack of effective mechanisms for detection of economic crimes in Poland, and most of the abuses are detected by accident. There are no ethics hotlines in Polish companies that can be used for anonymous reporting to executives about observed abuses. Another report finds that 16% of Polish companies—twice as much as in other countries—find out about the committed crime accidentally. Fifty-two percent of crimes were detected through controlling mechanisms in companies, but only 3% from people from the outside of organization's structure who were cooperating with another relevant group, such as suppliers or customers.[29]

Those results confirm the previous information noted by Rogowski in his paper. The findings of survey research of members of the boards and supervisory boards of the biggest Polish companies state that in about two-thirds of the companies there do not exist any procedures enabling employees or other stakeholders to offer early anonymous warnings by reporting any irregularities to corporate governance entities.

Is the lack of popularity of whistleblowing mechanisms in Poland and Poles' attitude to these mechanisms a result of historical experiences, or is it caused by mistakes made during its implementation, low citizens' awareness of such mechanisms, or fear of inadequate protection of the whistleblower? It seems that we should seek those causes in each of the mentioned phenomena.

3. The Value of Courage and the Cost of Silence; Examples of Whistle-blowers from Poland

The legal protection of denunciators differs across the world. In the United Kingdom, the Public Interest Disclosure Act from 1998 about disclosure for the public interest protects denunciators from retaliation and job dismissal. In the United States, the LaFollette Act from 1912 was the first act of particular whistleblowers' protection. This gave federal employees the right to provide information directly to the United States Congress. Currently in the United States, many laws at both state and federal levels exist that protect whistleblowers. The most important are still actualized Whistleblower Protection Act from 2007 and Sarbanes–Oxley Act from 2002.[30]

On the websites of Against Corruption Program (Program Przeciwko Korupcji) that runs under the Stefan Batory Foundation, we may read that whistleblowers in some countries, especially in

Anglo-Saxon countries, are covered by legal protection separate from the general rules of law. In Poland, whistleblowers do not have any protection (in case of civil law agreements) nor may try to assert their claim in accordance with the code of labor. However, as there is no particular reference to whistleblowers (no specificity for this mechanism), it does not provide them with sufficient protection. The Stefan Batory Foundation in 2010 conducted research among judges of labor courts in Poland. It was aimed at gathering opinions on the effectiveness of labor law solutions for protecting the employees who revealed irregularities in good faith in their organizations. The final findings confirm that opinions collected in the survey research force us to question if the Polish legislator achieved the objective recommended by the European Council to create legal conditions that truly protect a person who knows about irregularities and is not afraid of their disclosure.[31]

Without an effective legal system that protects a person who reports irregularities in a particular organization's performance, the whistleblower is always exposed to bearing the costs connected with a decision to inform a particular entity about those irregularities. Such a person is exposed to mobbing, professional exclusion, job dismissal, and ostracism. The person is perceived as a pariah who "fouls his/her own nest."[32] The price of such a decision is not typical just for Polish citizens. Many laws, including the Sarbanes–Oxley Act in the United States, the Public Interest Disclosure Act in the United Kingdom, and laws in other countries deliver protection for whistleblowers. Despite such legislation, many international employees fear repercussions.[33]

A decision to disclose irregularities has its consequences, but hiding in silence also has its cost. The price occurs in such forms as frustration, specific "moral hangover," questioning one's axiological attitudes, or a specific moral discomfort. We should remember that the fundamental characteristic of a human being is goodness. Goodness is what elevates us from animals. Moreover, disclosure of unethical and immoral behavior and opposition to them is specific to human nature. The renunciation of unethical behavior disclosure results in our participation in unethical dealings. Recent research conducted in Poland informs that among many professional groups 52% declare that they would not disclose any information. Nineteen percent of this number would be constrained by the threat of job dismissal, 14% by the lack of appropriate legal protection, and 19% by the lack of belief in the effectiveness of police and courts.[34]

Despite the constraints of the legal system in Poland and despite the negative association with the term "whistleblower," there are many examples of people who act in good faith, for morality, and for higher values of protection against all odds.

For instance, *Rzeczpospolita* magazine described the case of Leszek G., a 34-year-old miner who, in 2009, used a camera to record the practice of falsification of the measurements of methane concentration.[35] He collected proof of law violations in a Wujek-Śląsk mine in which 21 of his colleagues died. As a result, he became redundant (earlier he was forced to perform physically demanding tasks after he refused to falsify methane concentration measurements).

Another example is a Warrant Officer Dariusz Warchocki from the 56th Regiment of Combat Helicopters, who revealed that there were irregularities in training and document falsification. Finally, he decided to leave the army. In the period of notice, his supervisor prohibited him to fly and deprived him of extras to his salary.[36]

Dąbrowski gives the following examples of Polish denunciators:[37]

- Bożena Łopacka, a former manager of "Biedronka" shop (Jeronimo Martins), revealed a practice of falsifying work-time records and forcing employees to perform work that was not in the scope of their duties. It resulted in prosecution of the company as well as a lawsuit that went on for very long time.
- Tadeusz Pasierbiński, gynecologist and obstetrician, who currently works in a small medical facility in Silesia, decided to disclose corrupt practices that occurred in a hospital he used to work at. He was punished by his supervisors with numerous disciplinary sanctions. In addition, he was sued in medical court and lost his tied accommodation. After dismissal, he fought for reinstatement in his profession, fortunately with a positive result.[38]

Conclusion

Economic crises of recent years and numerous corruption scandals across the world severely damaged social trust in corporations and their leaders. The business world should not forget that according to Aristotle's Nicomechaen Ethics, the purpose of a business activity is to ultimately make a manager a better person and make the world a better place.[39] From an Aristotelian point of view, it is possible to simultaneously create wealth, be ethical, and be happy too.[40]

We should also remember that capitalism is not fundamentally an immoral and selfish system. It has been and may continue to be a flourishing economic system provided that people abide by the rules. What rules? Famed Scottish economist Adam Smith states them as follows: "Tell the truth. Keep your promises. Be responsible for your actions. Treat other as you would like to be treated—with compassion and forgiveness."[41] And be wise.

Implementation of whistleblowing mechanisms in organizations is a small step that should be taken toward the creation of a formal ethical infrastructure. Recommendations may be formulated to make whistleblowing a more effective mechanism for abuse detection. Such recommendations will be focused on making whistleblowing available via the Internet (including e-mail), keeping such activity confidential and protective for whistleblowers, available 7 days a week, 24 hours a day. Whistleblowers should be provided with the opportunity to report in their local language, ensuring anonymity. These choices should be provided by an independent organization, specifying inappropriate behaviors to be reported, providing feedback for whistleblower, and offering the possibility for whistleblowing by suppliers/customers.

However, even if an organization built this into its internal infrastructure, it would not be enough to ensure its integrity. An organization does not work in a vacuum. It requires an appropriate legal system that can effectively protect whistleblowers. In cooperation with numerous organizations, TI has prepared draft principles for whistleblowing legislation that examine existing legislation and provide a solid paradigm for international, regional, and local utilization.[42]

The formal ethical infrastructure as well as its external mechanism, however, cannot protect a company from wrongdoing. Each regulation, formal system, and knowledge base has its limitations. Within the process of ethical and moral decision making (behaviors of both an individual and an organization), there is only a human being with his or her knowledge experience, character, value system, moral, and social intelligence.[43] That is why, as noted by Wankel and Stachowicz-Stanusch, the education for integrity is also necessary.[44] This "lesson in integrity" manifests itself in structuring a moral framework applicable from the microstructures of individual job teams to the macrostructures of international business. In all cases, human beings need to be grounded in integrity, ethics, and high moral standards. They must identify corruption at all levels and choose not to live with it. It is incumbent upon business and educational systems to develop sound theoretical programs made real and practical with case studies, behavioral modeling, introspection, and analysis that harkens back to the Socratic method of inquiry, keeping a constant eye toward the greater good of humanity itself.[45]

The author hopes that a combination of education for integrity, the internal ethical infrastructure of organization, and effective and good laws will result in a situation whereby righteous citizens acting in righteous organizations and in a righteous environment make the world a better place for them and for their descendants.

Key Terms

Whistleblowing—the disclosure by organization members (former or current) of illegal, immoral, or illegitimate practices under the control of their employers, to persons or organizations that may be able to effect action.[46]

Whistleblowing—the disclosure of information about a perceived wrongdoing in an organization, or the risk thereof, to individuals or entities believed to be able to effect action (TI).

Autonomous whistleblowing—autogenous and independent social phenomenon; a spontaneous disclosure of irregularities, particularly when they affect the safety of the employee, but also when they threaten wider social environment.

Legal-backed whistleblowing—the phenomenon occurring if there exists an infrastructure that enables to inform about irregularities in an efficient way, as well as to verify this information and support in possible lawsuit.

Internal whistleblowing—a situation occurring if the irregularities are revealed inside an organization and discussed only within it.

External whistleblowing—a situation whereby the suspicion of irregularities are reported by an organization's member outside the organization (to the appropriate entities) while omitting the appropriate persons or units of his or her own organization.

Public whistleblowing—a situation when both the employer as well as the appropriate entities of supervision have been deliberately omitted and the problem of observed irregularities was presented to, for instance mass media, in order to disseminate this information broadly and to attract a particular attention.

Study Questions

1. What activity, despite the historical circumstances of a specific community, may influence the popularity and effectiveness of whistleblowing mechanisms in a particular community or nation?
2. What influence does a national culture have on the effectiveness and application of whistleblowing in a particular community?
3. What actions may be taken by an organization in order to increase the whistleblowing effectiveness?
4. How may an organization protect itself from the "black" whistleblowing?

Further Reading

Alford, C. F. (2001). *Whistleblowers: Broken lives and organizational power*. Ithaca, NY: Cornell University Press.

Bowers, J., Fodder, M., Lewis, J., Mitchell, J. (2012). *Whistleblowing: Law and practice* (2nd edition). New York, NY: Oxford University Press.

Cooper, C. (2008). *Extraordinary circumstances: The journey of a corporate whistleblower*. Hoboken, NJ: John Wiley & Sons.

Deloitte, Polski Instytut Dyrektorów, Rzeczpospolita. (2007). Współczesna rada nadzorcza 2007, raport z badań, s. 16. Available at: http://www.deloitte. com/assets/Dcom-Poland/Local%20Assets/Documents/Raporty,%20 badania,%20rankingi/pl_WspolczesnaRadaNadzorcza_2007.pdf.

Devine, T., & Maassarani, T. F. (2011). *The corporate whistleblower's survival guide: A handbook for committing the truth.* San Francisco, CA: Berrett-Koehler Publishers.

Freedman, W. (1994). *Internal company investigations and the employment relationship.* Westport, CT: Quorum Books.

Greenberg, M. D. (2011). *For whom the whistle blows: Advancing corporate compliance and integrity efforts in the era of Dodd-Frank* (Conference Proceedings). Santa Monica, CA: Rand Corporation.

Johnson, R. A. (2002). *Whistleblowing: When it works-And why.* Boulder, CO: Lynne Rienner Pub.

Kohn, S. M. (2011). *The whistleblower's handbook: A step-by-step guide to doing what's right and protecting yourself.* United States of America: Lyons Press.

Kohn, S. M., Kohn, M. D. & Colapinto, D.K. (2004). *Whistleblower law: A guide to legal protections for corporate employees.* Westport, CT: Praeger.

Lipman, F. D. (2011). *Whistleblowers: Incentives, disincentives, and protection strategies.* Hoboken, NJ: John Wiley & Sons.

Miethe, T. (1998). *Whistleblowing at work: Tough choices in exposing fraud, waste, and abuse on the job.* United States of America: Westview Press.

Near, J.P., Rehg, M.T., Scotter, J.R. & Miceli, M.P. (2004). Does type of wrongdoing affect the whistleblowing process? *Business Ethics Quarterly, 14*(2), 219–242.

Westin, A. F. (1981). *Whistle-blowing! Loyalty and dissent in the corporation.* New York: McGraw-Hill.

Whannel, G. (2008). *Culture, politics and sport: Blowing the whistle,* Revisited. New York, NY: Routledge.

CHAPTER 4

Integrity and Anticorruption Actions in an Organizational Context

Peter Odrakiewicz

Introduction

This chapter seeks to discuss integrity and anticorruption actions in an organizational context, and suggesting innovative methods of integrity and corruption—prevention management in diverse organizations. It is an opening and invitation to further exploration for finding better ways of integrity competences in organizations of acquisition and management, in addition to building corruption-preventative contexts with the aim of constructing corruption-free organizations that benefit their owners, shareholders, and community stakeholders.

How can we define integrity, and integrity in an organizational context? In fact, there is no simple explanation to this term. Organizations can understand it differently. Integrity can be defined as a philosophy of consistency of actions, values, methods, organizational principles, expectations, and results. Integrity, as defined in the 2007 edition of the Merriam-Webster dictionary, is a "firm adherence to a code of especially moral or artistic values (incorruptibility), an unimpaired condition (soundness), and the quality or state of being complete or undivided (completeness)."[1] Types of integrity include integrity of character and professional integrity.

Aristotle said: "Men acquire a particular quality by constantly acting in a particular way." One of the keys to maintaining integrity is the ability to act not in one's own interest but in the interest of others. Integrity is not something you are born with. It is something you learn and strengthen over time. It is a conscious choice you make that you have total control over.[2] Integrity is one of the most important and often-cited terms of virtue. To put it in plain managerial words, integrity can be defined as the formal relation to one's self and in an organizational context, it always has something to do with acting morally. In an organizational context we should examine the integrity principle of consistency. Is it possible to evaluate the manager's behavior in the organizational context on the basis of a body of his or her integrity standards? The principle of integrity could provide us with ideas on how to solve these problems.

Integrity issues in organizations are closely related to the notion of ethics. The practical goal of integrity issues is to solve the problem of how to select the best decision in an organizational context in an ethically difficult business context. The main known tools for application of the principles of business ethics are principles and codes of ethics. The implementation of various concepts and ethics programs, for example Corporate Social Responsibility (CSR), is not sufficient to maintain integrity in an organizational context.

Integrity issues are becoming increasingly important due to the internal business benefits and efficiency in searching for new customers, cooperating firms, and partners. It can be foreseen that issues of integrity in an organizational context are going to become increasingly important in the next few years. This is primarily caused by the crisis facing both organizations and sovereign states—mostly debt-ridden states—where organizations operate and there is reduced confidence in many companies caused by recent financial and socioeconomic crises.

Impediments to integrity skills acquisition in organizational contexts can be the result of the following: poor integrity management, a lack of consultation with employees and owners or their representatives, and CEOs or company directors who knowingly or unknowingly perpetrate a toxic management environment as they aim to implement a "bottom line profit" philosophy at all cost. Lack of knowledge and integrity competence transfer delivery in organizational settings can result in people delaying or refusing to communicate a philosophy of integrity in the managerial process. The personal attitudes of individual employees, which may be due to lack of motivation or dissatisfaction at work, can lead to corrupt practices in situations of insufficient or inappropriate integrity and anticorruption training in organizational contexts. Integrity, as defined in this chapter, suggests a person whose self is sound, undivided, and complete.

According to Wankel and Stachowicz-Stanusch, recent examples of "corporate, national and international ethical and financial scandals and crises have created a need to bolster the ethical acumen of managers through business education imperatives."[3] Their book, *Management Education for Integrity*, explains how curricula should be streamlined and rejuvenated to ensure a high level of integrity in management education, providing numerous examples of new tools, teaching methods, integrity sensitization and development exercises, and ethical management education assessment approaches. They suggest fostering integrity in business curricula, a critique of ethics education in management, measuring best practices in management education for integrity capacity, encouraging moral engagement in business ethics courses, management education for behavioral integrity, and a scenario-based approach as a teaching tool to promote integrity awareness.[4]

Corruption and Anticorruption

The Asian Development Bank (ADB), describing the term corruption, uses it as a shorthand reference for a large range of illicit or illegal activities. Although there is no universal or comprehensive definition as to what constitutes corrupt behavior, the most prominent definitions share a common emphasis upon the abuse of public power or position for personal advantage. *The Oxford Unabridged Dictionary* defines corruption as perversion or destruction of integrity, in the discharge of public duties, by bribery or favor. The *Merriam Webster's Collegiate Dictionary* defines it as inducement to wrong by improper or unlawful means (as bribery). The succinct definition utilized by the World Bank is the abuse of public office for private gain. This definition is similar to that employed by Transparency International (TI), the leading NGO in the global anticorruption effort:

Corruption involves behavior on the part of officials in the public sector, whether politicians or civil servants, in which they improperly and unlawfully enrich themselves, or those close to them, by the misuse of the public power entrusted to them.[5] The author concurs with the ADB judgment that these definitions do not give adequate attention to the problem of corruption in the private sector or to the role of the private sector in fostering corruption in the public sector. As a shorthand definition, ADB defines corruption as the abuse of public or private office for personal gain. A more comprehensive definition is available on ADB's website.[6]

Corruption involves behavior on the part of officials in the public and private sectors, in which they improperly and unlawfully enrich themselves, those close to them, or both, or induce others to do so by misusing the position in which they are placed. Some types of corruption are internal in that they interfere with the ability of a government agency to recruit or manage its staff, make efficient use of its resources, or conduct impartial in-house investigations. Others are external in that they involve efforts to manipulate or extort money from clients or suppliers, or to benefit from inside information. Still, others involve unwarranted interference in market operations, such as the use of state power to artificially restrict competition and generate monopoly rents. More narrow definitions of corruption are often necessary to address particular types of illicit behavior. In the area of procurement fraud, for example, the World Bank defines corrupt practice as the offering, giving, receiving, or soliciting of anything of value to influence the action of a public official in the procurement process or in contract execution.[7]

Concurring further with the ADB sources, it is often useful to differentiate between grand corruption—which typically involves senior officials, major decisions or contracts, and the exchange of large sums of money—and petty corruption, which involves low-level officials, the provision of routine services and goods, and small sums of money. It is also useful to differentiate between systemic corruption, which permeates an entire government or ministry, and individual corruption, which is more isolated and sporadic. Finally, it is useful to distinguish between syndicated corruption, in which elaborate systems are devised for receiving and disseminating bribes, and nonsyndicated corruption, in which individual officials may seek or compete for bribes in an ad hoc and uncoordinated fashion.

Concurring with Wankel's and Stachowicz-Stanusch's claim over the last decade, "we have been witnessing a dramatic contrast between the CEO as a superhero and CEO as an antihero. The new challenge in business education is to develop responsible global leaders." Relatively little is known, however, about how management educators can prepare future leaders to cope effectively with the challenge of leading with integrity in a multicultural space. Their recent volume *Handbook of Research on Teaching Ethics in Business and Management Education* is authored by a spectrum of international experts with diverse backgrounds and perspectives. It suggests directions that business educators might take to reorient higher education to transcend merely equipping people and organizations to greedily pursue their materialistic gains, gains which may have dire effects on the preponderance of people, nations, our planet, and the future. Their book is a collection of ideas and concrete solutions with regard to how morality should be taught in a global economy. In the first part, the editors present reasons why management education for integrity makes up an important challenge in an intercultural environment. This contribution is an overview of a spectrum of approaches to developing moral character in business students in this epoch of dynamic technologies and globalization.[8]

There is an enormous role for all types of international organizations in integrity support. Additionally, there is an undisputed role for these organizations in the process of supporting business anticorruption activities. According to the UN Global Compact conference on anticorruption in 2008, representatives of international businesses met in Bali on January 30, 2008 for a special meeting entitled *Business Coalition: The United Nations Convention Against Corruption as a New Market Force*. The meeting was held on the occasion of the Second Conference of State Parties to the United Nations Convention Against Corruption (UNCAC). Business and nongovernmental organizations' representatives in Bali adopted a declaration calling on governments to establish effective anticorruption mechanisms to review the implementation of the UNCAC. This declaration forms an integral part of the report adopted by the Conference of States Parties, which forms the core of anticorruption policies.

Jointly organized by the United Nations Global Compact, United Nations Office on Drugs and Crime (UNODC), Organization for Economic Co-operation and Development (OECD), International Chamber of Commerce, World Economic Forum, Partnering Against Corrupt Initiative (PACI) and TI, the meeting underscored the commitment of the business community to the fight against corruption. It also provided an opportunity for the business community to express its views on the role that business can play to ensure the effective implementation of the Convention.

Participants discussed the need to work toward the alignment of existing business principles with the fundamental values enshrined in the Convention, and to develop mechanisms to review companies' compliance with the realigned business principles. They also agreed to include effective whistleblower protection, due diligence in the selection of agents and intermediaries, as well as to address facilitation payments, described as "one of the cardinal inconsistencies of existing business principles," in their anticorruption policies and strategies.[9]

Stachowicz-Stanusch points out that in management philosophy, corruption and its variants have been studied across a number of disciplines, including psychology, sociology, economics, law, political science, and of course management. The current discussion about corruption in organizational studies is one of the most growing, most fertile, and perhaps, most fascinating ones. Corruption is also a construct that is multilevel and can be understood as being created and supported by social and cultural interaction. As a result, an ongoing dialogue on corruption permeates the levels of analysis and numerous research domains in organizational studies. Thus, she sees a major opportunity and necessity to look at corruption from a multilevel and multicultural perspective. Second, in the global society of the world today where organizational boundaries are becoming increasingly transparent and during the Global Crisis, which has been rooted in the unethical and corrupt behavior of large corporations, a deeper understanding of corruption, its forms, typologies, ways to increase organizational immunity, and to utilize the best practices to fight against—as well as uncover—corruption are particularly significant. This means that individuals, groups, organizations, and whole societies can be used to sustain a sense of purpose, direction, and meaning, as well as to find the best process for creating a moral framework for ethical behavior in a world of flux. Stachowicz-Stanusch provides an authoritative and comprehensive overview of organizational corruption. She contributes an essential reference tool to carry out further research on corruption in organization. Her work uncovers new theoretical insights that will inspire new questions about corruption in organization; it also changes our understanding of the phenomenon and encourages further exploration and research.[10]

Impediments to Integrity Promulgation and Anticorruption Practice

There is a multitude of impediments to acquiring integrity skills and to the application of anticorruption practices in organizational contexts. These impediments can result from poor integrity management, a lack of consultation and communication with employees, or a toxic management environment often unknowingly perpetrated by owners who implement a "bottom line profit" philosophy with the silent approval of corruptive practices. Impediments to communicating integrity standards and practices can be found in individual attitudes; for example, a refusal or unwillingness to communicate integrity philosophies because of personality conflicts, personal attitudes toward integrity and ethics, or a lack of motivation or dissatisfaction related to work. Sometimes, impediments beyond individual personalities may be the problem, such as language or cultural barriers,[11] or ineffective or inefficient channels of communication which are needed for the implementation of integrity management training and guidance. Awareness of such impediments is the first step for educators and managers in acquiring the necessary tools for managing integrity and anticorruption approaches in an organizational context.

Integrity learning challenges us to face new experiences and enables us to develop a global mindset. Self-examination of values—personal, cultural, or organizational—can come from new experiences, from our leaving the safety of what we know and experiencing something new and different. A global mindset allows us to transcend the constraints of our experiences and belief systems and to see the world for what it really is. In order to approach the fast-paced global world, people need to work across disciplines and think holistically. Integrity and anticorruption education in organizations for an increasingly global frame of reference will require educators and managers to inculcate those in their charge with adaptability and flexibility, while balancing this with the tools of instilling ethical reasoning and a commitment to one's own individual moral equilibrium. The process of refining these emerging global integrity competencies will be accomplished through the use of E-learning, blended learning, social media, and personalized learning environments. The process of teaching integrity in education and management is by acquiring global integrity competence benefits from such procedures as videoconferencing and collaborative blog-based methodology.

Integrity, ethics, and anticorruption in management and management education are intertwined. Ethics is the foundation for codes of conduct. It is a branch of philosophy that addresses questions of morality. These questions can be answered by adhering to a set of behavioral guidelines. A workplace, being the source of bread and butter for many, can also satisfy people's self-actualization needs. Work often provides a *raison d'être* beyond the simple maintenance of a standard of living. Following ethical practices in the workplace is ultimately a personal choice. It is a choice that cannot be forced upon employees; it can only be explained and expected as a part of an overall integrity management strategy. A workplace is a cluster of individuals, and hence it is an amalgamation of attitudes and imaginations. This diversity can sometimes dilute the adherence to ethical standards of conduct. It takes the zeal of an evangelist to have the workforce imbibe ethics while facilitating the growth of the organization in a holistic way.[12] Having integrity is not a state in which one is debilitated by a strict adherence to a normative code; integrity is indivisible from the growth of both individuals and the organization.

Modern organizations today do focus mainly on profitmaking. There is, however, a new trend to resurrect integrity and ethics to the workplace. Various multinational corporations today have incorporated ethics and integrity training for all their employees, from those working at the junior level to the CEO. Their employees understand what ethics are and how they can benefit the company in the long run. Many organizations, both in the public and private sectors, have designed their own workplace ethics training programs. These programs offer practical solutions to employees facing ethical dilemmas. Despite these advances in corporate training, many employees lack business ethics awareness and knowledge about their role in integrity as an organizational philosophy. These programs focus on two core messages: first, ethical dilemmas are part of the world of work; and second, there are written policies and guidance on how to work through these ethical dilemmas which are available to employees. These resources give a contextualizing framework to the employees upon which they can make ethical decisions. A rewards system for ethics and values, alongside one's performance, is another way of ethics promotion among the employees, and is being employed by many organizations.

Organizations which promote integrity, values, and ethics have many advantages *vis-à-vis* other organizations. First, employees of organizations which emphasize ethical conduct experience less integrity-related stress, as they are less inclined to compromise their personal or organizational values. Secondly, in such organizations, misconduct is more often immediately reported to individual managers in the hierarchy responsible for resolving ethical misconduct issues. Thirdly, instances of misconduct are minimized and the overall level of employee satisfaction in such ethics-focused organizations is higher than in organizations without a similar emphasis. Ethical issues in the workplace can be resolved if proper procedures are in place. Upholding ethics promotes a better working environment, and at the same time, a good reputation for the business. Both of these contribute to higher work productivity and profits.[13]

The Role of Managers in Organizational Contexts

The terms *ethical* and *moral* are used in two ways. First the term *ethical* is used as a synonym for the moral quality of conduct. When, for example, we speak of people being "ethical" or "unethical," we often mean that they habitually or intentionally act or fail to act in "good faith," and that they consistently do, or fail to do, what is right. "Ethical" may also refer to a "class" of judgments pertaining to morality that is distinguishable from other classes such as factual, perceptual, and logical judgments; here the terms *ethical* and *moral* do not denote that which is unethical or immoral, but pertain to ethics or morality as opposed to that which is nonmoral or nonethical.[14]

The role of managers is to incorporate integrity and anticorruption training programs in organizational contexts into the modern communications arena using social media, such as LinkedIn, Facebook, and Twitter, real life case studies, work-study-internship examples, and blogs on integrity-related discussions. Additionally, managers and instructors can employ nonstandard approaches such as community visits to local companies with integrity-related and anticorruption-focused interviews that are carried out as a part of the training, and are later conducted during get-togethers and anticorruption integrity sessions. These interviews will in fact become organizational integrity teaching materials for real life, as interview videos, interview transcripts, and portions of analytical works, such as papers, reports, or studies.

Similarly, in European Union countries that accredit and license governmental and nonprofit agencies, students are required to study business ethics as a part of their academic curriculum, regardless of the type of degree, whether business, or management, or economics. However, the process is not very well-structured in many schools where business ethics courses are offered as electives only, and are not part of the overall integrity and ethics education program, or part of an institutionally organized instructional approach and educational philosophy.

It is highly recommended that groups of employees do one or more of the following: participate in integrity and anticorruption exercises or scenarios using role-playing or social media; create integrity and ethics discussion groups on line; conduct and record video interviews on the topic of integrity and ethics. All of these are active methods for employees to use in order to acquire a basic orientation toward and knowledge of issues related to integrity and anticorruption. Employees will get the feeling that they are part of the solution related to the challenges of integrity management. In the field of integrity in organizations, ethical policies are typically recognized as protecting individuals from ethnic and gender discrimination, sexual harassment, physical brutality, violations of confidentiality, nepotism, inhumane research, and other violations of civil and human rights. Policies addressing professional competence, such as the setting of standards for good teaching, tenure, and promotion, are not typically identified as pertaining to ethics. Both types of policies, however, typically pertain to morality in that both attempt to direct conduct toward what is "right" or conduct which is in keeping with policies pertaining to morality. Unfortunately, our tendency to restrict professional ethics to matters pertaining to the protection of civil and human rights, and to treat issues related to competence as nonethical, obscures significant professional, moral, and ethical problems and dilemmas.[15]

It is worth pointing out that without effective integrity and anticorruption training during college and university years many managers may be severely lacking in much-needed integrity and anticorruption competences.

Personal Values, Morals, and Workplace Ethics

As individuals are the instruments who carry the process of making ethical decisions, many factors influence this process. These may include things as far-removed as early childhood understanding of ethical behavior, through to the examples set by parents, teachers, and spiritual leaders, to the behavior of organizational leaders and formal organizational codes of conduct.

Even though most instances of ethical and integrity misconduct are motivated for positive business or corporate performance reasons (financial, productivity, efficiency, effectiveness, etc.), good people sometimes do bad things, believing that they are acting in the corporation's best interest. However, more evidence has come out in recent years indicating that many instances of executive misbehavior have been extremely costly to the firms or institutions with which such persons were affiliated.[16]

A substantial amount of the research related to culture and business ethics has been done by Geert Hofstede himself or by others using one or more of his cultural dimensions of cultures, that is, the concepts of power–distance, individualism versus collectivism, uncertainty avoidance, long-term versus short term orientation, and masculinity–femininity. These have been particular to different cultures. Such studies include ethical attitudes of business managers in India, Korea, and the United States, the effects of Hofstede's typologies on ethical decision making and on sales force performance, and many more.[17]

Integrity and Ethical Standards in the Workplace

Even though the issue of ethics has been discussed for centuries, it is only during the past couple of decades that the topic has come to prominence in business literature. Ethics theorists divide the field of ethics into three general categories: metaethics, normative ethics, and applied ethics. Applied ethics has become a staple of business education. The two other categories of ethics—metaethics, which ponders the likely sources of our ethical principles and their meaning, and normative ethics, which deals with the more practical task of attempting to arrive at moral standards that regulate right and wrong conduct—have largely been left underexplored by business researchers.[18]

Many organizations, public and private, suffer from a serious decline in integrity and ethical standards. According to Newman and Fuqua these declines are related to increased aggression and violence in the workplace, which are occurring with increased frequency.[19] Universities and colleges that fail to uphold high integrity and ethical standards in teaching, and that fail to ensure policies and procedures are also followed (as well as displayed and approved), in practice, may encounter the same problems.

Ethics Rationalizations and Managerial Positions in Workplace

Ethics rationalizations are a problem for those in managerial positions. In order to understand this problem, as part of education and training, or as an actual issue in the workplace, a situation and an explanation of its conditions are needed, such as this one:

Adopted from Gentile:[20]

"Jonathan has a new job. Just promoted from the accounting group at headquarters, he is now the controller for a regional sales unit of a consumer electronics company. He is excited about this step up and wants to build a good relationship with his new team. However, when the quarterly numbers come due, he realizes that the next quarter's sales are being reported early to boost bonus compensation. The group manager's silence suggests that this sort of thing has probably happened before. Having dealt with such distortion before, Jonathan is fully aware of its potential to cause major damage. But this is his first time working with people who are creating the problem instead of those who are trying to fix it. This may seem like a mundane accounting matter. But the consequences—in terms of carrying costs, distorted forecasting, compromised ethical culture and even legal ramifications—are very serious. And except in only the most extraordinarily well-run corporations, this kind of situation can arise easily. All managers should know how to respond constructively. Indeed, learning to do so is a key piece of their professional development. Senior managers must be able to change the cultural norms that give rise to bad judgment in the first place."

These challenges will arise frequently in modern organizations, and without proper integrity in organizational management, they can turn into company liabilities and long term problems.

Use of Case Studies in Integrity and Ethics Education and Training

The use of case studies is an established method of instructing integrity and anticorruption prevention. Case studies can either be textual or in video form. Experience has demonstrated that video learning materials are generally more effective. Regardless of the case study format, a review of the elements of the case study should be followed by employees' discussion and role-playing scenarios moderated by the instructor. Prepared material with suitable questions and presentations by groups of employees, with an integrity and anticorruption trainer acting as a facilitator of learning, may help in organizational context competences acquisition and integrity/anticorruption skills learning. The innovative methods of synchronous knowledge could be a good means of bringing more interaction into organizational managerial integrity training and competence acquisition, by increasing discussion and participation and by making learning integrity more interactive while educating workers and managers in an organizational context.

Ethics and Integrity in Managing a Global Workplace

Managing a global workplace with significant social, ethical, cultural, and infrastructural differences from one country to another is, and has always been, a major challenge for multinational companies.[21] The concept of a global business citizen is instructive. A global business citizen has been defined as "a business enterprise (and its managers) that responsibly exercises its rights and implements its duties to individuals, stakeholders and societies within and across national and cultural borders."[22] This extended conceptualization of corporate citizenship argues that responsible multinational companies are trying to wrestle in good faith with the challenges of globalization. Such a company is considered as "a global business citizen."[23]

Globalization brings a number of challenges for multinational companies. Most of these challenges are related to differences of social, cultural, ethical, and infrastructural issues from one country to another. From a universal principles perspective of corporate citizenship, multinational companies should think globally and act locally by applying basic ethical values everywhere they operate.[24]

There are elementary steps being taken to improve compliance with legal and ethical principles, especially in organizations, both public and private. Rule-driven approaches to compliance will, at best, only have an impact on a limited number of operational areas, and will not create desired change throughout the organization. In the true spirit of capitalism, many consultants are developing and advertising ethics-based programs "for sale." Imposition of external constraints cannot, by itself, help organizations become ideal human environments. Fundamental structural changes are necessary in order to produce moral intentions, as well as both moral reasoning and behavior within every aspect of organizational life. Organizations, by their very nature, represent complex social contexts in which structural and relational characteristics are inherently value-laden. For example, consider the often competitive nature of interests among stakeholders of an organization.

It is a rare case when a given course of action will satisfy the interests of all relevant stakeholder groups equally well. It might be expected that production staff's concerns about working conditions, administration's concerns about profitability, and consumers' concerns about product safety and affordability might drive problem-solving processes in quite different directions. The functions of various organizational elements can dictate moral and ethical concerns. Therefore, diverse and inherent moral and ethical issues are embedded in the power structure of most organizations. It goes without saying that when power is unequally distributed among organizational members or groups, the emergence of moral and ethical conflicts is virtually inevitable. These are just a few examples of how the complexity of the organizational context can further complicate moral and ethical matters. The inherent limitations of mandatory integrity and ethics codes in such contexts seem clear. Organizations with genuine commitments to moral goals must actively pursue broader and more innovative approaches to building integrity and morality throughout the various dimensions of organizational structure and functioning.

The ideas of Tobias, in his articulated parallels between the *thriving person* and the *thriving organization*, have much relevance to the issues of individual and organizational morality and ethics.[25] He proposed several dimensions of human adjustment and maturity that have correlates in organizational culture—initiative, discipline, and accountability, to name a few. Tobias very effectively described the inextricable linkage between characteristics of members of the organization and organizational culture. In much the same way, managers need to recognize the notion of interdependence between *individual member* morality and *organizational* morality.

Conclusion

Mandatory ethical programs are an important part of an organization's framework. Clear guidelines established in formal ways create a baseline for expectations critical to the general well-being of the organization. Written rules in some areas (e.g., accounting) are mandated by law or by regulatory groups. Clear communication of certain principles and procedures are essential in many functional areas to meet externally- and internally imposed standards. Adherence to such standards is often so important that reporting and enforcement programs are critical components of operations.

However, the thoroughly moral organization must go well beyond principle-driven mandatory ethics programs. There are a variety of concept systems that one might use to discuss the nature of moral functioning at the organization level. Leadership topics often included moral and ethical dimensions. The key role of values and norms in organizational culture are closely related to integrity, moral, and ethical concerns and should be taught using innovative case studies approaches that use synchronous delivery methods such as role-playing, video-interviews, integrity project-participation, and intensive social media used in management education. More research needs to be conducted on the viability of synchronous competence acquisition methods and integrity competences in organization acquisition. Also, greater support is needed in using social media or similar synchronous and similar learning methods in integrity and anticorruption knowledge acquisition, by using real-life examples from organizations in order for an organization to gain integrity and anticorruption intellectual capital.

References

Andersen, J. F., & Andersen, P. A. (1987). Never smile until Christmas? Casting doubt on an old myth. *Journal of Thought, 22*(4), 57–61.

Carnegie Forum on Education and the Economy (1986) *A nation prepared: Teachers for the 21st century.* Carnegie Forum on Education and the Economy, Washington.

Goodlad, J. (1990). *Teachers for our nation's schools.* San Francisco: Jossey-Bass.

Holmes Group, (1986). *Tomorrow's teachers: A report of the Holmes Group,* East Lansing, MI: Author.

Richmond, V. P., Gorham, J., & McCroskey, J. C. (1987). The relationship between immediacy behaviors and cognitive learning, in M. McLaughlin (Ed.), *Communication Yearbook* 10 (pp. 574–590). Beverly Hills, CA: SAGE.

Internet Sources

Kell,G. (2006). Business Against Corruption, Case Studies and Examples, UN Global Contact Office, New York, http://www.unglobalcompact.org/docs /issues_doc/7.7/BACbookFINAL.pdf, accessed 22.01.2012.

Kell, G. (2006). Business Against Corruption, Case Studies and Examples, http://www.unglobalcompact.org/docs/issues_doc/AntiCorruption/UNGC _AntiCorruptionReporting.pdf, retrieved by the author on 28.12.2011.

Miller B.A. (2011). http://www.articlesbase.com/leadership-articles/leadership -how-important-is-integrity-in-todays-business-world-is-integrity-an -afterthought-1063750.html, accessed 27.11.2011.

www.tnv.com.pl retrieved by the author on 28.02.2011.

www.tnv.com.pl/gpmi, accessed on 13.03.2011.

http://www.unodc.org/documents/commissions/WGGOVandFiN/Thematic _Programme_on_Corruption.pdf, accessed Jan 20,2012.

http://www.oecd.org/dataoecd/26/31/45019804.pdf, retrieved by the author, 02.02.2012.

http://www.unglobalcompact.org/docs/issues_doc/AntiCorruption/UNGC _AntiCorruptionReporting.pdf, accessed 28.12.2011.

http://unglobalcompact.org/, retrieved by the author on 12.11. 2011.

http://www.adb.org/Documents/Policies/Anticorruption/anticorrupt300 .asp?p=antipubs, retrieved by the author on 23.01.2012.

http://www.unglobalcompact.org/docs/issues_doc/AntiCorruption/Bali
_Business_Declaration.pdf, accessed 01.09.2012.
http://www.amazon.com/gp/product1613505108/ref; retrieved on 20.01. 2012
http://www.adb.org/Documents/Policies/Anticorruption/anticorrupt300
.asp?p=antipubs, retrieved by the author on 14.02.2012.
http://amazon.com/gp/product1613505108, accessed on 02.02. 2012.

Key Terms

Integrity—the quality of being honest and having strong moral principles that you refuse to change, the quality of being whole and complete.

Anticorruption—institutional and noninstitutional actions to prevent and eradicate corruption in an organizational context and public spheres.

Ethics—the study of what is morally right and what is not.

Management education—in all business and organizations, regardless of size, including private, not for profit, public, and mixed ownership this is the act of getting people together to accomplish desired goals and objectives using available resources efficiently and effectively following ethical guidelines, striving to create integrity, and sustainable organizations caring for their communities as much as possible.

Impediment—something that makes progress, movement, or achieving something difficult or impossible.

Study Questions

1. Discuss integrity and anticorruption actions in an organizational context by showing innovative methods of dealing with new challenges and by suggesting the most effective approaches in an organizational context.
2. How can business strengthen the process of building an integrity-proof, corruption-free organization of the future?
3. Should integrity in an organizational setting be a part of executive learning/future training as an aim for all organizations? If yes , how can this be achieved in your industry ?

Further Reading—Books

Carter, C. (2007). *Business ethics as practice: Representation, reflexivity and performance.* Cheltenham, UK; Northampton, MA: Edward Elgar.

Cloke, K. (2002). *The end of management and the rise of organizational democracy.* San Francisco, CA: Jossey-Bass.

Cohen, W. (2008). *A class with Drucker: The lost lessons of the world's greatest management teacher.* New York, NY: AMACOM/ American Management Association.

Conrad, B. K. (2003). *The Tao of legal ethics: Integrating the rules of legal ethics with codes of personal morals and integrity.* Columbia, SC: H/S Publications in affiliation with Ment-A-Tech Publications.

Dealy, M. D. (2007). *Managing by accountability: What every leader needs to know about responsibility, integrity-and results.* Westport, CT: Praeger.

Finser, T. M. (2007). *Organizational integrity: How to apply the wisdom of the body to develop healthy organizations.* Great Barrington, MA: Steiner Books.

Frederickson, H. G., & Ghere, R. K. (Eds.). (2005). *Ethics in public management.* Armonk, NY : M. E. Sharpe.

Garsten, C., & Hernes, T. (Eds.). (2009). *Ethical dilemmas in management.* London, UK; New York, NY: Routledge.

Garten, J. E. (2002). *The politics of fortune: A new agenda for business leaders.* Boston, MA: Harvard Business School Press.

Jackson, K. T. (2004). *Building reputational capital: Strategies for integrity and fair play that improve the bottom line.* Oxford, UK; New York, NY: Oxford University Press.

Johnson, L. (2003). *Absolute honesty: Building a corporate culture that values straight talk and rewards integrity.* New York, NY: AMACOM, American Management Association.

Kolthoff, E. (2007). *Ethics and new public management: Empirical research into the effects of businesslike government on ethics and integrity.* Den Haag, Netherlands: Boom Juridische.

Langlais, K. J. (1997). *Managing with integrity for long term care: The key to success for building stability in staffing.* New York, NY: McGraw-Hill.

LeClair, D. T. (1998). *Integrity management: A guide to managing legal and ethical issues in the workplace.* Tampa, FL: University of Tampa Press.

Maak ,T., & Pless, N. M. (Eds.). (2006). *Responsible leadership in business.* New York, NY: Routledge.

Menzel, D. C. (2007). *Ethics management for public administrators: Building organizations of integrity.* Armonk, NY: M. E. Sharpe.

Murray, T. H., & Johnston, J. (Eds.). (2010). *Trust and integrity in biomedical research: The case of financial conflicts of interest.* Baltimore, MD: Johns Hopkins University Press.

Neef, D. (2003) *Managing corporate reputation and risk: Developing a strategic approach to corporate integrity using knowledge management*. Amsterdam; Boston, MA: Elsevier/Butterworth-Heinemann.

Perry, J. L. (Ed.). (2009). *The Jossey-Bass reader on nonprofit and public leadership*. San Francisco, CA: Jossey-Bass.

Petrick, J. A. (1997). *Management ethics: Integrity at work*. Thousand Oaks, CA: SAGE Publications.

Robbins, D. A. (1998). *Managed care on trial: Recapturing trust, integrity, and accountability in healthcare*. New York, NY: McGraw-Hill.

Siddiqui, M. (2005). *Corporate soul: The monk within the manager*. New Delhi, India; Thousand Oaks, CA: Response Books.

Sonnenberg, F. K. (1994). *Managing with a conscience: How to improve performance through integrity, trust, and commitment*. New York, NY: McGraw-Hill.

Spinello, R. A. (2003). *CyberEthics: Morality and law in cyberspace*. Boston, MA: Jones and Bartlett Publishers.

Srivastva, S. & associates. (1988). *Executive integrity: The search for high human values in organizational life*. San Francisco, CA: Jossey-Bass.

Storey, J. (Ed.). (2011). *Leadership in organizations: Current issues and key trends*. New York, NY: Routledge.

Traer, R. (2009). *Doing environmental ethics*. Boulder, CO: Westview Press.

Westra, L., & Lemons, J. (Eds.). (1995). *Perspectives on ecological integrity*. Dordrecht; Boston, MA: Kluwer Academic Publishers.

Whitton, H. (2005). *Managing conflict of interest in the public sector: A toolkit*. Paris, France: Organisation for Economic Co-operation and Development.

Further Reading—Journals

Dobni, D., Ritchie, J. R. B., & Zerbe, W. (2000). Organizational values: The inside view of service productivity. *Journal of Business Research 47*, 91–107.

Ferrell, L. (2004). Successful programs for teaching business ethics. *Presentation at the Teaching Business Ethics Conference*, Boulder, CO, July 21–23.

Fritzsche, D. J. (1987). Marketing/business ethics: A review of the empirical research. *Business and Professional Ethics Journal 6*, 65–79.

Gowen, C. R., III, Hanna, N., Jacobs, L. W., Keys, D. E., & Weiss, D. E. (1996). Integrating business ethics into a graduate program. *Journal of Business Ethics 15*, 671–679.

Kelly, M. (2002). It's a heckuva time to be dropping business ethics courses. *Business Ethics 16*(5 and 6), 17–18.

McCabe, D. L., & Treviño, L. K. (1993). Academic dishonesty: Honor codes and other contextual influences. *Journal of Higher Education 64*(5), 522–538.

Reidenbach, R. E., & Robin D. P. (1991). A conceptual model of corporate moral development. *Journal of Business Ethics 10*, 273–284.

Swanson, D. L. (2004). The buck stops here: Why universities must reclaim business ethics education. *Journal of Academic Ethics 2*(1), 1–19.

Treviño, L. K., & McCabe, D. (1994) Meta-learning about business ethics building honorable business school communities. *Journal of Business Ethics 13*, 405–416.

Verschoor, C. C. (1998). Corporations financial performance and its commitment to ethics. *Journal of Business Ethics 17*, 1509–1516.

Woo, C. Y. (2003). Personally responsible. *BizEd* (May/June), 22–27.

- The design or selection of uneconomical projects because of opportunities for financial kickbacks and political patronage.

- Procurement fraud, including collusion, overcharging, or the selection of contractors, suppliers, and consultants on criteria other than the lowest evaluated substantially responsive bidder.

- Illicit payments of "speed money" to government officials to facilitate the timely delivery of goods and services to which the public is rightfully entitled, such as permits and licenses.

- Illicit payments to government officials to facilitate access to goods, services, and/or information to which the public is not entitled, or to deny the public access to goods and services to which it is legally entitled.

- Illicit payments to prevent the application of rules and regulations in a fair and consistent manner, particularly in areas concerning public safety, law enforcement, or revenue collection.

- Payments to government officials to foster or sustain monopolistic or oligopolistic access to markets in the absence of a compelling economic rationale for such restrictions.

- The misappropriation of confidential information for personal gain, such as using knowledge about public transportation routings to invest in real estate hat is likely to appreciate.

- The deliberate disclosure of false or misleading information on the financial status of corporations that would prevent potential investors from accurately valuing their worth, such as the failure to disclose large contingent liabilities or the undervaluing of assets in enterprises slated for privatization.

Figure 4.1. An illustrative list of corrupt behaviors.

Note: Courtesy of the Asian Development Bank, 2012.

Humanistic Management

The Foundation for Building Organizational Integrity

What is the role of companies in society? Can we derive purpose and thus a catalyst effect from gaining clarity on this question? The first contribution of this section dealing with more humanistic management revisits the crucial role of different purposes of management and more balanced management systems in general. It argues that an integrity-based enterprise can play an important role in global transcendence toward a better world. Beyond the normative call, the chapter illustrates the different journeys of three entrepreneurs who serve as exemplary role models. Their inner calling to leave behind classic business pressures and careers on certain occasions is inspirational. The fully intrinsic approach to integrity reaches unprecedented degrees of authenticity and credibility.

The chapter also demonstrates the crucial role of consistency. Integrity is a multifaceted notion. Thus, consistency emerges as an additional condition *sine qua non* when it comes to building the right type of organizations. The chapter adds yet another key element to integrity, which is found in an intensified action focus. We also need, to some degree, an entrepreneurship attitude where we get started, learn, and adapt fast. Trying to launch the perfect solution from day one is overly ambitious.

The second contribution of this section deals with a consulting model able to clarify core values and promote organizational integrity. Getting one's moral compass in order is key to avoiding friction in the wrong place and aligning the entire organization. Organizations that have the future in focus are concerned with the kinds of meaning that will sustain it for the long term. In this chapter, we explore how diverse challenges for different organizations amount to a common goal of enduring for future success. They are organizations that act beyond a goal of profitability and have a vision that generates clarity during times of turbulence or flourishing. Adding empirical depth to the chapter, three different consulting engagements with three heterogeneous organizations yield corroborative insights. The chosen organizations are all SMEs and the consulting engagements centered on each entity identifying and defining their core values and vision statements. Core values acted out by organizations represent expressions of integrity, which in turn constitutes the kinds of meaning that are most meaningful to each entity. A wholeness or completeness, or in other words integrity, in organizations is the result of actions based on a clear set of core values. By having a set of core values that function as organizing principles, the entity has clarity in the decisions it makes down to the routine practices of everyday operations.

CHAPTER 5

Faith, Hope, and Care

Integrity and Poverty Alleviation Through Enterprise

Kathryn Pavlovich

Introduction

Integrity is the developing currency of the twenty-first century. Integrity, organizational sustainability, and social responsibility are words now consistently seen in contemporary scholarship. Indeed, the concept of caring for each other becomes dominant in this relational, interdependent world. This is particularly evident in the growing interest in enterprise development which is now seen as the most successful mechanism for alleviating poverty in emerging economies.[1] The term *creating social wealth* has been introduced to distinguish this phenomenon from solely commercial enterprise. Creating social wealth embraces longer term intent of increasing the self-sufficiency and sustainability of the local community.[2] Thus, it embraces different principles of value that attend to the betterment of human society than conventionally seen with commercial entrepreneurship.[3] Indeed, could this form of integrity-based enterprise play a role in global transcendence in making a better world?

This chapter describes the journeys of three entrepreneurs who have given up their comfortable western lifestyles to work in emerging economies solely for the purpose of creating enterprises to assist in alleviating poverty and human suffering. None of these people would have called themselves entrepreneurs as their enterprises were not developed from an externalized "opportunity discovery" process.[4] Rather, these ventures discovered them through an inner "calling" that they could not ignore. With no formal management training, no business plans, and no marketing experience, they followed this inner guidance and have formed successful enterprises for creating social wealth. This chapter examines this "call" as not only being a journey of enterprise development, but also one of developing a greater sense of self through "integrity." It uses three case studies to illustrate and contribute to new theory regarding integrity in organizations. The following section reviews the literature related to integrity and enterprise development through work as a "calling."

Integrity as an Eternal Truth

There has been a surge of research into character strengths following the development of Peterson and Seligman's virtues in action (VIA) framework.[5] Significantly, Sosik, Gentry, and Chun's recent study found that integrity was the most significant character strength that contributed to executive performance and the ultimate success of the organization.[6] They found that executives with strong integrity had the courage to make brave decisions and to act fairly and consistently "with their decision in the face of adversity and multiple constituents with competing interests and agendas."[7] Without integrity executives were not able to receive the same levels of trust, support, and communication from their associates. Such a study demonstrates the important link between integrity and organizational performance. While there has been little agreement on the meaning of integrity,[8] a number of qualities emerge as consistent, as reflected in Becker's definition of integrity as a "commitment in action to a morally justifiable set of principles and values…."[9] This, along with other definitions, suggests that integrity requires a strong moral base, consistency, and wholeness.[10]

Becker argues that integrity is both subjective (personal) and objective (social).[11] Subjective integrity consists of personal integrity that is based upon one's own moral norms, and moral integrity that is based on someone else's subjectivism. Objective integrity is more than adherence to a subjective set of values (whether personal or moral). For Becker, integrity is embedded in a rational set of principles that extent beyond personal emotion. This conforms to the first quality which is adherence to a universal moral principle. These moral principles have been described by Parameshwar as "eternal truths" that guide us.[12] These eternal truths mirror the six virtues Peterson and Seligman synthesized from the 24 character strengths valued by moral philosophers and religious thinkers (bravery, courage justice, temperance, transcendence, and wisdom).[13] While their initial research included integrity as a character strength contributing to courage, in later work integrity has been deleted in favor of honesty.[14] Yet, as Sosik et al. found, integrity is instrumental for organizational success and hence is central for moral guidance.[15]

A second important quality of integrity is consistency in action. As Drucker notes, integrity is the "congruence between deeds and words, between behaviour and professed beliefs and values."[16] This requires an inner alignment to respond consistently across time and space,[17] demonstrating that integrity is not a static one-off performance but is recognized, built upon, and developed over time. Paine confirms that those with integrity "stand for something and remain steadfast when confronted with adversity or temptation."[18] Integrity, therefore, needs to be earned and yet can be tested and challenged at any time which could, from one poor decision, diminish a person's stockpile of integrity.

The final quality characterizing integrity is wholeness, which means integrating the mind, body, and spirit. Jacobs explains that a person who has integrity is a whole person and is "likely to respond to a problem without compartmentalization... blending reason and emotion, self-interest and social consciousness in his or her work... [Thus] integrity implies a conscious reconciliation of variables."[19] Palanski and Yammarino extend this reconciliation process by stating that wholeness is when one's moral dispositions complement each other.[20] Feeling whole therefore enables one to attain clarity of insight which supports adherence and consistency to the eternal truths. Being whole also means the boundary between self and other become blurred, allowing one to live in a relational world with more equanimity. Integrity allows us to detach from our "small-egos" and we are able to connect to something far deeper than ourselves, a central feature of transcendence.[21] In suggesting that integrity is an eternal truth, the integration of both life purpose and meaning builds a vital energy that assists in mutual transformation.

Enterprise as a Calling

Klein suggests that most of the literature on entrepreneurial opportunity discovery focuses on the entrepreneur being alert to opportunities in the external environment.[22] Recent research also views opportunities as a creation process which depends more on iterative, inductive, and incremental decision making.[23] However, both of these perspectives still view entrepreneurship as an objective phenomenon and there has been little research into entrepreneurship as a "calling," a subjective and inner directed sense of knowing.

A calling relates to having a perceived purpose in one's career or work life.[24] Dik and Duffy suggest that a calling is "a transcendent summons, experienced as originating beyond the self, to approach a particular life role in a manner oriented toward demonstrating or deriving a sense of purpose or meaningfulness that holds other-oriented values and goals as primary sources of motivation."[25] While there is some disagreement regarding whether a calling is an external summons, for example, from God, or from some inner directive,[26] most of the literature supports that it emerges from within as a result of intense self-reflection, regardless of the source.[27]

Elangovan et al. attribute three conditions to a calling which they define as, "A course of action in pursuit of pro-social intentions embodying the convergence of an individual's sense of what he or she would like to do, should do, and actually does."[28] Thus, a calling is action-oriented and links with entrepreneurship, as both are agency based. Second, there is clarity of personal mission where life and livelihood become one. This clarity helps identify the course of action and direction that create a meaningful purpose for those being called. This clarity emerges from a deeper awareness that disconnects the narrow confines of the 'small-ego' and connects with the great whole as part of the eternal truths.[29] Finally, a calling involves prosocial intentions in helping others. Elangovan et al. cite Buechner in describing a calling as "the place where your deep gladness... and the world's hunger meet."[30] This emphasizes the growing awareness of enterprise as a mechanism for global connectivity and poverty alleviation. Thus, a calling will have some moral principle or cause at the core of its intention to help others and make the world a better place.

Case Studies

This section describes the three case studies of integrity in action. The first case study describes a New Zealand entrepreneur, Kerry Hilton, who gave up his corporate life to set up an enterprise in Kolkata, India, solely to assist women leave the sex trade. **Freeset** now employs over 200 women in the textile industry and the central criterion for employment is the need to leave prostitution rather than the more conventional skill-based requirement. "Freeset is a fair trade business offering employment to women trapped in Kolkata's sex trade. We make quality jute bags and organic cotton t-shirts, but our business is freedom!".[31] Kerry says,

> "If you're in business, you try and get the best skilled people for the job, right? In Freeset though, we take on women out of their need to be free, not on their skill. We have one woman here who costs us a fortune because she breaks and ruins the textiles, she just can't sew. Now, that's not a good business model for making a profit but it's our social purpose that drives us."

The second case is set in South Africa. **Rain Africa**, a handmade labor-intensive bath and body range was created by Bev Missing who has a mission to provide employment in a region with high poverty, high unemployment, and high crime. She began by making soap for her bed and breakfast, but quickly realized that her dream of providing high employment could only be realized through the global distribution of her products. Thus, she set upon expanding retailing stores throughout the world. Currently, there are eight in South Africa, one in New York and Amsterdam, and others are planned. The products are handmade with care and passion using local, indigenous, and wild-harvested plants.[32] The products are presented in 100% handmade gift packaging that is recyclable. Currently Rain Africa employs 100 people in their manufacture. Bev's vision for Rain Africa is to provide employment, education, and healthcare for her people:

> "I want a full factory—humming and happy. I also want to have small local project groups and businesses growing from our

demand—small entrepreneurs employing people and selling us things we don't make, like ceramics for example. I would like to see some sort of community living set up: small but nice houses with communal orchard, vegetable garden, indoor bathrooms... sheer luxury for them compared to what they have now, a small day care facility for the kids, a trust fund for education scholarships for staff children. We already do team building things, but with a bigger budget, we can really do good things with the staff. Sadly all of this costs money which we just do not have—so to get to a point where we can do things, the company needs to become profitable and that means more stores and more economy of scale—a process and a challenge."

The third case study involves the enterprise of **Rose Circles**, begun by Australian woman Anne Godfrey who now lives in the small town of Parola in the Maharashtra province, 400 km north-east of Mumbai, India. The purpose of Rose Circles is to give work to the many impoverished women in India who are in situations without hope. Anne says,

"Our video [website] shows the conditions that these women live in and the reality is just appalling. And then the joy that they get from making these wonderful products of love because we have given them one thing that they didn't have in their lives, and that is hope. They are locked into an economy where they can't go into a market like we can in Australia. They don't have that possibility. If a woman's husband dies, the parents often kick her out because they can't afford to keep her without the wage of their son. This is the fate of many of the women that we work with. They don't have any hope to improve their lives without assistance."

Using off-cuts of fabric from large textile manufacturers, Anne helps the women, with no technical skills, to make quilts and other products that can be sold in the West. The rose symbolizes love, and Anne's hope is that this message will inspire other women to purchase these products to improve the quality of the women's lives in India. Rose Circles is therefore a project with a mission to economically uplift women in rural and marginalized areas around the world, beginning in India.[33]

The following discussion describes and theorizes how enterprise development requires integrity for success and how this expands global transcendence. The discussion begins with further explanation on the discovery process of a calling to work with the poor in an emerging economy. The discussion then examines the qualities of integrity and enterprise success.

Discussion

Discovery of "Calling"

These entrepreneurs confirmed that finding their calling was both internally and externally inspired. But rather than being one or the other,[34] they experienced this awakening from both sources. Kerry recalled, "I had this quiet knowledge. I discovered this incredible power of God calling me and it got to a stage where my life was about the poor and I just had to go and do something. When we landed here in Kolkata we were as naïve as anything. During the first night in our rented home, we realized we were in the middle of the largest red light area in the city. So it was very clear what I needed to do! You would have to say there was some guidance there, wouldn't you? So choosing Kolkata—it was a God moment for me and the rest just followed." This demonstrates how a calling requires listening to the small voice and in Kerry's case, it intensified over time. The "unsettling" deepened until he did something active and then the path became clear.

Anne's experience of discovering her calling was instantaneous. She recalled, "He [the master] was the defining moment in my life. He just walked in and I experienced divine love. It just smacked me over. I didn't want anything else after that. It just changed me. If a human being carries that much energy, you just want to follow. But we were shocked when we heard what he had in mind for us in India. We thought no one could live where he suggested as there were no redeeming features. It was 50 degrees and it was like a piece of rock with only one or two trees. But now, 10 years later it's been transformed into a lush and bountiful oasis that supports nature and people."

Bev's calling too developed over time. Like Kerry, she explained how both internal and external sources guided her. She also articulated the effects of not listening to the call, an unsettling that is evident in this quote. "It's that still small voice inside, your conscience. You know when you are going off the path because something doesn't feel right or there is a feeling of guilt or a feeling of discomfort. And sometimes it comes from outside sources. You may be reading and something just really hits you between the eyes and it says this or that. And it's not what you want to hear, but you just know it's true."

These comments illustrate how being called can be unsettling. It may be instantaneous, but more often deepens with awareness over time. It involves a quiet listening, and more importantly, it is about the actions that follow the call. In these case studies, these actions resulted in significant prosocial behavior in creating their enterprises. Further, the call directed their action into their social mission of helping others and thus confirms the three attributes that Elangovan et al. note characterize a calling: action based, clarity of purpose, and prosocial behavior.[35] This data also demonstrates that the discovery of a calling means that there was a quiet knowledge that this is what one was meant to do, possibly for the rest of their lives. Their calling absorbs both life and work and provides clarity, meaning, and absorption.[36] Bev confirmed that if she had to leave where she is, she would create a similar enterprise elsewhere. Kerry also stated, "This is not a stepping stone for somewhere else. I have no desire to go on and get a better job. Let me put it another way... There is nothing better, for me, than what I am doing now. Being able to witness freedom in action every single day of my life. I mean it's hard... we have women that die, that have suffered, we live with a lot of pain ... but I've got nothing better to do. This is it. Giving freedom for life, I mean it's incredible. Why would you want to do anything else? What else is better than this?"

Enterprise as Social Wealth

Anne, Bev, and Kerry all spoke of the need to be successful commercially alongside their social mission and these tensions were evident in all of these enterprises. Bev explained, "The manufacture of our handmade products is done very deliberately without machinery. It is expensive because obviously if you can cut a large number of boxes at once, it's a much cheaper option. But we don't, we do everything by hand and that's very precious to me and I fight vigorously to preserve that. But the accountants, they always want economies of scale. They want to see that you can do something cheaper and get better margins. But we won't sacrifice that hand-made touch because that's what the company is about—job creation." This illustrates how maintaining integrity can mean standing steadfast when challenged by adversity,[37] and that maintaining true to one's purpose is a core attribute of integrity through both adhering to one's moral principle and consistency of action.[38]

Anne noted that her intention was to assist in making the women independent. "We are training them to be independent of us, and they have leaders in their villages that can help them to sell their product, so we are not responsible for marketing everything. So our goal is to train the women with skills to make products that are saleable: to help them source materials from commercial people with off-cuts, and to give them some hope that they can sell on the international market." This stresses the importance of skill development for social wealth to be created in these local communities.[39]

Kerry discusses the need for being commercially successful in order to create social wealth. "There are a lot of social organizations who are trying to make products and then they have to go around asking people to buy them. But we began by making products that people were already buying. So that was our first starting point and our whole enterprise is run from a very business-like manner. The freedom for these women depends on whether we do good business or not. We have to make sure that the products we have on offer are good and are those that people want to buy."

The above comments illustrate three qualities that are needed in creating social wealth. The first is that *job creation* can significantly increase through handmade and locally sourced products. The unique, custom-made aspect of these goods offers a point of difference that is not evident in mass production processes. There is a quality of love and care that is imbued in handmade products that is difficult to imitate commercially. This is important for a more differentiated consumer market that seeks unique, fair trade, and ethically made products. Anne confirms this, "The customers who bought our garments were touched by the plight of these women in these photographs and they wanted to help. Many of the shop owners who bought my stock also said that they would prefer to buy from me rather than from someone who wasn't doing this social work." This supports a global study of 17,000 consumers in five Western countries that found nearly half (48%) indicated a preference for fair trade products over mass production.[40] This trend indicates a growing awareness by consumers of products that are made with care. Job creation also stimulated sustainable capability development within the local communities. As Bev, Kerry, and Anne noted, their primary purpose is to empower local people. While most of the women at Freeset are good machinists, Kerry also employs women who don't always have good technical skills. "While this is not a good business model for making a profit, we continue to make one anyhow so somehow we have a blessing on us," he noted. Finally, they observed that the way to achieve this social purpose was through competent and credible commercial practices so that they became examples of excellence regarding how business can be done through integrating both a social and commercial purpose.[41]

A second theme of social wealth creation became evident in some of the day-to-day stories of how these entrepreneurs made *transformational impacts* in these communities. Bev's story related to a young girl who recently came from a village. "My staff don't have two cents to rub together either, but they bought a new girl some clothes, some shampoo, and a hairdryer and tried to get her to look like something other than a 'wild woman from Borneo.' They have been really sweet and are gradually teaching her. She's bought herself a cellphone and we asked her how she knew who was calling her as she can't read. But she's worked out a little system for herself. She'd asked you to phone her and she would save it with an icon. So she will know that it's my number if it comes up with a question mark, or a star, or whatever." This demonstrates how small acts of compassion can result in large-scale outcomes.[42] These acts emerge from the moral principle of integrity, where the staff connected with the girl in need to assist in alleviating her suffering. This also demonstrates both the subjective and objective nature of integrity in that it emerged from personal acts and yet was imbued by a universal quality of care.

Anne's story of transformation relates to giving the women opportunities to see what can be achieved. "We train the women in Tapovan when they come and stay here. For them, this is a life changing experience because they have never seen running water and they just play in that water for hours. Back in their villages, they have to walk 10 kms for their water and then carry it back on their heads. Here they just turn on the tap and they are just amazed. It gives us so much joy to see them so happy." This reinforces the reciprocal nature of energy transfer that accumulates over time. In giving to the women, feelings of joy are returned.

Kerry recounted a story following his frustration with an alcoholic and sometimes abusive husband of one of the women, and demonstrates that transformation is a two-way process. After a bad night Kerry said to the woman, "We have to put a stop to this. He is not good for you and we have to get rid of him. I will sort it out. She stops and quite calmly says to me, 'so Kerry, you love me enough to help me, but you don't love him enough to help him?' And it hit me, that she understood this stuff better than I did. So there are always little moments like that when I have to correct myself. So here I am thinking that I would show them, and actually they show me." This example illustrates the depth to which integrity can be challenged. With integrity being the ability to consistently maintain adherence to a moral principle,[43] this instance demonstrates the subjective nature of personal integrity[44] with both parties perceiving the situation somewhat differently. Yet it also demonstrates how objective integrity through reflective thought can help in the reframing of the situation for deeper mutual understanding.

Creating a Just Society Through Enterprise

These comments illustrate a strong sense of justice and a desire to create equal opportunities for others. Anne, Bev, and Kerry noted that alongside being called to develop their enterprises, they also felt a strong sense of need to help the poor emerging from their own privileged backgrounds. Yet what they found was that they learnt as much about their own freedom as what they were giving. Kerry said, "The poor give me a gift... they teach me in every moment in every day. It's not just about freedom for these women and it's also about freedom for me." They stated that working with the poor helped them work out what was important in their lives, and materialism and consumption did not rate highly. Thus, working with the poor helps settle a balance (justice) in terms of creating social wealth in the local communities, while also building a deepening awareness of what is important for the entrepreneurs.

Transformation Through Integrity

This final section integrates theoretical aspects of integrity and how it may contribute to the development of a more just and equitable world. The first quality of adherence to an objective *moral principle* was particularly guided through the enterprise development as a "calling." All three participants spoke of this calling becoming clearer from some form of summons—either from God or from an inner directive. Significantly, these calls resulted in an action orientation in the form of a commercial enterprise with a social purpose. This prosocial behavior provided the entrepreneurs with a clarity of purpose which became totally absorbing, where their work and play became intertwined in this purpose.[45] Bev said, "I feel a responsibility to make a difference. There are so many people in this country that go without. So maybe deep, deep down there's a guilt or a sense that I need to fix it or give back a bit of what I had and they have never had." The strength of the call and their dependency on such a moral principle may indicate why the enterprises are successful.[46] This ideal of job creation for creating freedom, hope, and independence for those less able became an overarching eternal truth which guided their moral behavior. Thus, the objective-based integrity guided their personal subjective actions.

In having this clear moral guidance, the second quality of integrity, *consistency*, was readily achieved. As noted, the commercial aspects of their enterprises created challenges, but their adherence to the social mission of their calling never wavered. Again, this involved both objective and subjective integrity through the clarity of purpose providing a framework within which subjective integrity could reside.[47] This suggests that having a strong moral purpose and clarity of action helps to guide the second quality of consistency. Thus, moral principles are the conditions under which consistency can be practiced. Being consistent means being the witness as well as the actor for ongoing transformation and learning. This requires a reflective nature to absorb where and how consistency is being acted out. This example of Kerry's illustrates his own reflective learning of integrity regarding how he walks alongside the women he works with. "That's really important to me, to be able to listen, to learn, and to walk alongside. It's not about resources, it's about relationships," he says. He gave other examples too regarding his need to listen more deeply, and many of the central tasks are now managed by the women themselves. "One day I realized that they knew more than I did," he reflected.

The final feature of *wholeness* is an outcome of the condition of moral principles and consistency of actions. The data had many references to how integrity expanded wholeness, which is a key attribute in transformation. Wholeness is relational; in being whole we relate in full presence to those around us. We have a growing awareness of the dynamics that result from our interactions. In being whole, we experience joy and harmony. Thus, wholeness is an outcome of relational depth. Anne's explanation of wholeness is evident in this comment that touches on empowerment. "When the women come here, we sing and dance together and they feel this wonderful feeling that comes up from inside them and that empowers them. That was dormant in their lives with no hope. When they feel their own power again, that affects the other women too. I guess it's a bit like lighting a candle and that candle lights others. So I am in India to be someone who can catalyze that. And it's fulfilling me."

Integrity therefore assists in care toward others. It's built on universal moral principles, requires practice for consistency, and creates wholeness as an outcome. Integrity based upon care is therefore a relational activity. It is a process and yet also a value to live by. Integrity through care touches hearts and this connectivity expands and deepens our awareness of each other to live in more equanimity in a relational world.

Conclusion

In this chapter, I have examined how the development of a prosocial enterprise shapes the relational space through integrity. The case studies of Kerry, Anne, and Bev have provided the context to explore how integrity is both an objective and subjective experience. The data contributes through providing insights into the three principles of integrity. These contributions focus on moral principles as conditions for the development of integrity as evident through their calling for enterprise development. In some ways, their purpose as a calling has intensified the expression of this moral principle. Second, the chapter demonstrated how the development of integrity is a practice through consistency of actions. This again has been intensified through the action focus of entrepreneurship. Finally, becoming whole is an outcome of integrity where life, work, and values become absorbed into a new relational awareness of being human. This aspect too is developed through the prosocial aspect of social wealth creation where personal ego becomes subsumed with relational equanimity. Thus, integrity, through conditions, practices, and outcomes facilitates a spiral of shared care and responsibility to flow out for global transformation.

Key Terms

Calling—"a course of action in pursuit of pro-social intentions embodying the convergence of an individual's sense of what he or she would like to do, should do, and actually does."[28]

Character strengths—seminal research that classifies 24 positive psychological traits that characterize being human.[48]

Eternal truths—the moral truths that bind all humanity such as justice, compassion, meaningfulness, and courage.

Integrity—"commitment *in action* to a morally justifiable set of principles and value."[9]

Purpose—being guided by positive action that serves others.

Transcendence—strengths that forge connections to the larger universe and thereby provide meaning.

Study Questions

1. Define the three qualities of integrity that emerge from this research.
2. How comprehensive are these three qualities?
3. Find examples of these three qualities and describe how they build integrity within organizations.

4. How does the notion of a "calling" create organizational integrity?

5. Discuss the relationship between enterprise development as a calling and poverty alleviation.

6. Find further examples of enterprise development and poverty alleviation. What are the issues and solutions that may stem from this?

Acknowledgements

I wish to thank Anne Godfrey (Rose Circles), Bev Missing (Rain Africa), and Kerry Hilton (Freeset) for their contributions to this study, and for allowing their personal thoughts and actions to be publicly revealed for research purposes. Without such grace, our academic inquiry would not be as rich.

Further Reading

Dacin, P., Dacin T. and Matear M. (2010, August). Social entrepreneurship: Why we don't need a new theory and how we move forward from here. *Academy of Management Perspectives* 37–57.

Elangovan, A., Pinder C. and McLean M. (2010). Callings and organizational behaviour. *Journal of Vocational Behavior* 76, 428–440.

Stoner, J. and Wankel, C. (2007). *Innovative approaches to reducing global poverty.* Charlotte: IAP.

CHAPTER 6

A Consulting Model that Clarifies Core Values and Promotes Greater Organizational Integrity

William B. Mesa

Introduction

Humanistic organizations are concerned with the kinds of meaning that will sustain it for the long term. The increasing need for organizations to act with integrity is imperative given the documented decline in ethical culture and behavior.[1] The kinds of meaning that are most important to an entity are ultimately acted upon by the entity—whether the actions are beyond goals of profit or focused on profitability shaped by business values.[2] This chapter explores how humanistic organizations are those that act beyond a goal of profitability and have a vision that generates clarity during times of turbulence or flourishing.

This case study of three different organizations provided the opportunity to observe, document, and analyze 4 months of consulting with each entity. Each organization is classified as an SME. The consulting engagements centered on the organizations identifying and defining their core values and defining their vision statement.

Core values acted out by an entity represent expressions of integrity which in turn make up the kinds of meaning that are most important to the entity. Integrity, a wholeness or completeness in organizations,[3] is the result of actions based on a clear set of values. By having a set of core values that act as organizing principles, the organization attains clarity in the decisions it makes down to the routine practices of everyday operations.[4] How the organization acts out its core values is primarily based on the idea that they are structured in an ordinal fashion. That is, a certain core value or set of values are prioritized over others. It is this ordinal nature of the entity's core values that provide a structure of meaning for the purpose of seeking enduring success.

Diverse Organizations with Similar Needs

There are a variety of reasons as to why an organization will seek out to define their core values and vision. Five reasons are: change in organizational status, change in top management, change in profitability, change in the competitive environment, and initiation of change.[5] For this case study, each organization wanted a degree of clarity on their reason for being. They wanted what Collins and Porras superbly expressed as attaining "enduring success."[6] With the possibility of enduring success, however, each organization faced different challenges prompting the need for clarity and purpose.

Serving Pets and Their People…in Unique Ways

The Pets Services Industry business (PSI) serviced client needs for pets. In speaking with the owner over a series of meetings, he came to the conclusion that he wanted his business to maintain the dynamic culture of his management team, yet still grow the business. He had successfully foiled franchise competitors over the years and was on the way to developing the largest specific pet service business in the state. What continually concerned the owner in spite of growth and healthy profits, however, was the desire to maintain growth but not at the expense of losing the close connection between employees. A reasonable and common challenge faced by nearly all successful SMEs as they move beyond the "small" or even "medium" definition. Bureaucracy emerges which, in the eyes of the leadership team, threatens the closely shared identity of the business. Probing more through inquiries, the owner revealed that there was a lack of clarity in deciding what new ventures to pursue, but also on how that would impact the business. Enduring success is a goal, but the immediate challenge was clarity on how to manage growth.

Be, Sing, Become.....IMPACT

The Performance Arts Organization (PAO) earned a reputation of excellence, but at the same time found itself to be in stasis with respect to patron and audience growth. Like most performance organizations and nonprofits, members participate, whether paid or volunteer, to be what Peter Drucker coined "human change-agents."[7] The artistic director, board members, and nonmembers proposed that the chief challenge of the ensemble was brand identity and needed to be revitalized. As such, the quick fix would be to create a new logo or a new brand and advertise it. While such efforts may attain some returns, they are short lived. Most importantly, they do not address the real need of seeking and sustaining the kinds of meaning that will provide direction. Upon discussing with the artistic director and board president, the real issue surfaced. We discovered that the organization didn't have an identity crisis, but instead had not fully identified or articulated what was most important in all matters of performance, administration, rehearsal, and fund-raising. The organization lacked clarity of vision in fulfilling what seemed to be an obvious reason for being: to perform, more than a redesign of brand or name was in need.

Wine for the People

Winemaking is an artesian process which is rich with practices characterized by tacit knowledge.[8] Such is the case with the winery. Previous consulting services yielded the identification of indirect costs for the winery (WC) thereby providing a frame of reference toward managing costs but not at the expense of compromising quality. Upon identifying indirect costs for the client, he found there was a basis to improving profitability, and perhaps the first time in 5 years. Yet from working with the owner, the winery needed to establish focus in seeking profitability balanced with artisanship.

Note that each organization faces a different challenge: one of maintaining identity while attaining growth; one of finding clarity of vision and being relevant to patrons; and one that needs to preserve their way of winemaking but not at the expense of pursuing only profit. All are challenges to the kinds of meaning that will sustain each entity. Why an organization preserves and draws from their values is a manifestation of integrity and characteristic of practices that set the foundation for a humanistic management.

Integrity in Organizations

Each consulting engagement focused on the organization identifying their core values and vision. As noted above, the entities sought enduring success and also clarity in confronting each of their unique challenges (see Figure 6.1). In the process of consulting with each entity, the pattern of integrity expressed through core values emerged as a salient pattern.

As a topic, "Integrity" has yielded research ranging from trust in organizations[9] to a resource that is managed.[10] Importantly, integrity has been defined as a wholeness, soundness, or completeness in the organizational context[11] and within the individual context.[12] All perspectives, however, differ on how integrity is expressed through actions leading to integrity being labeled as a virtue or implied as a type of business character.[13] Virtue, though connected to integrity, should be examined separately, yet part of the wholeness that makes up integrity.

Recently, the concept of virtue ethics has emerged as a priority topic in management journals. Virtue has been identified as a basis of consistent

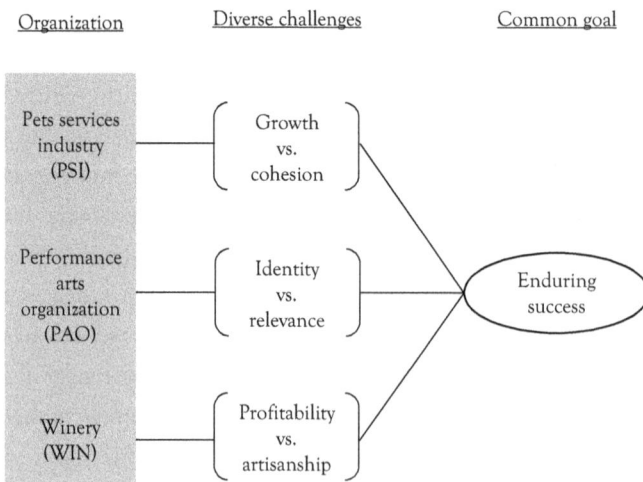

Figure 6.1. Organization challenges and a common goal.

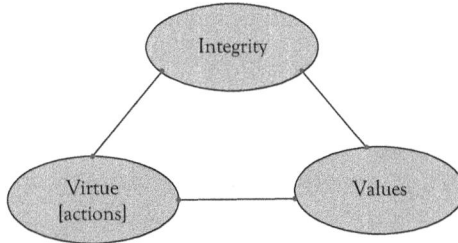

Figure 6.2. Interrelatedness of integrity, virtue, and core values.

actions or habits yielding excellence over time. Alasdair MacIntyre describes virtue as "practices" developed over time that hold intrinsic value.[14] Managing through a virtue context contributes to contexts where employee attitudes and behaviors contribute to a positive environment or mitigate negative circumstances.[15] In summary, virtues contribute to human flourishing[16] and a basis for action during challenging or routine times.[17]

Identifying distinctions between virtue ethics and the characteristics of integrity is essential toward understanding how an organization acts through its daily practices as manifesting integrity or falling short of acting with integrity. Specifically, the foundations for the existence of integrity—a wholeness and completeness—within an organization are dependent on why the mundane pattern of actions (the virtues) resonate or do not resonate of integrity.[18] Core values serve as guiding principles since individuals act out on what is important to them.[19] In other words, a type of end, or *telos*, is essential toward linking behavior and actions (virtues) to integrity.[20] Organizations are driven by purpose that shape how work is accomplished.[21] Values serve toward ends, purpose, mission, and vision. Virtue, integrity, and values provide a trinity of concepts that are interrelated. Figure 6.2 exhibits the attributes of each defined variable of virtue, integrity, and values.

Expressions of Integrity in Organizations

Given the above patterns, integrity is expressed via acting out a set of core values. Integrity is a wholeness and is derived by actions that provide a completeness.[22] Values are organizing principles that serve as signposts to why decisions are made or how mundane work practices are acted out. The connection between what is valued by the organization—core values—and acting out such core values represents expressions of integrity.

What determines the basis for a decision or action? If values are instinctive drives then such drives work competitively toward a point of balance.[23] Pirson and Lawrence suggest that individual actions are fundamentally shaped by four drives: the drive to acquire, the drive to bond, the drive to comprehend, and the drive to defend.[24] The four drives, however, are independent of each other and thus, inherently competitive toward each other as are instincts. Each drive will be more important than the other depending on the circumstance the individual faces. The problem with instincts or the four drives is that obeying them may be like obeying people. We tend not to if given a choice.[25]

Evidence emerging through the consulting engagements with the three SMEs suggests an alternate vantage point. While there is clearly a manifestation of the four drives in organizations, the competitiveness of each drive suggests that integrity is not a structural wholeness but dependent on circumstances and personal preference. In contrast, the consulting engagements provided evidence that suggests an ordinal structure to the core values identified and acted upon by members. Participants acted on a set of organizing principles.[26] This ordinal structure resonates of Augustinian thought as an "order of loves."[27] For purposes of this case study, evidence suggests that each organization leaned on certain core values placed above the rest but not at the expense of the other values.

The Consulting Engagements

Consulting offers a rich outlet to study, observe, and validate findings of how organizations accomplish their purpose. And since the consulting engagement is for the purpose of serving a client's needs, it also serves toward the application of action research.[28] Working as a perceived colleague, yet being a third party, consulting as action research allows for observations on how each entity developed their core values.[29] The consulting engagements also provided the best of what action research provides: a value outcome for the client that is applicable and relevant to business.

The process used for developing the core values for each entity was based on Appreciative Inquiry.[30] My approach to extracting out a set of core values and vision statement is essentially a synthesis of visioning and purpose;[31] appreciative inquiry in bringing out the "best of what is" in the organization;[32] and the researcher–client relationship where both work in developing solutions. Table 6.1 displays the characteristics of each business in the case study along with other case study components.

Integrity in Action: Core Value Sessions

Sessions with the entities were characterized by long hours of addressing questions and arranging data. The four questions used for each of the core values sessions are as follows:

1. Think of a time in your entire experience with your organization when you have felt most excited, most engaged, and most alive. What were the forces and factors that made it a great experience? What was it about you, others, and your organization that made it a peak experience for you?

2. What do you value most about yourself, your work, and your organization?

3. What are your organization's best practices (ways of management, approaches, traditions)?

4. What is the core factor that "gives life" to your organization?[33]

Each question is designed to solicit responses that focus on "the best of what is" within the organization. Participants work together toward a common end, but not through a process of "problem analysis" that focuses on what is wrong. Rather, the approach is to focus on the inherent strengths and a tacit understanding of what is most important to the participants. Table 6.2 outlines session responses and how the volume of responses trickles down to a set of core values and vision.

The first question always prompts the most enthusiastic of responses since reflection on a peak experience brings up memories of how excellent work can be accomplished. In each situation, many of the responses from the first question ultimately end up as a core value, an ideal within a core value, or in support of a core value. As an example of using pattern matching and theme analysis through tree diagrams, Figure 6.1 illustrates for the PAO the process of questions to final core values in Figure 6.3.[34]

Table 6.1. Organization Characteristics and Consulting Data Methods*

Organization characteristics	Core value consulting sessions	Post session consulting interviews	Data methods
Pet Services Industry Business (PSI) Employees—40 Type: Profit	4 sessions 4 hours each 5 attendees; management team and owner	8 sessions 1 hour each Owner	Pattern Matching (Cao 2007; Yin 1994; Cresswell 1998) Data Trees (Jonsen & Jehn 2009) Regular review and confirmation/corrections by participants (Vries, Manfred, & Miller 1987; Yin, 1994; Cresswell 1998)
Performing Arts Organization (PAO) Members—65 Type: Non-Profit	4 sessions 4 hours each 15 attendees; board, non-board, and artistic director	8 sessions 1 hour each Artistic Director	Pattern Matching (Cao 2007; Yin 1994; Cresswell 1998) Data Trees (Jonsen & Jehn 2009) Regular review and confirmation/corrections by participants (Vries, Manfred, & Miller 1987; Yin, 1994; Cresswell 1998)
Winery (WIN) Owner and 3 part-time employees. Type: Artisan/Family	3 sessions 3 hours each 1 attendee; owner	3 sessions 2 hours each Owner	Pattern Matching (Cao 2007; Yin 1994; Cresswell 1998) Data Trees (Jonsen & Jehn 2009) Regular review/corrections by owner (Vries, Manfred, & Miller 1987; Yin, 1994; Cresswell 1998)

*All entities had at least 3 consulting sessions followed by post consulting interviews. Applied pattern matching, data trees, and post interviews to interpret and confirm results.

Table 6.2. Responses by Session from Themes to Core Values to Vision Statements*

	PSI	PAO	WIN
Session 1 Responses	**42 Responses**	**147 Responses**	**12 Responses**
Session 2 Deriving Values	Four Themes Work Environment People and Servant Leader Customer Service Pet Compassion	Seven Themes Excellence in performance Audience interaction Process-rehearsal Being part of the group Variety of repertoire Organization/Board Community	Six Themes Removing snobbery from wine Educating customers Urban winery in a community Making visitors feel like family Reward of having people enjoy the wine A crafted good for others
Session 3 Finalizing Values	Seven Core Values Passion for pets Respect for others Accountability Service Excellence-customer driven Integrity FUN work environment	Four Core Values Pursuing excellence in the craft and performance of music Providing eclectic experiences for audiences Respecting individual members and their contribution Positively impacting the community	Three Core Values Education about wine and its virtues Neighborhood family winery where visitors are welcome like family Artisanship of a crafted good from practices handed down the family
Session 4 Establishing Vision and Purpose	Serving pets and their people, in unique ways	Be, Sing, Become….IMPACT!	Wine for the people

*All entities, PSI (Pet Services Industry), PAO (Performing Arts Organization), and WIN (Winery) developed themes from the early consulting sessions that eventually emerged as core values. From core values, a concise vision statement was developed. Note that several responses by each entity filtered down to essential core values and a concise vision statement.

Appreciative inquiry

Question 1   **Question 2**   **Question 3**   **Question 4**

Responses	Responses	Responses	Responses
• Concerts outside the normal concert • Unique/themed concerts • Variety of repertoire—on stage concerts, letters home, Russian concert • Variety of experiences (not restricted to programming) • Multiple performers: orchestra, soloists • Moving works of choral music • Group experience • Stepping out of our comfort zone, when it works—it's magic, variety of talent in the organization • Personal connections • Experience of being chosen as a member—anticipating in excellence	• Contribute in any way possible • No unredeemable weak links • Everyone's contribution is valuable • Make people around feel/know they're valued and important • Having a chance to contribute • Excellence • Vision of musical excellence and call to pursue that • Pushing my musical talents, improving • Sharing musical experience, love of it when the audience feels it • Educational—young people	• Rehearsal process • Rigor of rehearsal • Rehearsal time • Strict attendance policy • Serious rehearsal • Performance quality • Auditions • Open to having new members share talents • Accept all peoples, all walks of life; all professions, not restrictive • Social interaction • Open communication • 2 way street—respect, integrity, trust • Board members are chorale members • Open to new ideas • Board volunteer members	• Variety—spice of life: • Music, • People, • Cultures, • Venues, • Other organizations Variety of repertoire excellence • Performance • Process • Relationships • Do not settle • Celebrate • Quality Goal: Audience connection • Commitment to excellence • Caring • Communication • Greater plans to serve our community

Excellence   Audience   Process   Being in group   Repertoire   Organization   Community

Pursuing excellence in the craft and performance of music

Respecting individual members and their contribution

Providing eclectic experiences for audiences and members

Positively impacting the community

Be, sing, become.....IMPACT

Figure 6.3. Tree diagram.

A consistent set of responses suggested what was most important to participants in the organization. An organization's consistency to its values and aspirations is critical toward expressing integrity.[35] This also corresponded with the organization's general goals or approaches to conducting business since what is most important is acted upon.

A feeling of disorientation, rather than focus, was experienced by the participants. This disorientation was important for each of the sessions. Participants initially perceived their responses as having limited correlation yet recognized that organizational life offered much in terms of current and potential fulfillment. Experiencing dissonance in the process represents a form of sense-making that leads to a plausible set of core values.[36] The sense-making process that took place during the sessions reflects an expression of integrity in the organization for three reasons: First, by wrestling with the questions and trying to establish themes and patterns, participants regularly sought out cues and retrospectively created meaning.[37] This type of behavior is necessary at the organizational level under circumstances of conducting routine business. It suggests a bridge between behavior and character,[38] whether circumstances are mundane or extraordinary.[39] The problem faced by the participants was equivocality, not the need for more information.[40] When faced by a variety of outcomes, guidance toward establishing priorities is essential toward defining what matters most. This represents an expression of integrity: the acting out of core values given a consistent history of doing so (retrospectively answering the questions).[41]

Second, the identity of each participant was challenged in the process of extracting core values out of several responses.[42] The end (*telos*) of defining core values was plausible to participants rather than a "right" answer to be achieved. It was a process of sharing narratives where personal narratives represent expressions of integrity.[43] The appreciative inquiry process required individuals to negotiate their personal narratives to those of the group and to those of the organization. In this way, participants did "act out" what was most important to them and in the process aligned their values with that of the organization.[44]

Third, the sessions were social and led toward plausible outcomes.[45] Participants had to work with others and come to an agreement on what constituted the core values of their organization. It was one thing for individuals to tacitly know and have a general sense of what was most important to them as individuals and as groups. It was quite another to concretely define the values. The conduct of the participants was contingent on the conduct of others in the group. That type of interrelationship of conduct expresses the soundness and integrity of the organization.[46] As an expression of integrity, the process challenged participants to solidify the structural components of the organization's core values and vision as a team.

For the winery, I served as facilitator/guide but also the social dynamic of focusing on cues since the owner was the sole participant. The process, however, worked the same way as with the other entities. His sense-making was no different since I was available as both the facilitator and the collaborator in the process of developing a vision of *Wine for the people*.

Using the approach of asking "WHY" five times about why it is important what the organization provides, there was first a general sense of the disorientation experienced in defining a vision.[47] After many iterations in the process, a rewritten vision statement would strike an immediate response of agreement. The group would sleep on the vision statement and days later would still represent what the entity is all about.

To summarize, the process of developing core values and vision was an occasion for sense-making.[48] It was also an expression of integrity because what people tacitly knew was challenged. Participants needed to transform imprecise values into concrete values while working out that process with others. Since integrity is a wholeness the core values and vision process as sense-making challenges the underlying assumption of what people hold to be important and to act on what is important.[49]

Integrity in Action: Post-Session Consulting Interviews with Owners and Directors

As part of the consulting engagement, I met regularly with the owners and director for each organization. That time provided the owners and director to reflect on how the established core values were "holding up" in mundane everyday work. Habits, particularly in the mundane or remarkable, eventually shine as virtues or vices, either of which sustains the completeness of integrity or undermine it.[50]

During the time of post-session interviews I had with each organization spanning two months, the following outcomes were apparent and represent some of the practical outcomes of establishing a set of core values and vision.

1. **Clarity on strategic direction**
   - The direction of the entity had greater clarity and focus.
   - Distinctions between distractions versus opportunities emerged.
   - Clear strategies in tandem with improved operations.

2. **Acting deliberately**
   - There was a point of reference and reason for acting and deciding.
   - Priorities for operations had a rationale since they are based on values.
   - Cohesion within teams and groups based on agreed values.
3. **Core values crystalize**
   - Issues surfaced that challenged the relevance of the core values.
   - Internal conflicts require management and employees to apply what is most important in the business—the agreed upon core values.
   - Perceived conflicts deflated during the core values session since participants realized others held similar points of view and opinions.

Acting out the core values was an expression of integrity and completeness in the organization. The actions of the owners and director indicate that they are concerned with the kind of meanings that will yield enduring success for the organization. Since human activity and creativity creates a world of things, values also provide vitality to routines and processes.[51]

In the interest of space, the following are only samples of events for all three organizations. For the PSI organization, the first notable difference was the clarity the organization had about the direction of the business. The owner (Ben) comments:

"I've been wondering, actually all of us, about what really is the purpose of our work? We knew it was important, but identifying it and making it a continual pursuit as a vision statement and core values is great. I can't believe how clear a direction and purpose we have. In fact, we're now working on a new marketing campaign. One based on the direction and values that are most important to us and our customers."

Another instance was a challenge to the core values set by the group and the continual process of sense-making. In this situation, it was a simmering conflict between two managers. The owner continues:

"Will it keep us from growing? I wonder if this type of thing will keep us from growing into a world class company. Can we attain that status or do we need perfect employees?"

As owner and leader, he wants it to be a place where employees have fulfilling careers. He also wonders if he is at fault, another component of sense-making where one questions their identity.[52] When I followed up a week later on the conflict he responded:

> "They're doing better. We agreed that respect for our team and accountability were at stake. If we create a problem then we need to create a solution. And, the root of the issue was just a lack of respect one had over the other."

Overcoming a challenge to the core values creates cohesiveness of the assumptions and beliefs of the entity's culture.[53]

One final event stands as an exemplar on Ben's approach to conducting business. In one interview he said that a competitor approached him and asked if he would be interested in buying 25% of his client list. Surprised, Ben asked why. The competitor (smaller than Ben's operation which is three times larger) said his truck used on the job needed major repairs and he was out of operating cash. He also didn't want to borrow additional funds. Ben's response:

> "It's the guy's bread and butter. I couldn't take away or even consider buying that list and further create a bigger hole for him. That could send him out of business, just to fix the truck and have him try to recoup the costs and customers in the future. It wasn't right."

He acted consistently with his values and the values the team defined. Some items are worth noting about this incident: First, Ben exhibited what Michael Porter in *Competitive Advantage* calls being a good competitor,[54] one that creates a good competitive landscape where all organizations can thrive rather than one that seeks out predatory approaches and diminishes the value of the market and ultimately to the consumer. Second, Ben exhibited integrity out of habit. His order of values is set and he acts on them by habit yielding excellence. He acted based on an emerging ordinal structure of the core values. His habits cultivated virtue, which further strengthens the completeness of integrity.[55] Third, by virtue of Ben's actions, we find that he is concerned with the kinds of meaning that will sustain the business and the competitive landscape.[56]

For the PAO, a positive environment for processes and board meetings emerged where core values mitigated years of board latent conflict.

"Honoring people for who they are is that vital part of the process. I mean, the process can only be as good if people know they are respected, that what they have to contribute is important, that people enjoy being part of the chorale, that I respect them and want their best and of who they are. Because people have dignity as humans, that process is vibrant and has life. It's full of life.

Take orchestras—some are cogs in the wheel. They are equipment, supplies. They [musicians] are sour and well don't feel appreciated. We are not like that. What people contribute is vitally important and they know it."

Here, the artistic director, Mark, enacts the core values as one would a code of ethics, but it is more than ethics that are at stake. The positive climate of the ensemble is maintained.[57] Acting out the core value created greater cohesiveness in the ensemble.

Another instance on clarity follows:

"One thing I really appreciated about your process is that it diffused a lot of conflict in the board. Our meetings are so rife and dysfunctional. Members would sit and not comment during meetings even after our gracious president asked, any thoughts. Then out of nowhere, a member flares out with a comment, then sits silently and stews. This was essentially our way of having meetings.

Your process changed all of that. When the board members saw that everyone agreed on issues, they realized they were fighting based on misconceived ideas and assumptions. When they realized that so and so is thinking and thought along the same line as me, it was, 'Wow. I don't have to fight that person.' The meetings now have changed, people comment, interact because there is a common agreement that what they all value, they actually valued prior to the meeting. It took the process to discover that assumptions held eroded the moral integrity of interacting in the meetings and pursuing common goals for the good of the choir."

The appreciative inquiry process alone reduced latent conflict and encouraged closer collaborative meetings by improving their language and communication.[58] In this instance, an order of values emerges where respect for individuals is a priority. This contributes to a closer connection to the organization as a whole.[59]

Finally, the winery owner exhibited qualities of his established core values for the business. His artisanship coupled with his desire to remove the snobbery associated with wine (to educate) permeates how he conducts business.

In all of our interviews, when Peter speaks of making wine he trails off in various directions. His knowledge of making wine is highly tacit, which accounts for the "rabbit trails." But when working with him on the process of making wine, his desire to educate people about the realities of the effort and care taken into the process override stale explanations. On one occasion I had the privilege of observing how he blended one of the winery's signature labels. Peter continues:

> "Have a seat. Blending today will be a challenge since a restaurant downtown needs more of the label (wine) before scheduled. This will be interesting. You need two glasses so you can sample. This barrel (at the end of a row of barrels) has been sitting a couple of years, it should do for what we need. [Sniffs, looks, sniffs a sample]. This is important, if the blend doesn't work, the label is not there…and if it is not there, what's the point in making it? You know? [Explicative] this has to be good….it helps business, but most of all, I want people to enjoy what I've made."

Making wine is not just smashing grapes. Peter's approach was anything but precise, but it was qualitatively superior to what a mechanized approach could produce—at least for the very way and means as to how it was produced. This is important to realize since how Peter conducts business is reflective of how he makes wine and that improves my understanding about how certain entities conduct business.[60] For Peter, the lengthy process of making wine is how he conducts business, and this poses a challenge to attaining and sustaining profitability. His current status shows emerging profitability, but he also wrestles to balance that with the intent of the winery—to educate others on wine and preserve the way of making wine. There is excellence in practices, but there is also the personal integrity acting out the enduring tenets he originally set out when he opened his business. The profitability is testimony to his hard work and craft and yet, Peter still unifies his individual interests to what is good for the community.[61] His primary value is to educate the public: wine for the people. He is concerned with the kinds of meaning that contribute toward wine as being a part of the experience his customers feel when they have a glass of his artisanship.

Ending Comments

In each area of consulting, the core value sessions and the interview sessions, a consistent pattern of acting out values that express a completeness of integrity is evident. During the core values sessions, participants found their general sense of identity and what they believed to be challenged. The sense-making process was an occasion to challenge their values and act out with integrity. For organizations to develop integrity, the values of persons or entities must be challenged. This suggests that there not be permanent solutions to the intrinsic tensions organizations face. Rather, it is confronting tensions and challenges that build up virtue [actions] based on values that strengthen integrity.[62]

Key Terms

Core values—the enduring tenets of an organization, the most important values to the organization. They serve to guide in decision making.

Appreciative inquiry—the practice of focusing on what the organization does well rather than focusing on the negative or weaknesses.

Sense-making—making sense of situations that are vague by searching for plausible solutions or outcomes.

Study Questions

1. The three organizations in the chapter each had a set of challenges toward enduring success. What are your organization's challenges that serve toward your focusing on enduring success?

2. What shapes the decision-making process for major decisions and for routine decisions? Is what shapes the decision different in each? If so, how?

3. What constitutes virtue—actions and practices—in your organization?

4. What do you think are the core values in your organization? Would they also be held by employees?

5. From the case studies in the chapter, virtue and values work in tandem in building integrity. What does this process look like in your organization? Why?

6. Without core values, what serves as guiding your organization toward enduring success?

7. What types of sense-making are you engaged in, or your organization, where a set of core values would greatly help and thereby build the integrity of your organization?

Further Reading

For Nonprofits Working on Vision and Strategy

Collins, J., (2005). *Good to great: The social sectors.* Boulder, CO: Jim Collins.

On Organizational Culture and Management Perspectives

Schein, E. H. (1992). *Organizational culture and leadership* (2nd ed.). San Francisco, CA: Jossey-Bass.

Maslow, A. H. (1998). *Maslow on management.* Stephens, D. C., & Heil, G.(Eds.). New York, NY: John Wiley & Sons, Inc.

For Insights on Future Organization Design and Practice

Chodhury, S. (2003). *Organization 21C: Someday all organizations will lead this way.* Upper Saddle River, NJ: Financial Times Prentice-Hall.

On Action Research and Appreciative Inquiry

Reason, P., & Bradbury, H. (2001). *Handbook of action research: Participative inquiry and practice.* Thousand Oaks, CA: SAGE Publications.

INTRODUCTION TO PART III

Values and Virtues as Milestones for Integrity in Organization

This section kicks off with an interesting point and an overdue correction. Chinese managers and professors at local business schools or universities have tried to catch up with Western management styles for far too long. But similar to importing latest technology, the flows of knowledge may reverse. This chapter argues about a more local discussion of what integrity's forms are and how to make progress. Insights could well be helpful beyond the Chinese setting. Therefore, even the literature of integrity is carried out with the Chinese culture and Confucian thinking in mind. The used case study does not only add an empirical element to the analysis, it serves as a solid foundation for the induction of recommendations. The derived insights on "face saving" issues, contextual factors, as well as changes over time may not be limited to the Chinese context. They can serve as a fresh source of inspiration on how to improve the management of integrity initiatives beyond the Chinese setting.

Our international journey continues beyond the Chinese culture space and sheds light on Southeast Asia in the ensuing chapter. Also in this context, there is no ambiguity about corruption playing a negative role. To go one step further, the lack of integrity is portrayed and understood as one of the key reasons why developing countries fail to catch up economically. The chapter also clarifies that the substantial investments made in the past decades to curb corruption globally have generally failed to make a permanent dent in the level of corruption across countries. We thus need more insights about actionable knowledge and solutions, which this chapter aims to offer. Local expertise represents an essential requirement when making progress so that some of the represented countries like the

Philippines and Indonesia can leapfrog from the low rank in the Transparency International index. The chapter relies on in-depth case studies, subsequently analyzed and critically discussed, to provide rich insights. It presents education, not necessarily isolated legal reforms as a promising way forward.

The third chapter in this section clarifies that education as the panacea is not just the case in Southeast Asia. While taking the reader on a journey to Latin America, the authors again emphasize that a fish rots from the head down. The leaders of organizations can make or break future success. What they need, in turn, is to develop their own skills and competencies as well as see their staff embark on equal progress. Courses in ethics, humanistic management, integrity, and other more or less general topics with a strong normative nature help in clarifying responsibilities for everyone. All can become more aware of the vulnerability, which explains why we need progress in the first place. Training enhances awareness and critical thinking. Education in turn must be open to highly realistic approaches to changing people's behavior. Organizations do not change overnight just because a few employees have attended a short course. Education must embrace the complexities inherent in understanding leaders and managers, their pressures to behave in a certain way, as well as how progress can be made.

CHAPTER 7

Managing Integrity in Chinese Organizations

A Confucian Perspective

Yi-Hui Ho
Chieh-Yu Lin

Introduction

Most people shall agree with the importance of integrity in organizations. Integrity is essential for organizations because stakeholders delegate them with the duty of ensuring that organizations are held accountable for their actions. Organizations with integrity in its individuals or atmosphere are commonly believed to be inclined to desired outcomes and avoiding risk. Individuals with high integrity are likely to be honest and reliable. Without integrity, those who have capabilities are useless because they might use their skills to deceive others and thus undermine the benefits to the stakeholders of the organization. Past stories and examples about integrity failure keep reminding people of the consequences of the absence of integrity. Many of those incidents not only resulted in losses of billion dollars, but also led to disasters for individuals, organizations, or the society. Consequently, increasing numbers of organizations have laid a greater emphasis on their integrity practices.

This chapter focuses the discussion on the Chinese context. At the significant position that Asia is in global economic systems, more and more attention is drawn to organizations and business from Asia. In particular, an increasing number of multinational corporations have begun to access markets in the Greater Chinese Region, which includes Mainland China, Taiwan, Hong Kong, and Macau. As Chinese people from these places and those overseas constitute more than one-quarter of the world's population, studies regarding issues in Chinese organizations may bring about an increasing worldwide interest. As integrity is the key to business achievement, it would be helpful to learn more about how integrity exists in Chinese organizations in order to be successful in the Greater Chinese market.

This chapter therefore first discusses the diverse definitions of integrity in academic literature, and analyzes dimensions of integrity as well as the interpersonal connections from the standpoint of Chinese culture and Confucian thinking. Also, the chapter provides approaches to manage integrity in Chinese organizations with a case illustration. Finally, possible challenges and cautions of managing integrity in Chinese organizations will be addressed.

Diverse Definitions and Dimensions of Integrity

The word *integrity* is originally from the Latin word *integri* that denotes wholeness or completeness. The importance of personal or organizational integrity is self-evident; however, there is still no consensus on its definition. Numerous studies define integrity from different perspectives. Zauderer summarizes the unique elements of integrity definitions, such as "Consciously struggle to subdue the evil inclination" from The Old Testament; "Live according to the principle of The Golden Rule" from The New Testament; "Maintain concern for the community, engage in political and social life to improve the community, inspire others to do good deeds" from Aristotle; "Establish, affirm, and exemplify moral duties and obligations toward others, treat others as ends and not as means" from Immanuel Kant; and "a consistent commitment to do what is right, especially under conditions of adversity, confront all moral considerations before taking action" from Mark Halfin.[1] Each definition above obviously has different interpretations of integrity.

In addition to the definitions above, integrity can be defined as "the quality of being honest and morally upright,"[2] that has two major components: personal and impersonal. Personal integrity implies specific or universal goodness for individuals; impersonal integrity, which is often overlooked, denotes the capacity of organizations and systems to be moral. Integrity capacity is therefore the personal, collective, and system ability that consists of four dimensions: process, judgment, development, and system factors.[3]

Integrity can also be regarded as being consistent with what is said and done, being consistent with social norms, and being consistent over time—being consistent even at the cost of risks to self. Gosling and Huang suggest the dimensions of integrity to include wholeness, consistency in the face of adversity, consistency in word and action, and ethics and morality.[4] Becker proposes the philosophy of objectivism and discusses definitions of integrity from different perspectives. One of the arguments interestingly interpret integrity as "(1) I value (reason, purpose, and self-esteem); (2) I am (rational, honest, independent, just, productive, and proud); (3) my values, goals, and behavior are congruent; and (4) I am willing to do whatever is necessary to live according to my most cherished values."[5]

In addition, Koehn discusses integrity from the viewpoint of personal consistency and compliance with moral norms or expectations of Confucian integrity, Buddhist and Christian integrity, and Jungian integrity. She interprets integrity as "the compassionate the receptive work of making the self whole and enduringly happy through critically and assiduously separating who we truly are from the false ego...."[6] Although these above definitions are still inconsistent, the importance of integrity to organizations is never ignored in literature.

Integrity in Chinese Culture

From the perspective of Chinese culture, integrity also has diverse meanings that make it difficult to simplify in the Chinese way of thinking. To illustrate, traditional Chinese culture basically results from the influence of three major doctrines: Confucianism, Taoism, and Buddhism.[7] Among the three doctrines, Confucianism, which has more than 2000 years of history particularly forms the essential basis of Chinese culture, and has also significantly influenced many other countries in East and Southeast Asia.[8] To understand how integrity was perceived and acted out in Chinese organizations, an analysis of Confucianism will be helpful and necessary.

Confucius was the most influential philosopher and teacher in ancient China who had a position parallel to that of Socrates in ancient Greece. His teachings and philosophical sayings, *Confucianism*, are the central ideas and thoughts that instruct Chinese people on practical principles and rules to daily life. Confucius did not put his philosophy into writing; however, his disciples and students handed down and compiled the *Analects of Confucius* which is considered the most reliable book about Confucian teachings and has been one of the important texts for successive Chinese generations. Because of its everyday application, Confucianism deeply influenced not only Chinese culture but also expanded to the East Asian region for over 2000 years.[9] Confucian teachings related to personal and organizational integrity will be illustrated as follows.

Dimensions of Confucian Integrity: Ren, Li, Yi, Chiu, and Shin

Confucian integrity guides practical ethics without a religious angle. It includes the following five major dimensions: *Ren, Li, Yi, Chiu,* and *Shin.*

Ren, the core value of Confucian integrity, has several different interpretations in Confucian teachings. According to the *Analects of Confucius*, Confucius interprets *Ren* with a variety of definitions based on his disciples' backgrounds and conditions. *Ren* is commonly translated as "kindness" or "a benevolent and humanitarian attitude." It is based upon empathy and understanding others rather than commanded rules. Because of the belief in empathy with others, Confucius also explains *Ren* as "what you do not want done to yourself, not to do to others" to his followers. In sum, *Ren* is the basis of Confucian integrity,[10] and consideration for humanity is the center of *Ren.* A person with *Ren* can be regarded as a person with integrity, also called *jun-zu* in Chinese.

Li can be translated as rite, propriety, good manners, or politeness; it is the rules pertaining to rituals and forms of social regulations and refers to all actions taken and behaviors demonstrated by people to build an ideal society. Confucius emphasizes the practice of *Ren* by being *Li* and indicates that *Ren* is to subdue one's self and return to propriety. If a person can subdue him or herself and return to propriety, others will also ascribe *Ren* to him or her. Moreover, a person with integrity shall not stare at, speak out, or do what is contrary to propriety because these behaviors violate *Li*.

While *Ren* is the pinnacle of Confucian integrity, *Yi* is the means to perform and achieve *Ren*. *Yi* can be translated as righteousness, right conduct, or being just. According to Confucius, a person with integrity is aware of *Yi* rather than advantages. It implies doing things right and ethically with good reasons rather than pursuing self-interests. In addition, when performing *Yi*, Confucius reminds that people need to consider their identity and duties, and take different subjects and situations into account instead of using the same standard.

In terms of *Chiu*, Confucius thinks that a person with *Chiu* has no perplexity. *Chiu* can be translated as wisdom or intelligence, which refers to a person with wisdom as one who will not be of two minds when making a judgment of right or wrong. *Chiu* can also be explained as knowledge that one will use to make the right judgment based on what he or she realizes. In addition to learn things to gain knowledge, *Chiu* also means knowing other people to benefit one's interpersonal relationships. For example, it will be useful and necessary to know other people and understand their desires when communicating with the boss, promoting your subordinates, or negotiating with business partners.

Shin can be translated as trustworthiness, and it is the merit of being reliable and trustworthy with one's words and promises. Most Chinese companies regard *Shin* as the basic criterion for their customers and suppliers; therefore, when doing business with Chinese companies, being reliable and trustworthy is usually considered essential, probably as critical as signing a business contract. *Shin* also denotes building mutual trust with business partners, which is believed to benefit long-term relationships and business success in the Chinese society.

In short, these 5 dimensions of Confucian integrity emphasize the basic characteristics of being a person with integrity, called jun-zu in Chinese. However, in addition to achieve these 5 dimensions, a person with integrity has to maintain the harmonious relationships between individuals and the society, family, and each other. It results in a worldview in which a person is regarded as the core of a network of relations.[11] The concept of Five Luns illustrated below indicates how interpersonal relationships are considered and exerted in Chinese organizations.

The Five Basic Interpersonal Relationships: The Five Luns

Confucian integrity emphasizes harmonious relationships within society, family, as well as individuals; thus Confucian integrity can be regarded as harmonious ethics. The five basic relationships (the five *Luns*) within society and family which Confucius proposed include ruler and subject, father and son, older and younger brothers, husband and wife, and between friends. These relationships are maintained on the basis of mutual duties and obligations, and the family relationship is particularly the core of Confucius ethics.

The five basic interpersonal relationships have also influenced the practices of business management in Asia.[12] In particular, the relationships between ruler and subject, and father and son have been applied to the leader-and-subordinate relationship in business. Furthermore, the relationships between older and younger brothers and between friends have been used as the base to investigate the relationships between colleagues in a business context. It is these networks that are used to secure personal or business relations.[13] Also, Chinese people are inclined to long-term orientations.[14] They are not only likely to build harmonious, but also long-term relationships with others. Because of the emphasis on the harmonious and long-term relationships between persons, creating an organization with harmonious and long-term interpersonal relationships seems to be preferable in Chinese organizations.

These networks have become a permanent part of business though some researchers criticized the likelihood of such relationships resulting in inertia.[15] Lee also proposes that Confucian ideology may lead to relationships being more important than a contract.[16] The necessity of maintaining interpersonal human relationships, also called *guanxi* in Chinese, may cause problems for Western companies which have tried to initiate operations in China.[17]

Approaches of Managing Integrity in Chinese Organizations

This section illustrates how Chinese organizations may manage integrity based on the five dimensions of Confucian integrity and the five basic interpersonal relationships discussed above. The following discussion consists of integrity leaderships, organizations functioning as families, and a case illustration.

Integrity Leadership: An Essential Approach

In addition to maintaining the five basic interpersonal relationships and achieving the five dimensions of Confucian integrity, the role of leaders in Chinese organizations is also critical because they take responsibility for how integrity is exerted in Chinese organizations. Integrity in leadership is commonly considered to be the foundation of the ethical culture in organizations,[18] which is particularly obvious in traditional Chinese culture. Because most Chinese people tend to respect elders and listen to their leaders, they will mostly take their leaders as role models and follow their leaders' words and deeds. On the other hand, leaders and elders in the organization will take care of their subordinates and younger brothers and sisters. The close interpersonal relationships are thus well established and maintained. Those who are leaders and elders in Chinese organizations not only need to be good at their professions at work, but also have to be self-behaved and self-disciplined and stand by their words and behavior. Managing integrity in Chinese organizations also means doing integrity leadership. As Confucius says, "If the ruler is upright, his people will do their duty without the ruler's commands. If the ruler is not upright, although he may command his people, they will not obey." He also notes that leaders shall "Go before the people, work hard and encourage them to follow."

Confucius also suggests that rulers who demonstrate personal integrity and propriety will be better for leading by displaying integrity than establishing regulations and punishment. Laws and punishments may be useful to make people fall in line in Chinese organizations; however, Confucius says "if you govern people by laws and punishments, they will try to avoid the punishments, but your people will have no sense of shame. If, alternatively, you govern people by virtue and propriety, they will have a sense of shame, and will become good." Moreover, a leader with integrity needs to be moderate and humble, willing to listen to others, and take suggestions.

Organizations Functioning as Families for Building Integrity Culture

There is a traditional Chinese saying that "the strength of a nation is derived from the integrity of the home." Chinese people are inclined toward collectivism and think highly of their family. The role of the family in Chinese society thus shall not be ignored. Because of the emphasis on family relationships, the family's functions are often extended to the working environment. Leaders of Chinese organizations are often considered the father in a family; senior employees, or those who have worked for longer time than others, will become the elder brothers or elder sisters. Consequently, the tight working relationships between leaders and subordinates as well as between colleagues are established based on the family relationships, which makes members in the group identify themselves as a family. Accordingly, people will be willing to look after mutual benefits and glorifying their family reputations. In that case, a company is not just a place to earn profit, but a place to feel a sense of belonging and being at home with family members.

As a result, leaders can bring up the culture of integrity in Chinese organizations based on the traditions of family binding and respect for their family's father and elder. To be recognized and taken care by their leaders and elders, employees have to be aware of what their organization believes and values, and are likely to be involved in the culture of integrity. Leaders' beliefs on the culture of integrity can be a channel to guiding values in Chinese organizations.

Once the integrity culture is established, the additional benefit of considering organizations as families and building integrity within the organization is that the integrity atmosphere will gradually disseminate throughout the organization and become the consensus for everyone to follow. To honor his or her family, one will not easily go against the integrity values which his parents and siblings believe in. Moreover, as the old saying goes "birds of a feather flock together," it may attract more people who recognize the integrity culture to join the organization.

A Case of Managing Integrity in the Chinese Organization

Numerous Chinese companies have undertaken integrity initiatives. This chapter takes Taiwan Semiconductor Manufacturing Company

(TSMC) as an example to illustrate integrity in Chinese organizations. TSMC, founded in 1987 in Hsinchu Taiwan, is the world's largest dedicated semiconductor foundry. It provides worldwide services for its customers from North America, Europe, Japan, China, South Korea, and India.

TSMC has been recognized as a corporation that has high reputation for its integrity value. It has received number of awards for excellent performance in its corporate social responsibilities (CSR) initiatives. For example, the CommonWealth Magazine awarded TSMC the "Most Admired Company in Taiwan" for 11 consecutive years as well as "Excellence in Corporate Social Responsibility First Prize" in 2007. TSMC has won the "Best Corporate Governance Award" in Hong Kong and Taiwan regions from IR magazine, "The Best in Taiwan of Asset Governance Awards 2007" from The Asset Magazine, "Corporate Governance Asia Recognition in Taiwan" from Corporate Governance Asia, and the "Most Committed to Corporate Governance" for the Taiwan region by the Finance Asia Magazine.

TSMC's success in balancing both earnings and CSR can mostly be attributed to its corporate values. Corporate values are considered a potential precursor to ethical behavior in organizations. TSMC's major corporate values consist of integrity, maintaining a consistent focus on core business, globalization, long-term vision and strategies, treating customers as partners, building quality into all aspects of the business, constant innovation, fostering a dynamic and fun work environment, keeping communication channels open, caring for employees and shareholders, and being a good corporate citizen. In particular, integrity is considered the most important core value among the top ten business values of TSMC.

TSMC's integrity culture is influenced by its chairman, Morris C. M. Chang, who believes that building integrity is essential in business. According to Morris Chang, TSMC is an organization which commits to the highest professional ethics and integrity,[19] and their efforts in building business integrity have drawn public attention. Based on the results of the Corporate Ethics survey in 2004, 20% of those surveyed propose Morris Chang as the corporate leader with utmost integrity, and TSMC as the company that has the best integrity reputation. Because employees in Chinese organizations tend to see their managers as role models and are more likely to follow what leaders believe, the integrity culture in TSMC is mostly attributed to the integrity leadership.

Business integrity is the core of the TSMC value which includes telling the truth, not indulging in exaggeration and showmanship, keeping promises, competing within the confines of law, prohibiting vicious attack on competitors, and objectively and fairly selecting suppliers.[20] The relations between these integrity values and the Confucian integrity are illustrated below:

1. *Tell the truth.*
   This is exact *Shin*, one of dimensions of Confucian integrity, which means being honest, reliable, and trustworthy. It is also paralleled to *Yi* and *Ren* that one should do the right things when stakeholders are concerned: by telling the truth.

2. *Do not brag. Believe the record of achievements is the best proof of the merit.*
   Being humble is usually considered a virtue in Chinese society. Most Chinese people agree that actions speak louder than words and admire those who are modest instead of boasting. Moreover, keeping a record of achievements can also be regarded as being *Shin*, which means reliable.

3. *Do not make commitments lightly. However, once a commitment is made, devote completely to meeting that commitment.*
   This is also paralleled to the Confucian integrity dimension of *Shin*, of being trustworthy to keep promises to stakeholders. This statement also reveals the importance of maintaining long-term and harmonious relationships with stakeholders.

4. *With competitors, compete to the fullest within the limits of the law, but do not slander them in order to gain. Also respect intellectual property rights of others.*
   This indicates the integrity of *Ren* that being respectful and caring about others, even toward enemies. It also reveals *Yi*, of making profit by honorable means, and *Chiu*, using the wisdom and advanced knowledge to win the game, and being *Li* to follow the rite and regulations in the competition.

5. *With vendors, maintain an objective, consistent, and impartial attitude.*
This reveals the virtue of *Ren* to exhibit fairness and respect to others. It also ensures the long-term cooperation and relationships with vendors, and takes care of mutual benefits between TSMC and its vendors.

6. *Do not tolerate any form of corrupt behavior or politicking.*
This statement clearly indicates the basic requirement of *Yi* in TSMC: doing things right instead of doing what is self-advantageous. Company politics are forbidden to maintain the harmonious relationships within the organization.

Following the integrity value, when selecting new employees, TSMC places emphasis on the candidates' qualifications and character, but not connections or access. They believe character and talent are the key criteria for recruiting new staff instead of using interpersonal connection, *guanxi*. When a choice is to be made between character and talent, character is always chosen over talent. In TSMC, a very talented person who is deficient in character will never be recruited. The company also facilitates employees' self-controls with practical ethical education and training to encourage monitoring and correcting their own behaviors.

To reinforce the integrity culture, TSMC has established an Ethics Code to guide employees, officers, and nonemployee directors. Most Chinese employees prefer company rules and values to be specified and clear so that they can easily follow; hence the Ethics Code with more detailed illustrations will be helpful to promote integrity conduct, prevent wrongdoings, and support compliance with applicable laws and regulations. The principles embodied in the code express TSMC's policies regarding discrimination, bribery and corruption, conflicts of interests, protection of company assets and reputation, and so on.

TSMC requires that employees should comply with all applicable laws, rules, regulations, and in-house regulations in every aspect of corporate activities at all times, strive to ensure that all corporate activities are in compliance with normal business practices and social ethics, and should maintain impartial, fair, and open relationships with all stakeholders of the company as well as conduct business in a fair manner with them. Complying with the Ethics Code is the responsibility of every TSMC employee. TSMC takes disciplinary action which includes termination of employment. To illustrate, some statements of TSMC's Ethics Code are listed below:

1. All employees must observe high business ethics standards when dealing with suppliers, vendors, subcontractors, customers, competitors, and other relevant parties, including the government.
2. All employees or their family members and close relatives must not give or accept any gift, money, or entertainment to or from any TSMC suppliers, vendors, subcontractors, customers, or competitors. Any form of bribery is strictly prohibited.
3. All employees must abide by the principles set forth in the code when it is a required courtesy to accept gifts, gratitude, or any form of hospitality, or where it is in accordance with accepted courtesy to maintain and promote normal business relationships by giving gifts to relevant parties.
4. All employees should follow common business etiquette and refrain from frequent and excessive business hospitality when entertaining or being entertained.
5. All employees should not give customers or vendors the impression that any form of hospitality or gift giving is required to establish or maintain a relationship with TSMC.
6. Gift giving and entertaining between managers and their subordinates should follow the above principles, and should be based on the principle of simplicity.

It is usually challenging to achieve integrity and maintain the culture of integrity. Success in building business integrity culture requires continuing efforts and considerable time and resource inputs; however, organizations that promote integrity values will benefit from stakeholders. TSMC's achievement in pursuing integrity culture not only promotes a better working environment for employees, but also earns positive reputations for business. As a result, healthy and long-term relationships as well as mutual benefits with all stakeholders are well-maintained. Moreover, because TSMC's business integrity is a non-negotiable and precise standard for employees to accomplish its CSR by committing to integrity, employees are less likely to make decisions or experience orders from managers or colleagues that are against TSMC integrity values. TSMC therefore establishes organizational integrity culture that intrinsically motivate the integrity mindsets of employees.

Challenges of Managing Integrity in Chinese Organizations

Although the Confucian integrity is commonly recognized and applied in Chinese business and organizations, challenges of developing and maintaining integrity shall also be addressed. This section discusses the "face" issue in Chinese organizations, context considerations when following rules and regulations, and the changing environment that affects the thinking of Chinese culture.

"Face" Issues in Chinese Organizations

When managing integrity in Chinese organizations, face saving issues have to be carefully considered. Exerting integrity practices or integrity leaderships usually implies correcting of mistakes or unethical action. As a result, there may be some instances of criticizing others in public or in meeting occasions, which most Chinese employees or even managers are likely to take personally. They may feel embarrassed, feel disrespected, and may be upset about losing face. In addition, having a sense of shame is also an important virtue in Chinese culture. If you make other people lose face, it usually turns out that the harmonious interpersonal relationships between each other may be terminated. For a better solution, it may be workable to correct mistakes in private with friendly tones to save the other's face and show your respect. If the mistake must be corrected in public, most people will prefer tactful or peaceful communications so that the harmonious atmosphere and their "face" will be saved.

In addition, being humble and modest is commonly admired in Chinese society. Therefore, many Chinese people may not be used to taking compliments or speak out their opinion and suggestions in public even though it will glorify his or her "face." In that case, foreign managers in Chinese organizations can try using private occasions to collect opinions from employees.

Considering the Contexts

Contexts can be regarded as the environment which is to be considered when managing integrity in Chinese organizations. Although following rules and regulations is a virtue in Chinese culture, it should be noted that sometimes rules may not be certainly well-applied to all circumstances. For instance, Confucius thinks that each person has unique characteristics so that he often advises his disciples in different ways and provides with different answers based on their diverse characteristics and contexts. As a result, there may not be a single or standard solution to the same question in Confucian teachings. *Ren*, the major Confucian integrity, refers to sensitivity and kindness to others. Confucius makes different interpretations on *Ren* to his disciples but in sum, it is about thinking what is going on in the specific case to do more good than harm, and considering the circumstances and conditions instead of focusing on rules to improve the conditions. While doing business with Chinese companies, multinational enterprises may take actions and consider the contexts that suit local circumstances and conditions or make decisions that bring a better outcome.

The Changing Environment

Globalization and the changing environment bring about foreign cultures and values. Different social, political, and economic systems within the Greater Chinese Region are also influenced by the Confucian integrity. Increasing numbers of Chinese organizations have learned about the Western cultures and therefore adopted Western thinking into business operations. For instance, *guanxi*, the interpersonal networks, is usually considered critical whether between or within Chinese organizations. Maintaining *guanxi* with business partners was an important way of getting things done in traditional Chinese culture and thus may be regarded as necessary and acceptable. However, the overemphasis of using *guanxi* in business may result in possible ethical concerns, such as to bribe customers in order to build *guanxi*. Nevertheless, based on the study of Pedersen, the importance of *guanxi* in Chinese business is gradually changing, especially in coastal cities.[21] An increasing number of people are starting to recognize that *guanxi* is not necessarily sustainable if only based on money transactions. Accordingly, some Chinese companies are now beginning to establish *guanxi* with other companies by means of contracts to ensure long-term and stable business relationships. Accordingly, traditional Confucius integrity may be continuously influenced by the impact of political and economic systems, changing environment, and foreign culture exposures.

Conclusion

Managing integrity is a critical issue for modern organizations, and integrity culture is a precious intangible asset which benefits all stakeholders of the organization; however, achieving integrity and building integrity culture is not an easy task. As the increasing important influences of the Greater Chinese market, this chapter analyzes the dimensions and meanings of Confucian integrity, the importance of interpersonal relationships, and integrity leaderships in Chinese culture, and provides perspectives on how integrity is managed in Chinese organizations. Moreover, the chapter attempts to provide some clues to the answer by analyzing the integrity value of TSMC, a Taiwanese semiconductor company with excellent corporate social performance and integrity culture. The chapter also contributes to the understanding of dimensions of integrity in Chinese cultures and integrity managing in Chinese organizations.

Key Terms

Ren—the core of Confucian thinking which means kindness or a benevolent and humanitarian attitude.

Li—rite, propriety, good manners, or politeness.

Yi—righteousness, right conduct, or being just.

Chiu—wisdom or intelligence.

Shin—trustworthiness.

The Five Luns—the five basic relationships within society and family including ruler and subject, father and son, older and younger brothers, husband and wife, and between friends.

Study Questions

1. What, in your opinion, are the determinants for multinational corporations to consider in their business integrity policies for the cultural diversity of their personnel?
2. Which elements do you consider to be the most influential in the success of managing integrity in your institution?

Further Reading

Cheung, T. S., & King, A. Y. (2004). Righteousness and profitableness: The moral choices of contemporary Confucian entrepreneurs. *Journal of Business Ethics 54*, 245–260.

Hsu, S. (2007). A new business excellence model with business integrity from ancient Confucian thinking. *Total Quality Management 18*, 413–423.

Taylor, R. L. (2011). *Confucius, the Analects: The path of the sage-Selections annotated & explained.* Woodstock, VT: SkyLight Paths.

CHAPTER 8

Building Integrity Among Organizations in Southeast Asia

Roberto Martin N. Galang
Manuel J. De Vera

Introduction

There remains little doubt that corruption plays a negative role in the economic and social development process. There is an expanding academic literature on the destructive impact of government corruption on economic outcomes,[1] detailing how its prevalence lowers foreign investments,[2] increases risks and uncertainty,[3] and promotes greater oligarchic control[4] among others. The debilitating impact of corruption on economic performance is not only due to the additional costs involved in the payments demanded by crooked government officials, but also through its inherent unpredictability that penalizes firms to a much larger extent than a simple increase in tax rates.[5] Unsurprisingly, corruption has been demonstrated to be among the key reasons why developing countries fail to catch up economically with their counterparts in the developed world.[6]

Despite its palpable negative impact, the substantial investments made in the past decades to curb corruption globally have generally failed to make a permanent dent in the level of corruption across countries. One reason could be that most anticorruption policy studies, such as those conducted in the Philippines and Indonesia, focus solely on the countries' politicians and government officials who abuse their office for public gain,[7] overlooking the fact that that corruption not only provides largesse for corrupt public officials, but also accords benefits to entrenched sectors of society by generating an uneven playing field that allows politically powerful firms to enrich themselves at the expense of poorly connected companies.[8] The fact that corruption in both the public and private sectors are strongly interlinked can be attributed to a government that facilitates wrong-doing in the private sector by creating a business environment where corporate theft goes unpunished.[9] Any reform seeking to eliminate corruption needs to systematically identify all of its different beneficiaries in order to organize sufficient political support from corruption's victims and overcome the vested interests that may oppose the government's cleanup efforts.

In addition, the presence of government corruption strongly influences the country's sociopolitical structures, through both the nation's formal laws and regulations, and in widely held social norms and belief systems of its people.[10] Societies that display a low tolerance for corrupt practices promote behavior of higher integrity, even in the absence of legal or organizational sanction.[11] But when sociopolitical structures revolve around familial and clan-level ties rather than the rule of law, the transmission of corrupt practices becomes more widespread, as deep social ties among individuals makes it socially unacceptable for peers to police each other's behavior.[12]

Given the deep interconnections between social norms, political structures, and public–private sector interrelations, it should be unsurprising that piecemeal attempts to directly root out corruption in particular government agencies or certain procurement processes fail to eliminate the behavior entirely. This has led certain sectors to question the process of anticorruption reform as being too limited to be able to produce permanent institutional reform.[13] What may work in their stead is integrity reform.

The idea behind the integrity reform is that most institutional reform campaigns focus on punishing corruption and other instances of government malfeasance. By focusing instead on integrity—defined as the set of characteristics that improves trustworthiness to stakeholders—the programs build on identified positive strengths and opportunities, rather than the negative aspects of institutional weaknesses. By design, integrity reform programs are broader and more constructive than anticorruption campaigns, intended to create organizations and institutions that improve accountability, deepen core values, form local competences, and not least of all, control corruption.

This chapter analyzes how organizations can build integrity in societies where corruption is rife. It is aimed at detailing a comparative case study of two recently launched integrity programs in Southeast Asia. Both of these programs are designed to change social norms related to corruption in the public and private sectors, which could potentially lead to an improvement of integrity across firms, even in the absence of reform in the national legal systems. One program is aimed at changing behavior at the level of industry practices, while the other seeks to change broader norms regarding what is socially acceptable behavior.

Southeast Asia provides an apt location for studying organizational integrity programs, because it is home to a number of economically dynamic countries which thrive despite (or because of) the prevalence of widespread government corruption. The Philippines and Indonesia are not paragons of virtue, ranking 134th and 110th, respectively, among the 178 countries measured by Transparency International's corruption perception index (CPI) in 2010. Yet, both countries have made strides in recent years in improving the level of organizational integrity among their firms.

The first case study revolves around improving integrity in the Filipino private sector, through the Integrity Initiative of the Makati Business Club, which is co-organized by the European Chamber of Commerce of the Philippines. The program is a private-sector led campaign that aims to promote higher ethical standards among companies through the creation of integrity validation systems and a set of awards that recognize companies for exemplary performance based on these metrics. The publicity generated by the award-giving process is hoped to improve the reputation of firms and to legitimize integrity related behavior across the country.[14]

The second case study is based on the Integrity Education Network and their development and rollout of integrity-based university courses in Indonesia. The aim of this program is to generate and teach courses to university freshmen that explain the differences in corrupt behavior, in hopes of battling the cultural embeddedness of corruption. The aim of this program is more ambitious, hoping that by changing norms relating to the national tolerance for corruption, firms and governments would be forced to improve their organizational practices.

Through this comparative case study, this chapter seeks to document the factors that could lead to the successful achievement of improved integrity and accountability among Filipino and Indonesian organizations. There are very few systematic investigations of the processes by which integrity initiatives can be made to succeed in contexts such as the Philippines and Indonesia, where broader social norms and weak regulatory environments collaborate to make anticorruption programs more difficult to implement.

The chapter is organized as follows. The next section provides a brief illustration of the context of Indonesia and the Philippines, particularly in terms of their recent history in combating corruption. The subsequent two sections provide a case description of the Integrity Initiative project in the Philippines, and the Public Integrity Education Network in Indonesia. The final section discusses the initial goals and achievements of the two cases, with a conclusion regarding the results of the study.

The History of Integrity Systems in Southeast Asia

The Southeast Asian countries of Indonesia and the Philippines provide an appropriate context for studying these twin integrity campaigns. These countries are the two largest archipelagic nations in the world. They are home to substantial Malay populations with broad cultural, linguistic, and religious diversity, and have a shared experience of centuries-long colonial subjugation under Western rule.[15] There are also striking parallels in their recent political history, with both countries gaining political independence shortly after World War II. In the 1960s and 1970s, these countries were ruled autocratically by Suharto and Ferdinand Marcos respectively, leaders who have recently garnered the dubious distinction of being the two most corrupt leaders of all time.[16] The fall of the Marcos dictatorship in 1986 and the end of Suharto rule in 1998 have allowed both countries to adopt the trappings of democracy: relatively fair elections, free press, and rambunctious political parties and civil society groups. Despite progress made on said fronts, the presence of widespread corruption remains a problem in both polities.

The end of the Suharto regime was brought about by the tremendous economic dislocation caused by the 1997 Asian financial crisis that started in Thailand, whose impact was felt in Indonesia more than in any of its neighbors.[17] The effect of the Asian economic contraction in Indonesia was aggravated by the fact that the interlocking networks of businesses controlled by Suharto, his relatives, and cronies created a centrally controlled system of patronage and plunder, which became bankrupt from the sharp currency depreciation and then simultaneously eliminated much of the funding for the government itself.

The visible impact of crony capitalism spurred a strong backlash against what Indonesians refer to by the acronym KKN—corruption, collusion, and nepotism—in the post-Suharto era. Ending public corruption has been at the forefront of national consciousness, brought about by the rise of a freer media and civil society groups that continually shine the spotlight on fighting corruption.[18] In the post-Suharto reform period, termed as *Reformasi*, Indonesia had four presidents, all of whom undertook efforts to address the problem of corruption in the country. Anticorruption legislation was passed in 1999, 2001, and 2002, with the last law creating the Corruption Eradication Commission (KPK—Komisi Pemberantasan Korupsi), an independent corruption-fighting agency with its own investigators and prosecutors, and a new Anticorruption Court to hear its cases.

These and other efforts to fight corruption in terms of both prosecutions and long-term institutional reforms gained more momentum with the rise of the new Indonesian president, Susilo Bambang Yudhoyono in October of 2004.[19] Yudhoyono achieved electoral victory by campaigning on an anticorruption platform, which he followed through with action during his tenure. By providing additional government resources to the government's anticorruption entities, particularly the KPK, the campaign led to a slew of high-profile investigations and prosecutions of top-level Indonesian officials. Though the campaign began in earnest, there has been much backsliding in recent years, with some of the major officials prosecuted in the anticorruption campaign being freed early.[20] Although Yudhoyono is seen as personally clean, Indonesians understand that he is hampered by remnants of prior Indonesian regimes in the parliament, judiciary, and in his own administration. Nonetheless, Indonesians see advances—albeit very slowly—in terms of anticorruption and have granted him reelection with a landslide victory in 2009.

In the Philippines, the fall of the Marcos dictatorship was also spurred by a crisis that was economic in nature. Just like in Indonesia, the impetus for the economic crisis began elsewhere, in this case the sovereign debt crisis that started in Mexico in 1982. And like its neighbor, the tangled web of business dealings among political cronies and Marcos dummies bankrupted the state treasury and caused the worst economic crisis in the Philippines since World War II. This economic crisis was prolonged by a simultaneous political crisis triggered by the public assassination of Marcos' main political rival, the exiled former senator, Benigno Aquino, Jr. The accession by the senator's widow, Corazon Aquino, in 1986 brought about structural reforms such as the enactment of a new democratic constitution, which included the creation of a Presidential Commission on Good Government (PCGG) to recover the ill-gotten wealth of Marcos and his cronies, an independent antigraft prosecutor in the guise of the office of the Ombudsman and an antigraft court called the *Sandiganbayan* in hopes of eliminating the scourge of corruption that characterized the Marcos dictatorship.[21] Numerous laws and investigative bodies have since been created to combat corruption, turning the Philippines into the country with the most anticorruption measures in Asia.[22]

Yet, the optimism surrounding the early institutional reforms brought about by the newly democratic reforms slowly ebbed as the political realities of patronage returned. Reforms enacted in cleaning up government offices, such as the notorious tax-collection arm, the Bureau of Internal Revenue, have taken a backslide in recent years.[23] Corruption scandals reaching all the way to the top political and administrative offices are continuously reported in the media, leading to the jailing on corruption and electoral fraud charges of two former Filipino presidents.

Nevertheless, the recent election of Benigno Aquino III into the presidency on an anticorruption platform in 2010 provides the country with renewed potential for combating corruption.[24] Thought to be personally clean like his predecessor mother, Aquino and his single-minded determination for combating government corruption have already drawn accolades from the local and foreign business communities.

Despite the presence of presidents with strong anticorruption mandates, the anticorruption programs being undertaken by the Indonesian and Filipino governments are producing few tangible results. The political realities of operating in rambunctious democracies permeated by numerous vested interests make such top-down approach toward corruption control difficult to implement. As such, parallel work is currently being conducted by the private sector and civil society in both of these countries to potentially solidify the current momentum in corruption reduction.

Integrity Initiative in the Philippines

The genesis of the Integrity programs in the Philippines began with a group of private sector and civil society participants who were looking for their own solutions to root out corruption in the country. The proponents behind the Integrity Initiative share membership with the Transparency and Accountability Network, started in 2000, and the Coalition against Corruption that was begun in 2004. These programs involve a multisectoral coalition of private, civil, academic, and public organizations that seek to prevent instances of government corruption. These umbrella organizations have launched numerous successful programs that utilize volunteer groups to ensure the transparency and accountability of government programs. Examples of such programs include the Textbook Count program, which monitors the delivery of public school textbooks nationwide; Medicine Monitoring, which validates the procurement processes of public hospitals; and the Bantay Lansangan (Road Watch), which trains volunteers to assess the quality of public road construction.

This template of utilizing citizen-volunteers to promote transparency and lower government corruption has generated tangible successes in those projects that are monitored by these coalitions. For instance, the Textbook Count program has been able to lower the price of textbooks by 63% and lower the delivery errors to less than 5% when previously up to 40% of government textbooks procured could not be accounted for.[25] More citizen involvement in other government procurement programs have led to savings as large as 58% for the Bureau of Correction in terms of their purchases of ammunition and subsistence for prisoners and 38% for the computer purchases within the Housing and Land Use Regulatory Board.[26]

Despite the tremendous success of these individual projects in lessening corruption in the public sector, these programs have failed to make a broader impact on the general level of corruption throughout the country. The problem lies in the fact that these programs focus primarily on specific aspects of government service delivery, without being able to provide the same level of accountability and transparency throughout the entire government budgetary and procurement process. For example, the Bantay Lansangan road watch project is only able to provide volunteers to assess the implementation of road building contracts, whereas much of the malfeasance during public works projects can occur during the planning, bidding, project design, or project identification.[27]

Utilizing the same spirit of volunteerism and transparency, the Integrity Initiative hopes to broaden the impact of prior transparency and accountability programs by directly engaging with the proponents themselves: the government and the private sector. The Integrity Initiative is a private sector-led campaign which hopes to diminish and eradicate the vicious cycle of corruption in the Philippines, whose presence obstructs the development of a globally competitive business environment in the country and exacerbates the problem of widespread poverty. Begun in December 2010, the focus of the program is the reestablishment of proper integrity standards across the various sectors of society, including business, government, judiciary, academe, civil society, church, and media. The broad goal of the program is to institutionalize honesty, transparency, and fairness in conducting business through internal and external integrity validation systems.

The main proponents of the project are the Makati Business Club—an umbrella organization consisting of the top companies in the Philippines who are mainly based around the financial capital of the Philippines in Makati City—and the European Chamber of Commerce in the Philippines. Numerous other Philippine-based business groups, civil and academic organizations, such as the Asian Institute of Management, the American Chamber of Commerce of the Philippines, the Bishop-Businessmen's Conference, the Financial Executives Institute of the Philippines, the Management Association of the Philippines, among others, have since joined the program.

The main program of the Integrity Initiative is project SHINE, a four-year anticorruption campaign funded by the German multinational company, Siemens. Project SHINE hopes to Strengthen High-level commitment for Integrity initiatives and Nurturing collective action of Enterprises advocating for fair market conditions. The idea behind the SHINE project is to invite different CEOs and leaders of private and public organizations operating in the Philippines to publicly commit to push ethical practices throughout their entire organizations.

The goal of the project is to harness the collective action among signatories to modify the existing business culture in the Philippines and revolutionize the way companies do business locally. As opposed to the original anticorruption programs advocated previously by the private sector, these programs do not seek to find and punish companies that engage in malfeasance or bribery. Instead, the Integrity Initiative seeks to provide companies and government agencies with positive role models by which they can better align their operations with. By highlighting positive behavior by public and private organizations, such a program advocating integrity rewards the discovery of innovations that resolve deep-seated social problems that can in turn make innovations in corrupt behavior less rewarding.

Currently, the primary task of the SHINE project is the establishment of an Integrity Pledge. The pledge is a formal but voluntary expression by each organization to abide by ethical business practices and to support the national campaign against corruption. Although any company, large or small, foreign or domestic, can sign the pledge, the signatory of the company must be either the country director or the CEO of each firm, in order to signal that the support for the integrity initiative starts from the top management itself. By the end of January 2012, more than 1,000 firms had already signed the pledge, paving the way for its formal presentation to the Philippine president, Benigno Aquino III, in a conference wherein the president himself would be expected to sign the pledge.[28]

Subsequent to the Integrity Pledge, the next step for the project would be to create a unified code of conduct for businesses in the country. This code of conduct will provide more concrete details to the commitments of each organization in achieving greater integrity which include steps to publicly communicate the organization's position against bribery, corruption, and other ethical standards throughout the firm; to provide clear guidelines in the acceptance and provision of gifts to clients and suppliers; to promote greater accuracy and transparency in financial reporting, among others.

The acceptance of this unified code of conduct among firms should eventually lead to a standardized system of certification that validates whether signatories are fully compliant with the integrity code of conduct.

Through the use of a reputable international certifying body, these standardized integrity measures will form the basis for continuing audits for firms, forming a similar stamp of approval akin to the ISO standards. This certification process shall be piloted in a few firms in 2013, with the rollout of the certification processes expected to begin in 2014.

Eventually, the program seeks to provide fiscal, bureaucratic, and financial incentives for companies that pass the stringent—and costly—integrity compliance certification process. Over the medium term, the Integrity Initiative hopes to create a system that rewards properly accredited companies and prioritize compliant companies in contract biddings, public–private partnership projects, customs procedures, and tax payments. For example, integrity-certified companies may be provided as "preferred supplier" status for private and government contracts, or similarly, companies may be able to access a "green lane" for speedier tax and customs payments.

Admittedly, this particular Integrity Initiative program of the Philippines remains in its infancy and it will take a few more years to assess whether such a laudable program will achieve its goals. However, this particular Integrity Initiative should be understood within the context of the other national integrity programs promoted by the Filipino private sector to promote fair business practices and lower the prevalence of private and public sector corruption in the country.

Integrity Education Network in Indonesia

In similar fashion, the Indonesia-Integrity Education Network program (I-IEN) seeks to promote the value of integrity throughout society and to create a population that is intolerant of corrupt practices within the public and private spheres. In contrast to the Filipino initiative that operates directly through the main proponents of corrupt activity, the Integrity Education Network in Indonesia works through the educational system in hopes of creating the next generation of leaders that will have a mindset toward corruption that is different from their predecessors. By disseminating and institutionalizing the principles of good governance throughout Indonesian society, the program hopes to indirectly influence government at all levels and deepen the social commitment to governance reform.

The program is organized by TIRI, Making Integrity Work, an independent, nongovernment organization that works with governments, businesses, universities, and other civil groups to finding practical solutions to improving integrity globally. Founded in 2003 in the United Kingdom, the group has international operations throughout Eastern Europe, Asia, Africa, and the Middle East. Its work in Indonesia with the Integrity Education Network as one of its three programs on integrity building; other programs include Integrity@Work, which works with government and professional organizations to improve organizational integrity, and GrantCheck which promotes transparency in grant giving and aid effectiveness. With funding support coming from the United States Agency for International Development (USAID) and the Netherlands government, the I-IEN is being implemented under the Kemitraan (or Partnership for Governance Reform), a multistakeholder organization which works with government agencies and civil society in promoting and advancing good governance in Indonesia.

The basic aim of the Indonesian program is to rework the university educational system to include integrity courses throughout its curriculum. Integrity education could provide a more systemic approach in the fight against corruption as it addresses the symptoms and root causes of negative or unethical behavior. Most important to the idea of building integrity measures through public education is that the system provides scope for institutional reform by providing the platform for discussion and engagement in constituting integrity systems. Anticorruption measures, which are generally imposed through punitive action, can be limiting as it only focuses on the outcomes of bad behavior and does not examine or question the prevailing context that engenders or promotes said behavior. On the other hand, integrity measures through public education provides a methodical view of why ethical standards and accountability are critical, as it allows for a deeper appreciation and understanding of why ethical behavior promotes social change for equity and economic growth.

As of February 2012, the I-IEN has attracted 95 universities in its membership. More schools are envisioned to join and develop new modules, methods, and teaching materials that introduce the universal values of integrity to the students, with their appropriate application to the local context. Member universities are expected not only to infuse integrity courses within their curricula, but also to organize public lectures, conduct research, craft comparative studies, and exchange professors in order to strengthen its integrity campaign. Member universities are also invited to sign an agreement for the application of an anticorruption curriculum.

Under the I-IEN framework, universities are encouraged to create subjects, such as courses on state administration, which not only introduces students to the leadership and technical skills necessary for a career in the Indonesian public service, but also provides a description of the problems posed to contemporary state administrators brought about by the presence of corruption. Such exposure accords students with a better appreciation of the societal dynamics that generate government corruption, in hopes of showcasing the importance of ensuring integrity as they exit into the workforce.

Among the members of the I-IEN, Paramadina University leads in this advocacy by being the first university in the network to design and implement a mandatory course on anticorruption for all its students. Started in 2008, this unprecedented initiative of Paramadina University has allowed its students to learn about the definition and causes of corruption, for which they will be trained to present a culminating project of capturing instances of corruption using investigative methods taught during the course. To further raise awareness of corruption cases, the best projects are then presented to the public with the involvement of the university rector, faculty members, and invited guests.[29]

On the whole, however, the educational program is not solely designed to introduce integrity as a future concept that is removed from their current lives as students. Part of the inclusion of integrity development within the university curriculum is to showcase how integrity needs to permeate behavior at all levels. For example, students are taught not to tolerate cheating in class examinations and are informed as to how cheating in college exams undermines the integrity of public life, as the broader social problems of public corruption and deceit have roots in minor dishonest activities such as cheating. By undermining the traditionally accepted beliefs regarding the tolerance of student cheating or of professors receiving gifts, students are also expected to inculcate positive values toward integrity and honesty, and make them understand that integrity is a personal decision that has social ramifications.

Neither is the work of the Integrity Education Network confined to the classroom only. I-IEN has utilized the network of universities to organize a number of Integrity Dialogues, where participants from different professions: intellectuals, NGO leaders, media practitioners, students, professionals, professors—including international speakers—are brought together to flesh out the propagation of integrity throughout different sectors of society. The most recent dialogue involved the analysis of integrity in business communication, with the aim of promoting studies involving practitioners and academics to find solutions to the integrity problem.

As an offshoot, students from Paramadina University have organized themselves into the Integrity Movement Through Social Media (IMTSM). IMTSM members, otherwise known as "Integrity Agents," seek to spread the concept of integrity among their student peers by harnessing their interconnections through social media, as well as through various offline media such as stickers, posters, and t-shirts. These students have already visited their counterparts in other universities in hopes of attracting more members to their movement. The challenge now for the I-IEN is how to sustain these initiatives and how they could mobilize support from their stakeholders in creating a critical mass to forge integrity systems that transcend beyond the education sector and into the government and private sectors. In November 2011, the I-IEN held its third National Annual Coordination Meeting (NASCAM) in Denpasar, Bali, to verify the progress that had been accomplished by members, as well as to formulate the future directions of its integrity programs.

The Future of Integrity Systems in Southeast Asia

As mentioned earlier, the design of integrity programs involve the mastery of the skills required to develop: (a) improvements in institutional accountability, (b) understanding of institutional core values, (c) key, local competences, and (d) corruption control measures.[30] Despite the seeming difficulty of implementing such a multipronged skill building campaign, the launch of the twin integrity initiatives in the Philippines and Indonesia has achieved quick and immediate successes. Within months of their launch, both programs have been able to garner a substantial amount of private sector signatories and academic partners in each program, respectively.

Notwithstanding issues on definition, the ongoing integrity initiatives have been able to broaden the public conversation on the importance of building integrity in institutions in both countries and on imbuing its participants with the desire to contribute in arresting corruption in a systematic fashion. The story in Indonesia is a telling example of the systematic nature of the campaign as the Kemitraan (Partnership for Governance Reform) enjoys wide public support through its bottom-up approach on integrity education recognized by both the private and public sectors. It is through the Kemitraan network that TIRI dovetails its integrity educational reform campaign, as detailed in the prior section. And parallel to this, under a similar program with TIRI called Integrity@Work, integrity education programs are also currently in place for government bureaucrats and middle management staff with the plan of setting up a training center within a university from which the outputs of the I-IEN and Integrity@Work can be synergized.

Although less systemic in its approach to promoting integrity across the different sectors of Philippine society, the Philippine initiative has similarities in terms of its tactics in advancing its membership to its cause. Due to its more focused emphasis on private sector organizations, the methods utilized by the Makati Business Club on attaining universal membership for its integrity initiative is based on tactical targeting of the diverse multisectoral associations that comprise the gamut of the Filipino private sector: for example, multinationals (American Chamber of Commerce, European Chamber of Commerce), financial corporations (Financial Executives Institute of the Philippines), procurement experts (Procurement and Sourcing Institute of Asia), marketers (Philippine Marketing Association), and so forth.

The systematic nature of such approaches, especially in comparison to prior piecemeal anticorruption programs, may truly be the way forward in achieving an effective private sector-led corruption control reform program. What remains to be seen is whether such public conversations can snowball into concrete actions beyond the signup sheets and membership drives. Organizers are cognizant of the fact that the more difficult task involves translating these broad definitions into action items, codes of conduct or integrity standards that are deemed acceptable across a wide swath of Southeast Asian organizations.

Part of said discourse requires the contextualization of these Western definitions of integrity within the Indonesian and Filipino cultural value system, especially that the fingerprints of Western corporations and NGOs are predominant in the funding and organization of both integrity programs. Though there may be a reason to assume that much of the values spouted by integrity initiatives against classroom cheating, bribery, or opaqueness of transactions can be deemed as universal, the implied definition of integrity as being based on personal and organizational choices—as opposed to being societally and collectively determined—harks toward Western cultural systems that maintain the primacy of the individual over the collective, as opposed to the more collectivist mentality prevalent among Asian organizations. The cultural translation of integrity behavior becomes more problematic when translated into particular activities, such as gift-giving, networking, or whistleblowing, which have different connotations and denotations depending on the context of the activity.

In essence, integrity articulation involves social expectations that the network organizers need to be sensitive to—especially on how it is translated into individual organizational commitments that promote and sustain behaviors characterized by integrity, especially in the case of integrity building in government. Moreover, the vagaries of political administration should not lend itself to a weak appreciation and understanding of integrity measures as this invariably impacts on the very accountability and competence of power structures. Without the eventual involvement of government, it may be difficult for these reforms to take root permanently.

From the experiences of Indonesia and the Philippines on integrity building measures implemented by private and nongovernmental organizations, another curious question would be as to how governments in said countries design and roll out parallel measures or complementary programs that can broaden and deepen the reach of integrity systems in its government agencies. Interestingly, inasmuch as these countries' governments are pursuing governance reforms actively, integrity initiatives are oftentimes similarly understood as anticorruption education, and vice-versa. While interpretations on anticorruption and integrity measures may have been inexplicably interchanged, it does not help that interest in the equally important task of instituting systems of accountability and integrating principles of ethical behavior within their particular government administrative context is not gaining much traction.

To illustrate, in 2001, the Philippine government created the Presidential Anti-Graft Commission (PAGC) which required government agencies to develop their own Integrity Development Action Plans (IDAP) as a program to build integrity in public institutions. The guidelines of the IDAP included 22 anticorruption measures or indicators, which included prevention, education, investigation, and enforcement, and strategic partnership all aimed at a multipronged strategy in fighting corruption. As a reportorial requirement, a government agency submits its IDAP to the PAGC using the indicators to a scorecard. Based on the results, the PAGC then would then make the determination of what particular integrity measure is suited for a particular agency.

Admittedly, as integrity-building measures take time to gain momentum, and with PAGC focusing most of its work in the investigation of corrupt government officials, little discussion was materialized on how the IDAP was to be implemented and how it was able to achieve its targets. Unfortunately, the PAGC was abolished in 2010, vanishing with it the chance for the public to see what the overall picture is when it comes to building integrity in the Philippine government.

In summary, the current approaches initiated by the Integrity Initiative and the Integrity Education Network provide an inspired step forward in improving private and public sector governance in Indonesia and the Philippines. The emphasis on transforming social norms and rewarding positive behavior, combined with a systemic approach in tackling governance reform, provides a more concrete roadmap toward achieving the ambitious goal of promoting more ethical practices across governments and private organizations. Given the current political climate prevalent in both countries, such a process could indeed translate into genuine reform as integrity norms are built and as these new norms tap into the growing voter sentiment regarding the corrosive nature of the lack of good governance.

Ironically, what may hamper the success of each program is that both initiatives overlook a crucial stakeholder in their respective reform programs, with the Filipino Integrity Initiative requiring greater grass-roots participation among the youth and with the Indonesian Integrity Education program missing the deeper involvement of the private sector. From our vantage point, the Indonesian experience on integrity education provides the better chance of creating an integrity infra-structure that can provide both scope and breadth for meaningful societal changes, because it systematically tackles the cultural roots of the problem. Duplicating each program in both countries could enhance the probability that the programs achieve fruition. Such a cross-polli-nation of programs across the two countries would go a long way in promoting integrity in both societies, which in turn would allow both countries to finally live up to their long-awaited promise of economic development.

Key Terms

Corruption—the pursuit of private interests through the abuse of organizational resources in nonconformity with generally accepted social practices.

Integrity the set of characteristics that improves trustworthiness to stakeholders.

Study Questions

1. Compare and contrast the traditional anticorruption measures enacted in different countries with the integrity building measures enacted in the Philippines and Indonesia. Which approach will more likely lead to more positive economic outcomes?

2. Compare and contrast the Integrity Initiative in the Philippines and Integrity Education Network Indonesia. Which approach will more likely lead to an improvement in integrity building in either countries?

3. Which aspects of the Filipino Integrity Initiative should be implemented in Indonesia? Which aspects of the Indonesian Integrity Network should be implemented in the Philippines?

Further Readings

Campos, J. E. (2001). *Corruption: The boom and bust of East Asia*. Quezon City, Philippines: Ateneo de Manila University Press.

Kimura, H., Suharko, Javier, A.B., & Tan, A. (2011). *Limits of good governance in developing countries* (pp. 39–70). Yogyakarta, Indonesia: Gadjah Mada University Press.

Quah, J. S. T. (2011). *Curbing corruption in Asian countries: An impossible dream?* Singapore: Emerald Group Publishing.

TIRI. (2012). The integrity challenge, Vol. 2012. Retrieved from http://www.tiri. org/index.php?option=com_contentand task=viewand id=490and Itemid= accessed 21.02.12.

CHAPTER 9

How Could an Executive MBA Ethics Course Contribute to Humanistic Management?

Gustavo González-Couture
Verónica Durana-Angel
David Schnarch-González

Introduction

Latin American (LA) organizations share universal management principles of efficiency and efficacy in order to endure. However, its complex context challenges managers in ways unusual in developed societies. With the analysis of these challenges in mind, this chapter describes the experience of an Executive MBA ethics course developed in the Universidad de los Andes (Bogotá, Colombia) that contributes to the moral awareness of its participants. The course shows that neither the rules (e.g., corporate ethics codes) nor the goods (e.g., favorable organizational goals) are sufficient to ensure an ethical behavior. It takes a joint effort by three ethical dimensions: rules, goods, and virtues. The experience shows how, through encouraging self-observation and self-reflection framed within the mentioned ethical dimensions students, at the end of the course, register a change in their perceptions about their exemplary behavior and their commitment; they became less naïve and more critical.

The Latin American Management Challenge

How to contribute to build sustainable organizations? When the key to this question lies in an adequate behavior of all members of the organization, then humanistic management is brought to the fore. Thus, accomplishing integrity (trust, transparency, and loyalty) in all of the organization's practices becomes the most adequate means.

A sustainable firm is usually thought of as being economically and financially healthy. Nevertheless, to be "sustainable" is a culturally laden concept and dependent on the economic, social, and political situation of a society or a country. For example, Latin American (LA) organizations share universal management principles of efficiency and efficacy in order to endure. However, its complex political context, its economic uncertainty, and the prevalent social inequality, challenges LA managers in unusual ways other than those present in industrial societies. Sustainability and corporate social responsibility have then different agendas from those of the former societies.

We do not define nor discuss Corporate Social Responsibility (CSR) in this chapter, a concept of varied interpretations[1] and difficult to offer a uniform view of.[2] We just illustrate that in spite of LA organizations sharing universal management principles of efficiency and efficacy with their northern counterparts, the complexity of LA's environment challenges managers to approximate CSR in alternative forms to those prevalent in industrial societies.

Organizations in LA "appear driven by contradictory objectives: becoming more competitive in the global arena while still coping with pressing issues such as underdeveloped physical infrastructure, little access [to high quality] education, social and economic inequalities, political uncertainty, and increasing costs of living."[3] Nevertheless, the CSR literature—mostly developed in the United States and Europe— fails to acknowledge such elements in their widely recognized visions and concepts about the subject. As Lindgreen et al. claim, "it is contested that literature developed in the U.S. context of what constitutes CSR and how organizations should act responsibly, may well be of limited utility in other contexts. In particular, cultural aspects are highlighted as important in determining what is required by, and expected of, organizations when addressing economic, legal, ethical, and discretionary concerns."[4] These cultural aspects are definite in order to understand common and uncommon issues that pervade organizations in different societal settings.

The context, history, and cultural aspects often determine what is required and expected of organizations with regard to economic, legal, ethical, and discretionary concerns.[5] However, CSR's foreign roots have not taken into account specific aspects about LA circumstances. For example, "one of the region's biggest social problems is poverty, yet the tools and methodology of CSR—created in the North—do not emphasize this issue as much as they should. Corporate tax avoidance is another social problem in LA, yet many LA companies professing allegiance to CSR would be shocked if tax avoidance became a key CSR issue."[6] Therefore, paying fair wages and taxes, complying with advertised quality, carrying out a full day's work, honoring contracts, caring for the environment, and giving shareholders their due share are amongst basic duties in order to build a sustainable organization under such mentioned uncertainty. This can be considered complying with essential dimensions of CSR in said settings.

In the same direction, Jenkins pointed out that the priorities that largely have driven CSR agenda in the "North" (environmental impacts, working conditions, and human rights) "lead to a tendency to see CSR in negative terms. In other words, with emphasis on things those companies should not do, such as employing children or violating human rights, rather than on seeking positive development outcomes, such as helping eradicate poverty."[7] The discussion, therefore, is concentrated in what CSR does not include and not in what it does. Then, while "paying taxes" are out of the CSR mainstream in industrial countries, such elements are among essential duties of CSR in LA.

These differences in the moral context of CSR are signaling differences too in how ethical decisions are taken within the complexity that LA organizations face. Awareness toward the differences present in CSR in the North from the South helps to understand why contributing to the ethical awareness of managers and business people in LA cannot just follow text books and methodologies used in the North. With this approach we are *not* suggesting a relativistic view of ethics. We accept universal ethical principles agreed to by most world religions, declarations of Human Rights, and work ethics present in most business. Within businesses, these principles are related to: honoring contracts, fair salaries, paying taxes, complying with advertised quality, and so forth, all of which pave the road toward sustainability.

Developing technical and professional competences in managers acquires then a humanistic dimension where, we insist, the resources are scarce, not all labor is qualified, and social and economic inequality is prevalent. Employment plays not only its expected economic role but also a very important social function. The resilience of firms, flexible work contracts, and social security schemes in northern countries allows said firms to take decisions mostly dependent on the market. Bankruptcy doesn't carry any social stigma; takeovers and mergers are common and somehow are ways of salvaging companies in ways not present in the South. While here, decisions have to take into account social consequences, employment being the priority.

How to approximate the training of managers willing to act under a humanistic approach within the LA setting? The educational challenge for management schools in these settings is to contribute to managers not only being proficient in conventional economic and management disciplines, but with special character traits, sensitive and responsive to the above mentioned complexity. Including the awareness that private corporate decisions and actions, because of the reasons mentioned, have a stake in the general interest of society (more so than in the North).

The interplay amongst business models, practices, ethics, culture, and regions, although researched on a regional scale, offers findings yes, but so general that they don't allow for managers to understand their firms and their own decisions with the necessary depth that sound ethical decisions require. So contributing to the moral and ethical awareness of managers requires pedagogical strategies that bring to the fore the ethical issues present in real situations lived by them. Furthermore, there is a need to expose them to ethical notions, concepts, and theories that allow them to better conceptualize and understand not only past experiences but also future situations where ethical dilemmas will be involved.

Having analyzed these challenges, we will now describe the experience of an Executive MBA (EMBA) course developed in the Universidad de los Andes (Bogotá, Colombia) that contributes to the moral awareness of its participants. The pedagogical strategy in the first place, seeks the student's self-reflection about their management practice in the past, persuading them to build cases from such practice in order to discuss in small groups, and then bring pressing issues to the whole class discussion; in the second place, by delving in classical and contemporary literature pertaining to ethics, a framework for notions, concepts, and theories is built around three dimensions of ethics: norms, desired goods, and lived values or virtues.

We consider that virtues are lived values, and that is why they are so significant; because they transcend the value discourse of "ought" representing concrete actions in complex situations. Virtue is the classical term in ethics used to describe the incorporation of good moral habits: in other words character building, something that only learning or discussing about values doesn't warrant.

The course seeks to complement the conventional management skills training with broader knowledge about the conditions of human action. Action that not only regards the deployment of material resources—the role of conventional management courses—but the arrangement of work such that it gives meaning to the organization's members plus satisfying their material and intellectual needs. We then describe the methodology of the course, how it operates and how it has impacted the students. To analyze the impact of the course on students, we used qualitative analysis of a database of 107 students who participated in the program along three cohorts (2009, 2010, and 2011)[8] and wrote essays about their experience concerning ethics (dilemmas, decisions, and consequences). Additionally, we complemented said information with a recent Internet-based survey from a handful of such alumni.

This program takes place in a fully internationally accredited management school.[9] Our description doesn't purport to prove if the experiment has been or not successful. It's the reader who will judge the suitability of offering mature executives a setting that seeks their reflection and self-knowledge about each one's management practice in the past and present plus contributing to their ethical awareness.

Why a Course of Ethics in an MBA Curriculum? How Does It Work?

The course: "Leader, His Ethic and Responsibility," belongs to the EMBA curriculum. It was clear from the start (2000) that this course had to transcend the information level; it had to somehow capture the students' attention in order to persuade them of a knowledge that not only affects their mind but their will too.

The EMBA at Universidad de los Andes is a master's degree in management for professionals in executive positions from different organizations and sectors. The EMBA's students are, on average, 38 years old, have more than 8 years of experience in executive positions or, in some cases, are entrepreneurs of their own firms. The groups constitute people in the first or second level of their organization's hierarchies who are very diverse in terms of geographical origin, gender, and the economic sector in which they have developed their professional careers. The program emphasizes a strategic orientation; it trains leaders to be aware of the needs of their organization and those of the context, as well as to develop human capital in their organizations and to deal with the challenges of technology and knowledge.

Along the EMBA's program, the course seeks to complement student's skills training—usually instrumental (finance, marketing, logistics, strategy, among others)—with improving the way these managers interact with their environment. This implies being more aware of the ethical impact of their decisions on others and on themselves. The course doesn't offer a toolbox similar to those offered by other disciplines; rather, it enhances critical thinking about the student's past and present decision making—in some cases, even behavior. The significance of the pedagogy and conceptual framework used is that "virtue theory shows firms that to pursue ethically driven strategies can realize a greater profit potential than those firms who currently use [only] profit-driven strategies."[10] Besides, it should be recognized that "the business of business is ethical business and that the crises that business and society face today are crises of leadership and ethics."[11] This is where a course of ethics starts playing a fundamental role in an EMBA, a role that is acknowledged by the students who have taken the course:

> "I consider this course to be central in the EMBA. It is the first time I am exposed to a topic which initially I thought very philosophical. But after some time I realized it was much more practical than many of our financial subjects."[12]

"I broaden my reasoning capacity with concepts that for a man that crunches numbers all the time were difficult at the beginning."[13]

Learning Objectives[14] Developed During the Course

1. Students will promote ethical behavior and practices and will act in a socially responsible manner in their organizations.
2. Students will strengthen their leadership skills to promote commitment and shared viewpoints.
3. Students will enrich their critical vision by sharing their own experiences with fellow students under a common conceptual frame.

Course Duration and Academic Intensity

The course is offered along the second of 10 modules of the EMBA; six 4-hour sessions held twice a month. Besides onsite sessions, it is estimated that each participant must dedicate approximately two-and-half hours a day of reading and exercises to go through the mandatory assignments of each session.

Teaching Methodology

The course seeks to contribute to the executive's knowledge and awareness about the following notions: norms, goods, and virtues. However, a greater effort is devoted to the notion of virtue. It is the Aristotelian classical notion whose complexity and clarity allows for a better understanding of ethics than what the notion of value can offer. This is why the course's main goal is to motivate the students to be aware of their own actions, thoughts, and feelings, and their impact on themselves and on those who surround them.

"Instructors never told us what was right; they just put us to think."[15]

"As readings progressed and so workshops and discussions in small groups and in the large class, I had the opportunity to have serious 'interior monologues' about how to improve my human and professional competencies."[16]

The course focuses on the students as persons and as citizens, not only as top managers. We consider that if people improve their awareness over their own actions, they will also improve their interest over the common good and wellbeing of communities.

The former is implemented thanks to a mix between a theoretical and a practical component, in an environment of mutual respect in which students feel free to express their opinions and stances. The instructor does not offer the solution to the dilemmas (unless pressed to do so in rare occasions), s/he only offers the means to facilitate this process among the students; s/he prepares the group atmosphere in order to foster reflection and discussion.

> "We shared a calm but stimulating atmosphere where nobody would reproach others. We all could express ourselves freely, our beliefs, and our selfhood."[17]

Theoretical Component

This component seeks to disseminate and clarify the main concepts and intellectual trends around ethics. It consists of readings, tests, and small group and class discussions. The readings must be done by the students individually and prior to each session. The tests are also done individually, using a Web City or Blackboard software that allows limited time and random questions: all based on an honor system. At the start, the amount of reading material seems large:

> "With my engineer's mindset, I thought the topics could have been approached with much less readings than what the syllabus proposed. But as time went on and we dealt with the readings, the tests and the class discussions, I started to appreciate the worth of the readings and issues discussed. I even enjoyed the most complicated readings… At the beginning I thought they were obtrusive but then the class discussions clarified questions and so the topics became interesting and understandable."[18]

Practical Component

The fact that the theoretical component is approached by students mainly by out of class study allows the instructor to use class time for discussion about concepts and their application. This helps to achieve the actual goal of the course: increase the students' critical thought and self-awareness about their actions, motives, and context. To do this, the class time is devoted to two main activities.

The first one involves working in small groups (four to five students) to discuss a written assignment that each student has previously prepared, in order to share and arrive at peer-assessment and comments. The findings of such team work are later presented to the whole class (of around 40 students). The possibility of working with small groups allows the participants to speak and carry on a dialogue about ethical and even personal issues in a more relaxed, detailed, and in-depth way.

> "I don't speak much in large groups. I prefer smaller groups where a continuous interchange of ideas takes place."[19]

> "We did accomplish sharing our ideas with others in small groups. Such interchange in small rooms allows in-depth conversations about what afflict us, and how we face those situations. Some things come out in the smaller groups rather than in front of the whole class."[20]

The second is to share with the whole class what the student has learnt from his or her team work and his or her individual readings and written assignments. This allows students to contrast their stance with other ways of thinking and also to be aware that they are not alone in their dilemmas or complex situations. Hearing what other people have to say, helps the student; he or she may even feel support by just having others listening to him or her. But an ideal balance between open discussions and formal lectures is not always attained:

> "At the beginning I thought discussion time was too long and didn't allow for enough time to consider the most important all-embarking concepts [in class]. But as time went on and I became aware that ethics is a practical science, about life, that way of interchange of experiences [in small groups] is and should always be the core of these type of courses."[21]

Finally, after the whole course has ended, students are asked to evaluate it: their involvement, their peers' contribution, the instructor's performance, the lessons learnt, and the reading's content. They are also asked suggestions to improve the course. This last evaluation together with their written assignments has taught us about the particularities that management faces in the LA region. Since most of the literature published in business ethics comes from northern countries, students have enough working experience and maturity in order to take a critical stance about how adequate that literature is to understand LA business reality.

The Conceptual Framework or Theoretical Underpinnings

Although the course offers students ample room for several ethical theories to be considered (deontological, utilitarian, consequential, stakeholder, virtue ethics) a preference is given to a systemic approach which combines three dimensions of ethics: norms, goods, and virtues. Following other authors,[22] we consider that ethical behavior is sustainable when it evolves from the interaction of these three dimensions. This is what we have called the Ethics Triangle (see Figure 9.1), whose dimensions and dynamics will now be described.

Goods

As Aristotle stated in the Book 1 of his Nicomachean Ethics,[23] goods are defined as aims which can motivate actions.

"Every art and every inquiry, and similarly every action and choice, is thought to aim at some good; and for this reason the

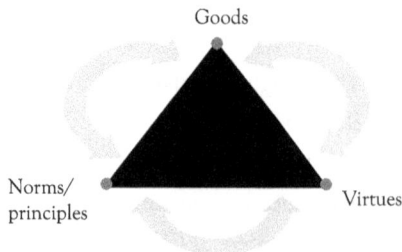

Figure 9.1. Ethics triangle.

good has rightly been declared to be that at which all things aim. But a certain difference is found among ends; some are activities, others are products apart from the activities that produce them. Where there are ends apart from the actions, it is the nature of the products to be better than the activities. Now, as there are many actions, arts and sciences, their ends also are many; the end of the medical art is health, that of shipbuilding a vessel, that of strategy victory, that of economics wealth."

Thus, goods represent the end to which an action can be oriented. According to Melè, there are three different types of goods: human or moral goods (e.g., friendship), useful goods (e.g., money), and pleasant goods (e.g., an ice cream).[24] All of them are desirables but only the first ones are appropriate for perfecting human beings. There are also "real" goods and "apparent" goods. The first ones are goods indeed, while the second ones seem goods at first sight but they could turn harmful to people and society. Amongst the purposes of studying ethics is precisely to understand the difference between "real" and "apparent" goods. Very few individuals consciously intend harm; it is their ignorance about goods being apparent that usually misleads them.

Polo highlights the role of each dimension and the importance of the interaction amongst them.[25] When goods are given precedence over the other two dimensions, breaking its connection with virtues and norms, we are at the threshold of hedonism. Seeking goods without the guidelines of norms/principles and the positive disposition enhanced by virtue—that is self-control—fuels valuing material and ephemeral things the most. There is no future, only present; "as the human ideal slips into the background there is no reason to postpone present consumption. All the projects undertaken are short-term."[26] Thus the need for all three dimensions to be interrelated and present at each action and decision if we want these to be influenced by ethics.

Principles and Norms

Melè indicates that "both principles and norms express the moral duty to behave rightly."[27] However the author distinguishes that while "principles are propositions taken as fundamental norms for directing behavior," norms are more specific guidelines and are deduced from principles.

Despite these differences, what it is important to underline is that principles and norms "give guidelines for evaluating alternatives, discerning the correct course of action, establishing priorities, and discovering the correct relationship between ends and means."[28]

This dimension of ethics is the prevailing one in organizations that agree to follow an ethical management and establish an ethical policy: codes of ethics, codes of business conduct, compliance officers, hot-lines, and so on. As Arjoon states, "more firms are adopting professional codes of ethics and corporate credos that focus on specific rules."[29] It is true that norms have the advantage that once established and accepted by members of the organization its compliance becomes an imperative. Penalties are usually enforced and if the fault is illegal, management usually reports it to authorities.

Normative ethics prevail in cultures of Anglo-Saxon protestant tradition. When the religious restriction fades away, as happens to be the case in contemporary western culture, organizations face a difficult situation: how to warrant a minimum ethical behavior? An employee's written oath that he or she will comply with the Code doesn't assure he or she will effectively behave in alignment with it. This is the compelling ethical problem, made evident by Greek Classical philosophy and by all world religions. In one of its most known formulations: "Why is it I act in ways I didn't want to?" or "Or why didn't I behave as I should have?"[30]

If we accept being free individuals, conditioned by external factors, and of course by our biophysical condition, that is, our genetic code influences us, then ethics has a role to play in our life. But if we surrender to the viewpoint of being wholly determined by these factors, not just conditioned, then we aren't truly free individuals and there isn't much sense of speaking about ethics.

Polo considers that norms and principles play a fundamental role amongst his theory of ethics, which is expressed by the ethics triangle.[31] However, as mentioned earlier when talking about goods, norms can be given precedence and when done so they curtail the growth of human beings. The normative dimension of ethics is supported in Kantian ethics. Its rationalistic underpinnings claim that it would be irrational not to obey norms. Only savage, uncivilized, and unenlightened beings fall short of obeying norms.[32] Rationalism reduces ethics to norms. The consequence of ethical rationalism is that norms become autonomous from the rest of the two other ethical dimensions (goods and virtues), since their knowledge makes them obligatory precepts.[33] However, norms should not be followed just because of a rational instruction, but because of their potential to improve and enlarge the person's actions. This is why Polo considers that when norms are carried out regardless of the role played by goods and virtues, human behavior is impaired.[34]

> "Isolated, ethical normativism begs to be grounded. Without virtue, complying with norms becomes inhuman and ethically lacking. To do without moral growth and govern behavior only by reason demotes moral norms into rules and regulations."

Not only goods and norms, each on its own, can take precedence over and above the other dimensions, but virtues too. This is what we set to examine in what follows.

Virtues

Due to the fact that norms and goods are not sufficient for action to be ethical, virtue plays a crucial role.

> "Virtues are fundamental in getting a full view of ethics, and accordingly of action. If we assign the control of the ethical system to norms, then the possibilities for action are reduced to strict compliance with norms. On the other hand, if we center ethics on goods, then projects for action are curtailed and we slip into consumerism. Both norms and goods need virtues to be organized from the individual. The individual cannot live enslaved, either by social norms or by bodily enjoyment."[35]

According to Koehn, a virtuous agent is one "habituated to desire to do what is good and noble."[36] Virtues mean good character traits; they "reinforce the will for good behavior [and] are acquired by repetition of good actions."[37] Aristotle wrote at the beginning of his Book 2 of his Nicomachean Ethics:[38] "For the things we have to learn before we can do them, we learn by doing them; for example, men become builders by building and lyre-players by playing the lyre; so too we become just by doing just acts, temperate by doing temperate acts, brave by doing brave acts." Thus, when talking about virtues, practice plays a central role.[39]

When talking about ethics, as Arjoon stated, it is also very important to underline the components of deliberation and freedom which are essential characteristics of virtuous action:[40]

"We do not display virtue when we do something that happens to be good, but we must act with a deliberate desire to perform our function as human beings properly. Ethics, understood in the above context, would not be perceived as a constraining force on human behavior as traditional approaches (for example, deontological ethics) promote, but rather, it would now be a liberating or inspirational force since it depends on the individual's ability to pursue excellence through virtuous acts."

The relationship between virtues and the common good is another key issue that must be emphasized. Virtuous people are good citizens, responsible parents, and positive leaders. All this allows society to function appropriately and to make the common good flourish.[41] "The intimate link between virtues and the common good is that both have the underlying philosophy that people are social by nature and cannot be understood apart from the larger community in which they participate."[42]

Empirical studies like those performed by Jim Collins demonstrate that virtuous leaders (level 5 leadership[43]) can explain the success and sustainability of companies.[44] Also, vices like arrogance can collapse companies.[45] However, as we mentioned above in relation to goods and norms, virtues must also be understood and practiced as part of a system: the ethics triangle. If they are separated from the other two vertices, they do not accomplish their configuring potential. Once again, Polo states that virtues must interact with goods and norms in order to enrich human behavior and configure an ethical action:[46]

"Virtues separated from human growth and from acquiring goods constitute a barrier to life that desires to eliminate external influences, building like a bunker unwilling to be affected by the outer world. With this, I insist, virtues lose their true meaning (virtues are not for establishing dispassionate individuals) when isolated from norms and goods."

It is important to clarify that although the term "value" is frequently used in the business ethics literature, we do not consider it as a pillar of our ethics triangle. As Melè indicates, it "is an equivocal term";[47] it is ambiguous because it does not refer to something in particular. Many things are related to its definition, because there are a lot of things which we can consider worthy or desirable. Therefore it can allude to a good considered valuable, or to a principle that the majority of human beings respect; in that case the word "values" is used as a synonym of principles. Besides, values correspond to a more theoretical field while virtues to a more practical one. As Melè states:[48]

"Values belong to the cognitive sphere, whereas virtues refer to character. Recognizing an ethical value is not equivalent to having acquired the corresponding virtue. For instance, the understanding that being generous is praiseworthy is a value, but the recognition of this value does not make one a generous person."

When we live values in everyday life, they become virtues. "Justice" is a value, but someone "just," that is who practices just actions, is a just person, therefore he or she is someone virtuous.

It is important to mention that these three dimensions which form the ethics triangle must be alive and interacting permanently. As Polo clearly explains, trying to support a theory of ethics only on one of the three vertices leads to an ethical reductionism:[49]

"From the inadequacy of prioritizing any one of the dimensions an ethical reductionism is set and so a complete ethics is begged. This complete ethics is one of virtues, norms and goods enforcing each other. There is no sense in speaking of virtues without norms, for the latter conflicting with the former strain up these to the point of deriving in stoicism. Too, there is no aspiration to higher goods above material things in the absence of virtues. Too, norms separated from goods are inhuman. Consequently then the completeness of ethics is accepted or a partial, reduced and inconsistent ethics is predominant."

Summarizing: The ethics triangle implies that being ethical requires the harmonious interplay of these three dimensions. The moral norm fulfills itself *through* action. *With* action we try to *acquire* goods. *From* action virtues or vices are derived. While human goods can motivate people for acting ethically, principles and norms provide guidelines to do so rightly.[50] However desiring the appropriate goods and being respectful of norms is not sufficient for making the appropriate moral judgments. It is thanks to virtue that a person is capable of "identifying the good in each situation and applying principles and norms correctly, as well as facilitating moral reasoning and decision making."[51] This is why goods and "norms are very useful especially to those whose virtues are weak, for determining what is morally unacceptable, for resolving ethical dilemmas and for acting as a guide to human excellence; [...] but are not sufficient for making moral judgments."[52]

Not much can be added to this, just the fact that virtue ethics, in contrast to most contemporary ethical stances, place full moral responsibility on the individual. It represents a different strand of thought from psychologism and sociologism where external factors to the free will of the person is claimed determine his or her behavior.

Research Methodology

The methodology employed in preparing this chapter was in-depth case study research.[53] The objective of the research was to analyze the impact of the course on students from the 2009, 2010, and 2011 EMBA cohorts. The next three stages describe the methodology followed by the authors:

- We analyzed 107 essays written by all students at the end of each course. Those essays were part of a final assignment mentioned above (Teaching Methodology section of this chapter). The content of this assignment didn't influence the students' final grade.

- As Eisenhardt suggests, we didn't start with a hypothesis to test or be refuted.[54] For this reason, no explicit assumptions or initial categories were made to analyze the content of the essays.[55] The data analysis was undertaken in stages, visiting and revisiting information iteratively, as recommended by Glaser and Strauss.[56] Based on this first approximation, nine categories emerged to explain and organize the students' responses. Those categories were refined by the researchers after two long discussion sessions. At the end, four categories (see Figure 9.2) were used to construct the results section.

- In order to deepen the information regarding the long-term effect of the course (the fourth category, "Generate changes in others"), the authors decided to gather new evidence. Two recent in-depth interviews and 12 responses (from former students that responded to an Internet survey offering their perception of the course a few years after having taken it) were added to the database and included in the analysis. It is important to note that while in the first stage of the research the response rate was 100% (107 students), in this stage only 14 people answered although an E-mail request was sent to all alumni.

Each of these categories describes the contributions that the course, through all its activities, might have made to its participants. The variation in answers allowed us to classify these contributions in two dimensions.

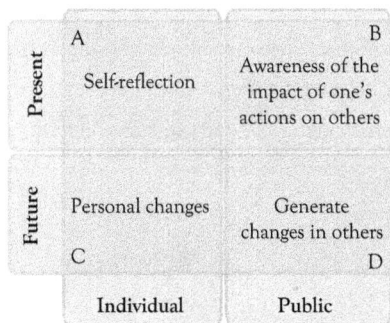

	Individual	Public
Present	A Self-reflection	B Awareness of the impact of one's actions on others
Future	Personal changes C	Generate changes in others D

Figure 9.2. Categories regarding course contribution on students.

The first, refers to a time interval (present–future), while the second dimension is about the contributions' possible range of impact (individual–public). By *present* we refer to what students felt just after they finished the course, while *future* calls attention to the participant's, at the time, behavioral or mindset change or intention of it in the long run, after the course had finished. By *individual* we refer to the course's possible effect only on the student while by *public* we signal its possible effect not only on the student but on how it drives his or her concern for others. Therefore, while categories (A) and (C) are focused on the individual, categories (B) and (D) focused on the public sphere. Similarly, categories (A) and (B) indicate what was in the student's mind at the time he finished the course, while categories (C) and (D) suggest sometime in the future (see Figure 9.2).

Results

The mentioned categorization—which emerged from the data—helped us to analyze the real contributions students perceived and appreciated. It was interesting to find that 58 out of 107 students perceived the course as a space for self-reflection (category A), which indicates the highest percentage (54%). In comparison, 38 out of 107 considered the course as an opportunity to be aware of the impact of our actions on others (category B), and as a motivator of personal change and self-control (category C), respectively. However, it's also pertinent to mention that 12 showed specific actions to spur change "in others" (category D).

The decrease in number of answers from the first category to the last one may be due to the time when students wrote the essay. As can be inferred from the research instrument (107 essays), it is difficult to establish at the end of the course how it will change the behavior of individuals in the future (many showed the "willingness" to change, but only some indicated specific examples of their change). Here the interviews and internet survey played an important role.

A. The Course as an Opportunity for Self-Reflection

Ethics has been a subject of multiple interpretations. Many of these—especially in common wisdom—confuse ethics with morality, religion, and law. The course participants came with many of these mindsets and most were surprised by the methodology given, which transcends just a conceptual approach on ethics. As a former student expressed, "my original expectation was less optimistic and was oriented to the acquisition of conceptual bases on ethics within the context of corporate social responsibility."[57] In the same direction, another affirmed: "I was expecting a series of lessons of philosophical positions and theories about ethics. I thought that we would talk about the 'good and evil,' and how to adopt those theories in our companies. However, along the course, I saw that beyond that, this course puts you in front of yourself."[58]

Contemporary business world moves fast and its noteworthy privileging "doing" over "thinking." Although managers take time to discuss strategies and tactics to improve market and organizational conditions, there is little room to reflect on personal stances. According to the participants, this course was a place to "get away" from the daily routine: "for the first time in my life I took time to think over."[59] Similarly, another expressed that "maybe the best part of these two months was to give me space to think transcendent things that I haven't had the time to analyze."[60]

Indeed, most students stressed that the course allowed reflection and personal questioning. This, however, was not easy for those who saw the "ethical responsibility" outside themselves: "I wanted to question my company. But the questioned one was me. How hard was that!"[61] Consequently, participants highlighted the course as a personal analysis and evaluation process, a complex activity for most: "Naïvely, I thought that I was transparent, secure and clear in my ethical principles. Nevertheless, when I came to read subtle authors like Banaji,[62] I realized that I'm not as fair as I thought."[63] Consequently, a representative part of the course "had strong internal confrontations" about their role in organizations and society (as shown further ahead).

A frequent answer marked out by students was the need for consistency. One of them illustrated the experience of many: "the course leads us to a comprehensive ethical reflection that could be summarized in one simple sentence: to be coherent between what you think, say and do."[64] The challenge, another concluded, is "to ask whether what we do is congruent with what we think and what we say."[65] The important thing, another expressed, is to be aware of one's own weaknesses: "Now I am clear that however strong my convictions and beliefs were, these are not a sure guarantee for a correct action through life. Fortunately I understood that I am vulnerable."[66]

To sum up, the course enables participants to break paradigms about "ethics," to question themselves, to create awareness of their moral vulnerability, and to establish mechanisms of creating congruency between thinking, speaking, and behaving. As a former student noted: "it is not possible to expect that a course like this will radically change the way individuals act, but it enables a space for questioning and reflection via academic orientation."[67] In the same direction, another expressed: "The course was designed to generate more questions than answers (...). I am aware that some of these questions probably will never have a final or absolute answer, but the process of reflection is what matters."[68]

B. The Course as an Opportunity to Become Aware of the Impact of Our Actions on Others

Within the interviews and the analysis of the essays written by the students, there were an important number of opinions that ranged between the role of leadership in organizations, to the implications of the actions made by individuals in other aspects of life different to organizations— family and less favored members of society.

Concerning the role of the leader in organizations, the respondents recognized its significance when identifying that "we have the responsibility of being a role model, because as leaders we are observed by everybody and everything we do is going to be magnified for good or bad."[69] It is worthwhile mentioning the assumption that, after the course the students were able to go beyond the implications that their actions have on their very personal environment, to a more public level where organizations are favored or punished depending on their performance. Likewise, one student highlighted that "[...] being the head of an enterprise or group of people is something of great matter, which forces me to move from a local to a general – public – scope [...] This means that our responsibility as leaders has to take [the whole of] society into consideration."[70] Also, many of the students viewed business ethics, plus being aware of their influence on others, as an opportunity for contributing to the improvement of the performance of their subordinates and other members of the organization.

However, the students also emphasized the fact that the course was useful in ways that it made them assume a sense of responsibility for their acts with respect to settings other than just their working organizations. Amongst the concepts considered in the course and referring to responsibility is that of "objective social responsibility" and "subjective social responsibility."[71] These are applied to the individual and do not refer to the sociological term of CSR already discussed above. A person's "objective social responsibility" has to do with the social class he or she belongs to: socialization, education, opportunities, and so forth. It summarizes what society expects from a person brought up and exposed to those factors. On the other hand, a person's "subjective social responsibility" is what each individual establishes as his or her responsibility toward others and society in general. In summary, this latter responsibility is the contribution the person feels and thinks s/he owes toward the common good.

Many students thought these concepts plus readings and discussions aided them to become aware of their responsibility as individuals toward society. As one of them states: "[...] I also learned that I have an objective responsibility for receiving so much from society, and I'm looking forward to develop my subjective responsibility in order to involve myself genuinely in some kind of project, that contributes to the improvement of the plexus of which we are part of."[72]

In addition, they acknowledge the increase of their awareness about the intellectual understanding of a variety of concepts that were useful to better comprehend their influence on others. They became aware of the fact of their freedom being a catalyst for contributing to the common good (but also being capable of damaging it). In fact, one of the students recognized that his expectation toward the course was to "learn how to implement corporate cultures which foster ethical behavior in business."[73] However, then he reconsiders that "my vision was incorrect in the way that I was just focused on an organizational level, releasing me from my responsibility towards society, family and myself ("freedom for") [...] the course has impelled my profound questioning of my responsibility as a leader, as well as an individual."[74]

In this way, students were able to see not only their behavioral implications as leaders in organizations, but also as active members of society. Their awareness about how they contribute (positively or negatively) to employment, to paying taxes, to making government officials account-able, and to safeguarding the environment are amongst the issues high-lighted by this category. Also, here we learnt about the concept of CSR being differently challenging in the LA region than it's in the North.

C. The Course Encouraging Personal Change and Self-Control

Although a great percentage of the students recognized that the course was useful, in the sense that it provided the space to think and reflect about how they make decisions in everyday life; fewer of them actu-ally perceived the course prompted personal change and self-regulation. However, those who thought the course had the stated quality or impli-cation, were also clear in specifying that it provided the opportunity to improve their decision making professionally and personally. As one of them states "reflection and self-control has improved my decision mak-ing in my personal and professional life."[75] Additionally, another student highlights that "[the course] deepens in the moral aspect of each of us and in internalizing those values, but through action and through habit."[76]

Another important point identified in the analysis is the fact that their main motivation to personal change is not to follow the agreements of social norms, or only to improve in an organizational context, but for their wellbeing and for their continuing and active learning about virtues. One respondent demonstrates that "[…] recognizing our vices is a virtue that can lead us to be not just better managers, but also better sons, par-ents, brothers and friends. This is the best lesson we have received."[77]

Furthermore, it appears to be that, in addition to the theoretical underpinning explained along the course, the interaction amongst its members and their experiences provides an opportunity to delve into and evaluate their actions. In this way they became "more critical about the attitudes of people."[78] In fact, it appears to be that the course provides "an indicator that aggregates to a panel of instruments; is a light that has to be activated as an alarm towards certain situations; an additional criterion to consider the process of decision making."[79] Therefore, the course not only seems to provide the opportunity to raise awareness about the responsi-bility of actions and their effect on others, but also the chance to evalu-ate and be critical about the student's environment (work and others).

Yet, it is not clear whether the students had the motivation to change, or if they actually modified their decision making process. However, what is certainly clear is that the students seem to consider that they are presently more prepared to confront ethical dilemmas, than they were before taking the course. One of them wrote, "Now I'm more aware of a lot of things that I have never thought before,"[80] and another stated "I feel strengthened as an individual and as a professional to challenge difficult situations in life. When I'll have to make a decision, I will do it in the correct manner, searching for virtues."[81]

In conclusion, the evidence showing how some of the students went beyond self-reflection, to self-control, and increasing awareness about the impact of their decisions cannot be proved statistically, but the students' statements give grounds for proving the importance of these kind of courses in an EMBA. Hopefully the seeds for change claimed by some students would grow both in the professional and personal realms.

D. The Course as Motivator to Generate Change "in Others"

It is noteworthy the little evidence we collected for changes in the way students act. Indeed, only 8 of 107 students reported changes in their actions at the end of their respective courses. And 5 of the 12, who responded to a recent Internet-based survey about the effects of the course a few years later, testified to variations in their ethical behavior.

Most of the changes informed, furthermore, are related to the concepts of the course: "I included several concepts and topics in my discussions at work."[82] In the same direction, another former student stated that he is trying to bring the content of the course as a leader: "Today I have a group of subordinates to which I am applying the concepts that I could internalize, for one thing is reading and another is putting those concepts in practice."[83]

On the other hand, some alumni emphasized that the main contribution of the course was to make them aware of the ethical dilemmas and how to respond to them: "When facing ethical dilemmas I go back to my EMBA and remember the cases seen in class to find the right path (with no shortcuts)."[84] "Now I think twice before accepting a lunch from a contractor,"[85] another concluded. Similarly, two of them developed a sensibility to distinguish such ethical situations: "I have now a 'peri-scope' that helps me detect ethical dilemmas in professional and personal situations."[86]

Conclusion

Selznick, in his pioneering work about institutions, speaks of organiza-tions becoming institutions when they are infused with values thanks to the "institutional leadership" of individuals who surpass the technical administrative management and are able to lead in order to maintain institutional integrity.[87] In his words:

"The integrity of an enterprise goes beyond efficiency, beyond organ-ization forms and procedures, even beyond group cohesion. Integrity combines organizations and policy. It is the unity that emerges when a particular orientation becomes so firmly a part of group life that it colors and directs a wide variety of attitudes, decisions, and forms of organization, and does so at many levels of experience. The building of integrity is part of what we have called the 'institutional embodiment of purpose' and its protection is a major function of leadership[...] it is more than an aesthetic or expressive exercise, more than an attempt to preserve a comforting, familiar environment. It is a practical concern of the first importance because the defense of integrity is also a defense of the organization's distinctive competence. As the institutionalization progresses the enterprise takes on a special character, and this means that it becomes peculiarly competent (or incompetent) to do a particular kind of work."

Such organizational integrity interplays dynamically with the per-sonal integrity of its members. One influences the other. "Sustainable organizations" is the current expression for what Selznick meant half a century ago for an organization becoming an institution. In the mean-while, institutional economics has taken precedence, given priority to the analysis of norms and rules and organizational arrangements. It is then understandable that corporations bet on codes of ethics or busi-ness conduct in order to warrant a predictable and acceptable behav-ior of its members. These are well intended policies that contribute in some measure to such an end. Nevertheless, the alarming proliferation of faulty leadership calls for measures to be effective starting at the education level.

Courses in ethics, be them for undergraduates or graduate students, might be as naïve as the above mentioned codes. If we accept we are morally free beings, in other words, we can choose right or wrong, we then need to endure prejudices, erring, and misjudging becoming part of our stock. And so mind and heart (will power) need to be educated in order to face our vulnerability plus amending our behavior. With this in mind, the most it can be done in an educational setting is to help the student become aware of such vulnerability. Expose him or her to the complexity of the moral world, without dismaying him or her about the want and possibility of right conduct. Otherwise there wouldn't be any room for ethics as a practical science to improve our action.

This is the basic premise of the pedagogical experiment described here. There are many ways of contributing to critical thinking of students. We have found that ethics contributes some to such thinking and moral awareness—awareness that is not only an intellectual feat, but one where the will has to be fully engaged.

This explains why the value discourse—an intellectual appreciation for positive moral behavior—isn't sufficient. Virtue, a disposition toward right behavior, attained from intended positive moral habits is the most amenable notion to deal theoretically and practically with ethics.

The change of behavior, the incorporation of virtues, and the improvement of character are impossible to warrant with a course. Exposing participants to several thought and discussion activities within a subject matter is the most we have intended. We conclude with a student's statement:

> "My perception of the course is that of being something very important. The subject shouldn't be treated only in a course, but all along the EMBA's curriculum, in order to approach the issues from different points of view. It isn't a secret we are in face of a value crisis in the ethical conduct of most of our leaders of the country. We belong to that group. If we leave the EMBA at least recognizing the need for making more thoughtful decisions, then a big step has been taken in the right direction."

Key Terms

Ethical education—the fostering of a class environment where self-reflection about the person's thoughts and actions takes place in order to improve decisions and behavior.

Moral awareness—the fact of being sensitive to ethical dilemmas, deciding about the best course of action, and acting for the good of all involved.

Goods—represent the ends to which an action can be oriented.

Norms—specific guidelines for discerning the correct course of action, discovering the correct relationship between ends and means. Its compliance becomes an imperative.

Virtues—a voluntarily acquired habit toward positive moral behavior. They transcend the intellectual dimension of values, thus, virtues are lived values.

Managerial challenges—all those problems and situations not amenable to easy solutions or courses of action.

Corporate Social Responsibility (CSR)—voluntary initiatives of corporations that show actions above legal compliance with Human Rights, Labor Justice, and Sustainable Environmental practices.

Self-reflection—to think about our own thoughts, feelings, and behaviors in a critical manner.

Study Questions

1. To what extent are Business Schools responsible for the future behavior of its alumni?
2. Should MBA curriculum include ethics courses?
3. Can Corporate Social Responsibility make up for ethics?
4. What are the ethical implications of leadership?
5. What is your position about the course methodology described in the chapter and its impact on students? How would you design an ethics course?

Further Reading

Audi, R. (2009). *Business ethics and ethical business.* New York, NY: Oxford University Press.

Banaji, M., Bazerman, M., & Chugh, D. (2003, December). How (un)ethical are you. *Harvard Business Review* 56–64.

Baumeister, R., & Tierney, J. (2011). *Willpower: Rediscovering the greatest human strength.* New York, NY: Penguin Press.

Bazerman, M., & Tenbrunsel, A. (2011). Ethical breakdown. *Harvard Business Review 89*(4), 58–65.

Bird, F. (1996). *The muted conscience.* West Port, CT: Quorum Books.

Bowie, N. (2002). *The Blackwell guide to business ethics.* Blackwell Publishing Ltd.

Paperny, J. (2009). *Lessons from prison.* Woodland Hills, CA: APS Publishing.

Pava, M. (1999). *The search for meaning in organizations: Seven practical questions for ethical managers.* Westport, CT: Quorum Books.

Integrity Priorities During and After the Crisis

This book unequivocally acknowledges the insight that the understanding and application of integrity may well differ across the globe. This last section adds an additional contingency view element to it. Also, crisis management is likely to be highly situational and, therefore, must consider local elements for maximum impact. We thereby differentiate remedies in times of crises, especially after the financial crisis commencing in 2007 on one side, as well as initiatives which could be triggered in calmer times. The first contribution in this final section deals with key reflections on augmenting integrity after radical changes. The empirical foundation is based on the Turkish healthcare sector. It has gone through a period of radical change, which has affected the roles of physicians, units, and healthcare organizations. These changes aim to increase efficiency and effectiveness of the system and make health services more accessible to the public. As mentioned in the main principles of the Health Transformation Program, contributions of all stakeholders matter if this initiative is to bear fruits. As outlined, the implications are not always positive when it comes to integrity. Thus, the litmus test of organizational change seen from an integrity point of view is whether negative consequences are anticipated. If not, such an approach can only be interpreted as being unprofessional and lacking a holistic nature. The next crisis context is not as focused and actually deals with the main financial crisis haunting our economies since 2007. The authors link the collapse of the Icelandic economy to a lack of good business ethics and integrity. Such an unethical behavior was demonstrated by the Icelandic business elite, politicians, and civil servants. This represents a counterintuitive insight presented by the authors; as traditionally rating agencies (such as Transparency International) have always rated Iceland among the least corrupt countries in the world. Iceland even adorned the very top spot prior to the crisis. By adopting and maintaining a comprehensive ethical approach in conducting business, organizations can maintain their legitimacy, create long term success, sustain growth, and remain good corporate citizens. While these are general statements, the chapter delves deep when substantiating them. The section's final chapter takes the crisis consideration to a higher level, and deals with a combination of political and religious conflict; along with elements of workforce diversity issues. In light of globalization processes, diversity of workforce and organizational membership are a reality in most parts of the world. The pervasiveness of this phenomenon notwithstanding, its ramifications on humanistic organizational practices, particularly on workplace integrity, have hardly been examined. We do not remain on the descriptive level in this context, but outline solutions. The underlying diversity amongst people and their often divergent agendas do not necessitate a fatalistic situation. Smart, active management can counterbalance some of the tendencies and overcome challenging situations. The authors thereby outline and discuss best practices. Based on the example of nurses' teams consisting of Jews, Arabs, and immigrants from former Soviet Union in medical centers, as well as a diverse college students population, the chapter distills an integrity-oriented human resource management model, followed by a critical evaluation of the proposed framework.

CHAPTER 10

Reflections on Building Organization Integrity after Radical Changes

Experiences of Physicians in Turkish Healthcare Sector

Burcu Guneri Cangarli
R. Gulem Atabay
Adviye Ahenk Aktan

Introduction

In Turkey, the Ministry of Health was established in the year of 1920 with the object of constructing and controlling legal arrangements in healthcare and supplying well-qualified health personnel in sufficient numbers. From 1938, legal arrangements and practices were developed in order to strengthen the central structure of healthcare management. The year 1961 saw the beginning of the socialization process of health services, and within this context, the Law on the Socialization of Health Services came into force.[1] Under this socialization context, clinics responsible for providing the first step of healthcare services were integrated into the entire healthcare system. The healthcare system witnessed several changes in the years between 1980 and 2002. In particular, in 1987, the Law of Fundamental Health Services, the first attempt to adapt the healthcare sector to open economy, was accepted. Moreover, with the bylaw of Green Card in 1992, healthcare organizations started to provide free-of-charge healthcare services to citizens who were unable to pay.[2] During the 1990s, major changes regarding gathering social security institutions under one roof and providing the same rights to all patients, establishing general health insurance, the expansion of primary healthcare within the framework of family medicine, the conversion of hospitals into autonomous businesses, and giving priority to preventive health services had been discussed, however, they couldn't be realized until the 2000s.[3]

Transformation Program in Healthcare was realized in 2003, aimed at creating a radical change in the sector focusing on eight main themes:[4]

1. Positioning the Ministry of Health as the planner and the controller—The Ministry positioned itself as a strategic institution, which carried out the central planning and controlling for the delivery of health services.

2. Establishment of a general health insurance by gathering different social security organizations under one roof—An integrated insurance model in which social security organizations for workers (SSK), the self-employed (BAGKUR), and civil servants (*Emekli Sandigi*) were unified as a single organization; the Social Security Institution (*Sosyal Guvenlik Kurumu*) was created.

3. Creation of a widespread, easily accessible, and friendly health service system—It included strengthening primary healthcare, establishing effective integration among the healthcare organizations, and providing healthcare organizations with financial and administrative autonomy.

4. The development of a labor force equipped with knowledge, competence, and high motivation—For instance, a new education program was developed for the specialization of family physicians and nurses who would work in the primary care area.

5. The establishment of education and science institutions supporting the healthcare system—An academic structure under Health Academy or Health Specialization Institution was aimed to be established to reorganize education hospitals, to plan the current education in medicine, and to make standardizations.

6. The assurance of quality and accreditation for qualified and effective health services—National Quality and Accreditation Institution was

established as an autonomous structure in order to develop systems for the measurement of health outcomes and to formulate performance indicators for health service suppliers.

7. The establishment of effective inventory management for medicine and equipment—Catching up to international standards in terms of standardization and authorization, and rational uses of medicines, equipment, and medical devices was aimed.

8. The establishment of effective health information system—it was aimed to integrate all the mechanisms of Healthcare system through effective information management.

The major driving forces behind the Transformation Program in Healthcare were achieving efficiency, productivity, and equity in the sector. The other driving forces for the program could be also considered as the "Health for All in 21st Century" policy of the World Health Organization, "Accession Partnership" document prepared by the European Union, and the need for harmonization of Turkish Health Legislation with the European Union's, in line with the "National Program" for Turkey.[5] Health Transformation Program was accepted on the principles of humancentrism, sustainability, participation, reconcilement, volunteerism, division of power, decentralization, and competition.[6]

Based on the components of the Health Transformation Program stated above, hospitals have witnessed the following results:

1. The unification of public hospitals under a single roof and giving patients the right to choose their hospital.

2. Giving patients the right to choose their physician.

3. The development of a performance-based wage system for the physicians—the rate of payment was related to the number of patients seen and the number of medical interventions.

4. Restrictions of physicians' work outside the hospital—the physicians were encouraged to work at hospitals on a full-time basis.

5. Total quality management and accreditation process—quality units were generated in each hospital chaired by the deputy chief physician. These units worked in a coordinated manner with the Ministry of Health.

6. Protection of patients' rights—patients' rights units were established to consider patient complaints in each hospital.

7. Computer automation—in accordance with procedures to reduce paperwork, bureaucratic procedures were simplified and the use of information technology was substantially increased.[7]

As seen, Health Transformation Program brought radical changes. Some researchers argued that the transformation period increased the productivity, accessibility, and quality of the healthcare services.[8] For instance, Diler found that the efficiency of the majority of hospitals increased after the realization of Health Transformation Program.[9] Celikay and Gümüs showed that the general satisfaction of citizens with healthcare services had significantly increased.[10] In contrast, other researchers stated that many important problems occurred with these changes.[11] For example, Görgün indicated the negative effects of the new performance-based wage system on the working conditions and motivations of physicians.[12] In the new system, performance evaluations were based on the number of patients seen and medical treatment performed. However, their results or quality were not taken into consideration. This may lead that physicians try to see more patients a day, but spare less time to each. Moreover, they may demand unnecessary treatments to increase their performance score. Also, as the scope of healthcare service was defined in terms of medical intervention numbers, it was also possible that less risky interventions carry the same score with more risky ones. Under this working condition, work peace may be broken among healthcare staff, and as a result, motivation of working collaboratively with other healthcare personnel is affected negatively. Accordingly, Görgün stated that the new performance evaluation system may create more competitive environment and stimulate unethical behaviors.[13]

Due to the conflicting research findings, Tatar emphasized the need for further empirical studies to evaluate the effects of Health Transformation Program on three crucial points: (a) the effect of the increasing role of the private sector on service quality, (b) the effect of a new performance-based wage system on the number of unnecessary medical interventions, and (c) state expenditures in healthcare.[14]

As explained, Turkish Healthcare System has been witnessing changes that radically affect the roles of physicians, units, and healthcare organizations. These changes aimed to increase efficiency and effectiveness of the system and make health services more accessible to the public. As mentioned in the main principles of Health Transformation Program, contributions of all the related parties and stakeholders are vital in the achievement of such a challenging aim.[15] However, some experts argued that an indispensible part of the healthcare system, the physicians, were affected negatively and their motivation and integrity have been damaged.[16]

To shed light on this issue, opinions of physicians, as one of the important stakeholder groups, were taken in interviews. In that regard, five physicians with diverse backgrounds, working history, and positions expressed their opinions about all these changes and their effects on integrity. Moreover, they defined physicians, units, and healthcare organizations behaving with integrity, and offered suggestions to stimulate integrity in the entire healthcare system.

Definition of a Physician with High Integrity

Sebnem, full professor in psychiatry, described the behaviors of the physicians acting with integrity thus:

> "Listening and understanding the person (patient) in front of you, helping that person and showing professional knowledge and skills in doing so, without regarding the congeniality and social background of the patient… and when you get out of your depth in terms of interest or knowledge, referring the patient to others (other physicians), asking for help, sharing your professional knowledge and lack of it… and resisting status quo and constantly improving yourself, anticipating that illnesses and symptoms may change, probably always keeping this in a dynamic process…"

Levent, a physician working in a private dialysis clinic, emphasized the importance of understanding the patients while describing a physician with high integrity:

"Someone compassionate, looking out for their (patients') rights, able to understand their concerns, making an effort to understand and resolve them, making things easy for the patients when they face difficulties, someone realizing it when things get difficult... and of course, among our obligations for the patient is continually trying to improve the scientific aspect of the job. Improving ourselves, offering the latest treatments, asking for necessary consultations, attempting to gain a wider perspective..."

Differing from her colleagues, Hatice, associate professor in medical education, approached the issue from a more emotional viewpoint and she evoked that:

"A physician must be very compassionate, and every step he takes, he must treat the patient as he would his own parents or children. I mean I should treat you kindly, knowing that your stomach hurts, and thinking how I would treat you if we were kith and kin. What's expected of us is empathy..."

Moreover, she defined stimulating factors for physicians to behave with integrity.

"In order to have integrity, I need to know everything positive or negative about myself, I need to know myself. What makes me unhappy, what I envy, what I can and cannot do well—I need to know all this. I need to love myself, and I need to have ideals. Having dreams and goals is particularly important for the medical practice, since you can easily fall apart if you can't set goals..."

Supporting the views of Hatice, Cem, associate professor in pharmacology, stated that:

"To a certain extent, it's about how you feel inside, what individuals expect from life, what they want to give to people, what they want to do in life..."

Definitions of a Healthcare Unit with High Integrity

While talking about a healthcare unit behaving with high integrity, Levent stated that:

"If you have a manager who strives to work out problems, intervening when necessary and supporting you continually in your unit, then your work atmosphere seems to be more pleasant and productive. In such a clinic, interpersonal relations will work better. If the manager sometimes puts in the effort in that unit, he or she may cover a lot of ground toward creating a more agreeable atmosphere. I experienced that when I was working [at the] university hospital; I saw how good a manager can be. It was really different. It wasn't just about his attitude toward situations; also important, of course, was the fact that he guided people, kept them open for improvement, moving them to be productive…"

Sebnem added that:

"The attitude of the supervisor is important. Knowing that you're liked by your supervisor… actually feeling a stronger commitment to your organization… It's then possible to tolerate feelings such as anger. It's also important how the supervisor handles a problem. What's the level of fairness the employee feels when the problem is being addressed? Some people feel commitment and integrity if they feel they can express themselves."

Definition of a Healthcare Organization Behaving with High Integrity

After discussing the characteristics of a healthcare unit behaving with integrity, Hatice defined the requirements for integrity in healthcare organizations where different units are needed to work in harmony. She evoked that:

"There needs to be symmetry of information. Ever since I was appointed to the position of the coordinator, I write journals, because whatever I do, others need to know about it, thus we can have integrity and continuity. But I know this is not the typical structure... You do something, and that stays with you; I do something, and it stays with me. Then we get together, and we don't tell each other about what we've done..."

While Hatice, as a coordinator, referred to her observations in terms of required mechanisms for organizational integrity, Sebnem stated her views on this issue as a subordinate:

"The sense of equity is important. If the sense of fairness prevails in the institution, and if people know they'll receive equitable compensation for their efforts, then no one sidetracks..."

In addition, Hatice and Cem emphasized the role of belonging in a healthcare organization with high integrity. Hatice quoted that:

"When individuals can't properly define themselves on their own, they're unable to do this with regards to the organization. And when they can't do that, a sense of belonging can't form. Inability to form belongingness is one of the obstacles in the way of organizational integrity..."

Cem added that:

"For one thing, the sense of belonging is very important. I love this hospital of mine. And because I feel I belong here, I even want to give of myself without paying much regard to financial matters..."

Physicians' Suggestions to Stimulate Integrity in the Entire Healthcare System

Cem started with the importance of stability in healthcare system. However, he believed that Health Transformation Program brought many uncertainties to physicians' careers. As expected, those uncertainties negatively affected physicians' identifications with the occupation and healthcare organizations:

"In this country, when I started in medical school, there was no medical compulsory service. I graduated and it was there. I passed the exam to specialize in medicine, and compulsory service was abandoned. I finished my specialty training, compulsory service returned... I mean there's a situation in which you can't see the future..."

In line with Cem, Levent also criticized the continuously changing healthcare system. He clearly stated that physicians' feelings of hopelessness prevent them from behaving with integrity.

"When you enter the profession, you'd like to think about how much money you make now and by the time you retire, about what your retirement pension would be, right? But uncertainties affect your future expectations... people don't see a light on the horizon; therefore, they lose hope... a friend of mine is thinking about getting into the restaurant business..."

Besides the importance of the factors such as "the system certainty" and "identification," "education" was also evaluated as another crucial factor affecting the level of integrity. Omer, assistant professor in pharmacology, strongly believed that behaving with integrity can be learnt.

"(Integrity) It can be taught. I mean, after all, we didn't even know how to speak when we were born; anything could be taught! ... Our professor used to say "when a patient with a fever arrives, don't try to reduce the fever right away. First, follow up for a couple of days, and then intervene only when necessary." This bit of information appears in none of the books on medicine. I never read about this in any book. That's the professor's comment. I could make a remark like this, too. When can I do it? When I see 45, 50, hundreds of patients, then I can do it. That's the mentoring system."

Although Hatice supports Omer's opinion, she indicated the potential negative effects of mentoring system on integrity, when the mentoring system was not well designed.

> "Medical training is a hierarchical one; we actually learn from those before us in a mentoring kind of relationship. While teaching, the mentor tyrannizes over the learner on occasion. (The underdog) learns to tyrannize as well. Having learnt to tyrannize, the downtrodden oppresses the next one... This damaging relationship is reflected on the patient, patient's relatives, sometimes a colleague... When I was in medical school, we'd take the advice of our consultant professors, and we were together until six in the evening, watching how they treat the patients... until we graduated... There are some professors whom we still keep in touch with... we still haven't drifted away... we learned so much from them... Much as we idealize and say that the student and the professor should work very closely, learn something from each other, we can't create an environment to allow this to happen. Other than that, what kind of solution could we come up with? How could we transfer these values? I don't know. The contact hours in education program are so few... we try to increase contact as much as possible but those contact hours to teach... teach the attitude... very few. They're very few in internships, too..."

When it comes to the evaluation of healthcare system from the perspective of stimulating integrity for physicians, healthcare units, and organizations, the physicians were pessimistic. They started with the negative attitude of the Ministry of Health toward physicians. Cem expressed that:

> "The ministry of health is, in my opinion, inadequate in protecting its staff (against violence by patients or patients' relatives)."

In line with Cem, Levent provided a long and detailed explanation regarding the negative attitude of the state based on his experiences. He referred that:

"Politicians, prime ministers, ministers of health have always made the physicians scapegoat for anything in the eyes of the public. I mean they obviously made people believe that the main factor for the failure of the healthcare system is the physicians. ... (About a problem experienced with a patient) I tried for about five months. First, I wrote a petition. I wrote to the person in charge at the dialysis center and to the managing director. It was referred to the Ministry of Health and the social security institution. We reported the incident, and a response came about five months later. When a patient files a complaint as soon as he's out of the door, before he even makes it to the stairs, they called. Believe me; they called us from the Ministry within two or three minutes. ... The money allotted by pharmaceutical companies for congresses has decreased, so did the number of people they send to these events. Therefore, you have less of a chance to attend congresses and improve yourself. In the past, let's say a hundred physicians would attend any given scientific conference, but now, perforce, only five or ten physicians do so. They eliminated the funds (referring to the ministry of health). Well, you eliminated these funds, but you need to compensate somehow for this. I mean you need to make congresses accessible. No efforts have been made in that aspect. The ministry does not endeavor to disseminate the proceedings of congresses..."

Besides the negative attitude of the state, working conditions of physicians, the new performance-based wage system, high workload, and lack of proper control mechanisms were heavily criticized by all five physicians.

Cem:

"Working hours... very important... I mean you can't expect performance by keeping a person in the hospital for 36 hours..."

Hatice:

"Now with the changes in the healthcare system, physicians see an average of one patient every three minutes... In any case, that doesn't even mean seeing a patient..."

Levent:

> "Time allotted for the patient is surely an important factor... the number of patients that you see in one day..."

Omer:

> "There are some clear figures. While 50 angioplasties were performed annually in a city before, the number has gone up to 150 after performance evaluation system. Did the number of patients go up?"

Hatice:

> "A small example... if a patient stays in the intensive care unit for three days on average, the performance score peaks... both my siblings are surgeons... they perform the surgery and discharge the patient on the same day, because they think the patient would be better off at home. Some other physicians tell them they're crazy because they're not making any money from the performance system then. Who ends up losing here? The physicians who do their job well..."

Sebnem:

> "What does a physician do during a cesarean delivery? She cuts open the woman's abdomen, then cuts the uterus, then intervenes with a second living being and gets 160 points for that. The point value for giving an injection is 90. When you equate the labor of the physician to a few points, you cannot separate money from healthcare... on the contrary; healthcare is money now... what else happened... all the labor of the physician goes down the drain. It's now comparable to a few points... Money should not be an issue in terms of healthcare. Healthcare should be accessible. But while we intended to remove money from healthcare, now healthcare equals money... because each intervention has a performance score... I mean, a physician performs cesarean delivery and that has a performance score. Now how's that point determined..."

Omer:

> "The performance evaluation system needs to be substantially overhauled. Let's say you charge 100 TL for a simple intervention, and 150 TL for a much more risky intervention, one that could be fatal. Which one would you do? Many physicians opt for the simple one. They don't want to deal with risky patients. ... Look, before here, I was a physician at Buca closed prison. I was a prison physician for six or seven years... I'd say to the inspectors who came there: 'you always examine things like, whether I have my tie on, whether my shoes are polished, whether my protocol log is in order, whether I clocked in and out on time, whether there are complaints about the infirmary in general. Yet you don't look into how many patients I referred to the hospital, how many of those patients had to go to the hospital, how many of them could be treated within the facilities of the prison, did I take any bribe from some patients to refer them there...'"

As seen, physicians clearly described the characteristics of a physician, a healthcare clinic, and an organization behaving with integrity. However, when they evaluate the Health Transformation Program, with its effects on health care system, they draw a pessimistic picture, and they indicated many major issues that can be reconsidered by the Ministry of Health.

Key Terms

Integrity—Calhoun indicated that integrity has three main dimensions:[17] first the integrated self-dimension, integration of the parts within the person such as desires, evaluations and commitments, into a whole; second, the identity dimension, loyalty to the personal principles as a matter of character; and finally the identity and clean hands dimension, maintaining personal commitment and purity in corrupting situations.

Health Transformation Program in Turkey—a program issued in 2003 with the aim of creating a radical change in healthcare sector.[18]

Performance-based system—one of the seven components of the Health Transformation Program in which the rate payment for physicians became related to the number of patients seen and the number of medical interventions conducted.[19]

Study Questions

1. What is integrity? What is the importance of integrity in healthcare sector?
2. Is there a harmony between the principles of Health Transformation Program with the notion of integrity?
3. What are the radical changes observed in Health Transformation Program?
4. Why might physicians' motivation and integrity be affected negatively due to the changes brought by Health Transformation Program?
5. If physicians behave with integrity, will it be sufficient to create healthcare clinics and organizations with high integrity?
6. If you were the Minister of Health, how would you evaluate the success of Health Transformation Program? what additional changes would you make?

Further Reading

Palanski, M. E., & Yammarino, F. J. (2007). Integrity and leadership: Clearing the conceptual framework. *The Leadership Quarterly 25*(3), 171–184.

Palanski, M. E., & Yammarino, F. J. (2009). Integrity and leadership: A multilevel conceptual framework. *The Leadership Quarterly 20*, 405–420.

Verhezen, P. (2008). The irrelevance of integrity in organizations. *Public Integrity 10*(2), 133–149.

Tatar, M., & Kavanos, P. (2012). Healthcare reform in Turkey. *Eurohealth 12*(1), 20–22.

CHAPTER 11

Business Ethics Following a Financial Crisis

Throstur Olaf Sigurjonsson
Audur Arna Arnardottir
Vlad Vaiman

Introduction

The authors claim that the collapse of the Icelandic economy in the fall of 2008 was partially caused by the lack of good business ethics. The empirical research that will be presented here (where 400 managers of the 300 largest Icelandic firms were surveyed) supports such an argument. Other recent studies also provide compelling examples of unethical behavior leading to an unstable business environment—unethical behavior not only demonstrated by the Icelandic business elite, but also by politicians and civil servants.[1] These findings have surprised many, both inside and outside of Iceland, since Iceland was ranked by rating agencies, such as Transparency International, as being among the least corrupt countries in the world prior to and immediately after the financial crisis of 2008.

In the years leading up to the financial crisis, Iceland did extremely well in Transparency International's Corruption Perception Index (CPI) rankings. This culminated in Iceland being ranked as the least corrupt country, according to the index, in 2005 and 2006. In 2008, after the collapse, Iceland was still ranked by Transparency International's CPI as being in the top ten least corrupt countries, sharing seventh place with the Netherlands.[2] The obvious discrepancy between the index and the actual experience in Iceland highlights that methods of measuring corruption have failed to reflect real economic conditions.[3]

In all areas of a business, ethics is fundamentally important. This includes an ethical approach to all stakeholders, such as employees, shareholders, customers, and the community. By adopting and maintaining a comprehensive ethical approach to conducting business, organizations can maintain their legitimacy and create long-term success. Moreover, the potential to grow, maintain long term profitability, and benefit society by being good corporate citizens have increased.[4] Therefore, business people with a strong moral character and strong ethics are also important for an organization, as they affect the business' prosperity and longevity. But when the business culture in society does not promote ethical behavior, to the extent of promoting unethical behavior, disastrous economic events can occur, such as the Icelandic financial collapse.

The following section will examine these issues, in order to shed light on the circumstances and developments that led up to the Icelandic financial crisis of 2008, where examples of poor ethical behavior in business are many. Next there is an overview of the methodology and data applied in the research and the results of research are given. Finally, the last section presents some recommendations.

A Fallen Star

As previously discussed, for several years Iceland has stood out as one of the least corrupt countries in the world. In 2007 an article published in US News & World Report[5] asked what Iceland was doing right. According to the CEO of Transparency International, the top countries had a "social contract between the government and the people" and a "culture of accountability." In the same article, Mr. Olafsson, chair of the Icelandic-American Chamber of Commerce, claimed that the Icelandic public is educated, well informed, and active in politics. Furthermore, he added that Iceland's compact size, relative isolation, and cultural characteristics had created an environment where people knew each other well and this made it difficult to be corrupt without drawing attention.[6] The collapse of the financial sector in Iceland only a year later shows not only that the Icelandic situation was more complex, but the close links between individuals and other characteristics of society were, in fact, weaknesses and not strengths. In particular, the close links between individuals established an environment for rampant nepotism. This significantly weakened the ethical business culture and created a culture encouraging unethical business practices and corruption.[7]

Nepotism and Business Culture

Even though Iceland was a founding member of the European Economic Area (EEA), and because of this enjoyed the benefits of membership in the form of free trade with the European Union, Iceland's political culture had a history of heavy state intervention in the economy. This culture had created a strong bond between politics and business.[8] Based on business owner's loyalty and political affiliations the political elite decided who would benefit from the "juiciest" business opportunities and who would miss out, particularly when it came to the privatization of government companies.[9]

One of the key features of the Icelandic business culture and one of the most important reasons behind unethical behavior and corruption in Iceland is nepotism.[10] For example, the banks were a highly sought after asset, and during their privatization their ownership was transferred to a limited number of closely connected Icelandic groups who, in the majority, had little experience running sophisticated financial institutions.[11] This was contrary to the original criteria of the banking privatization, which was to attract a small but diverse group of international investors. Domestic political interests became paramount in the privatization process, and the newly privatized banks became the governmental parties' largest donors.[12]

Many international experts, as well as the Icelandic public, have begun to see that the financial and economic crisis in Iceland was brought about by the business culture as a whole. This culture was not as strong, open, and transparent as that of many other developed countries[13] and recently more situations that illustrate Iceland's weak business culture have become apparent. The office of Special Prosecutor was established by law in 2009 with the responsibility of investigating suspicious financial acts in the period preceding the collapse of the Icelandic financial system. As of winter 2012, over 300 individuals have been named as possible culprits, in a nation of just 300,000 people.[14] In February 2012 the former Undersecretary of the

Ministry of Finance was sentenced to jail for over two years, being found guilty of insider trading.[15] The Icelandic parliament also established a Special Investigation Commission (SIC) in 2008 to investigate and analyze the processes leading to the collapse of the three main Icelandic banks. The Commission delivered its report in April 2010. Its findings were that major misconduct and fraud had taken place in the years before the financial collapse. A special 300-page chapter on "Ethics and Business Practices" was amongst the 3000 pages published. Amongst the conclusions was that the owners and the managers of the largest banks thought good business ethics and use of ethic codes (which all the banks formally had) as more of a hindrance than a necessity. By doing so, the bankers ignored law and just business procedures in all aspects of operating their banks and subsidiaries. The effects of this mindset spilled over onto the whole business culture.[16]

The strong connection between politicians and business owners, outlined earlier, made the system of checks and balances ineffective. The presence of powerful corporations in a small country such as Iceland aggravated the situation, as it resulted in imbalances in favor of business over the regulatory authorities, making them hesitant or incapable of overseeing complicated business transactions.[17]

Bad Corporate Governance

The dominance of major shareholders over smaller ones was another unfortunate development of the economic boom in Iceland. The result of this was that the largest shareholders in a corporation were receiving large amounts of funding from the corporation, along with favorable interest rates, to an extent that was not available to the smaller shareholders. Because of concealed ownership, rules of maximum lending were exceeded and the rules for collaterals were ignored. For example, cases have been found where large shareholders received loans amounting to 100% of the purchase price for stock, when the rules stated that lending for such purposes must not exceed 60% of market value. Furthermore, the largest shareholders received more favorable borrowing terms than the smaller ones and enjoyed additional dividend payments. Because of these conditions the large shareholders leveraged their positions, and bought more shares of the corporations that they owned in order to push up the share price. This was funded by the banks and there was little or no collateral. The dominance of this kind of business culture over weak regulatory authorities later proved fatal for the financial system in the country.[18]

Furthermore, the conduct of corporate governance within the Icelandic banks did not foster sustainable banking. A mismatch between incentive systems, risk management, and internal control systems appeared to have been unnoticed by the banks' boards.[19]

While the banking system in Iceland was expanding at a tremendous pace, foreign financial institutions, international rating agencies, and foreign media began criticizing the Icelandic banks for the lack of transparency in their operations, strategy, and media relations. The main point of their criticism was related to the lack of direct and unbiased coverage of the banking expansion in the Icelandic media. The reality was that nearly all the Icelandic newspapers and business magazines during this period were indirectly owned by the banks themselves, through their largest shareholders. The same shareholders, many of them board members of the banks, were also their largest debtors. Any attempts to criticize the banks or institute legislation against media monopolies were promptly quashed by the government. Moreover, although the banks had thousands of shareholders all around the country, they were quite inactive in challenging either boards or bank executives. Therefore, there was no media to act as a watchdog, and likewise, the politicians denied any wrongdoing on the part of the banks.[20]

Endemic Only in Iceland?

All these practices led to a significant exaggeration of business capabilities, where projects that many firms chose to participate in, and the new heights that the country's banking sector was trying to reach, were way beyond their means. Ignorance might be the cause of such business behaviors on some occasions, but when these behaviors and practices became a commonly accepted way of doing business, the business itself becomes unsustainable. As soon as the international financial "springs"—an abundance of easily available and cheap credit—dried up, the Icelandic economy collapsed like a house of cards: all due in part to the highly unethical and blatantly corrupt business practices described above.

It is important to mention that similar business practices were not exclusive to the Icelandic economy and Icelandic enterprises, but what distinguishes the cases illustrated above from the rest is the unprecedented direct and indirect involvement of the political elite in the way that business was conducted.[21] To extend the argument, both political favoritism (nepotism) and weak business culture are to blame for the demise of the Icelandic economy and significantly, in Iceland these two factors are strongly interrelated. According to Brynjarsson,[22] nepotism is the most significant reason for the weak business culture in Iceland. It influenced not only how business was being conducted but also the capacity of the civil service to exercise restraint and oversight over the private sector.

To summarize, it is important to reiterate that all of the questionable practices presented above may be explained by a weak business culture in the society. This weakness was compounded by a company-level lack of diversity and tight personal networks in managerial relationships and asset ownership. To aggravate the situation, political culture and a history of extreme state intervention in the economy created an unprecedented bond between politics and business, some sort of a symbiosis of the political and business elites.[23]

Data on Icelandic Business Ethics after 2008

In order to examine whether and how business ethics has changed since the dramatic experience of the 2008 financial crisis, data was collected in a survey from more than 400 managers of Icelandic firms, aimed at establishing the relationship between what went wrong and the development of improved business practices after the crisis. The respondents were presented with a set of 23 questions to evaluate in general terms the status of business ethics as of today in Iceland, and then to express which actions have been taken within their own firms in order to foster improved business ethics. The authors examined in which way the lack of ethics played a role in the financial collapse of Iceland according to the viewpoint of Icelandic managers, with a strong emphasis on how and whether the business community has learned from the crisis and improved its ethical standards. Empirical research was conducted amongst managers of the largest Icelandic organizations. The managers were asked questions aimed at establishing the relationship between ethics and the role of business in forming and developing the moral foundation. The questions were divided into three major themes: (a) business ethics as they perceive it today in Iceland, (b) whether the 2008 financial crisis has led to improved business ethics, and (c) a self-assessment of business ethics in respondents' own firms.

The survey was conducted through Internet between December 3 and 17, 2010, and out of the 1000 receiving the questionnaire 419 replied. Women were 40% of the respondents. The year of graduation mirrors the demand that has been for business education over the last decade—with 44% of the respondents graduated in the years 2003 to 2008, 16% graduated after year 2008, and 41% before the year 2003. This is reaffirmed in the age distribution of the respondents, where 20% are younger than 35 years of age, 38% of them are between 35 and 45 years old, 31% are between 46 and 55 years old, and 10% are older than 56.

Most respondents, or 37%, categorize themselves as top managers, middle line managers are 27% of the respondents, specialists are 25%, and others are 12%. Respondents come from a variety of industries with 27% from finance, 4% from accounting, 16% from production/fishing industry, 24% from services, 16% from retail, and 13% from IT. Table 11.1 provides an overview of the independent variables used in this research.

All questions have been measured either on a 5-point Likert scale (1 = disagree, 5 = agree), or "ranking questions" where participants were asked to rank by 1 = most important to 5 = least important. Additionally, three open-ended questions supplemented the questions that related to improvement of business ethics.

Has Icelandic Business Ethics Improved?

It was mentioned previously that the bad business practices exposed in Iceland were not exclusive to the country's institutions, but were found elsewhere as well. Consequently, after 2008 a widespread international discussion has been launched on the necessity of improving ethical standards in the business community.[24] But have these been simply discussions or has any action taken place? Has Iceland, having gained such a bad track

Table 11.1. Survey Participants' Data

Independent variable	Total number	Percentage (%)
Gender		
Male	252	60
Female	167	40
Age		
Under 35 years old	84	20
35–45	162	38
46–55	132	31
56 years old or older	43	10
Graduation year		
Before 2003	170	41
2003–2008	184	44
After 2008	65	16
Occupation		
Top level manager	150	36
Mid-level manager	110	26
Specialist	97	23
University teacher	17	4
Other	44	11
Industry		
Accounting	9	2
Financial/Banking	66	16
Manufacturing/Fishing	44	11
Professional services	57	14
Retail	41	10
IT	33	8
Other	168	40

record for its business practices, managed to rebuild more sustainable business behavior? Accordingly, it was of great interest to ask the participants in the survey whether or not business ethics has improved in Iceland.

It must be noted that the findings are disappointing. Only 30% of the respondents could agree with the proposition that business ethics has improved in Iceland since 2008. Women and younger managers are even more skeptical of any improvements (24% and 26% respectively). Respondents believe ethical standards are in a better shape now, during an economic downturn, than before the crisis in 2008. Only 19% claim things are worse now. Nonetheless, this means that managers believe practices are still pretty bad. There is a difference between who is believed to be behaving better or worse. Most believe women practice better business ethics than men (only 16% vote for men). A similar finding is regarding age, where older people are believed to have adapted better business ethics than younger ones (24% vote for the younger).

Iceland, as one of the Nordic countries has many common characteristics with the others. But have the other Nordic countries gone down the same route as Iceland when it comes to bad business practices? Respondents were asked to compare the situation in Iceland to the other Nordic countries. The answers do not evoke any optimism on the Iceland's behalf, since only 11% of the respondents agree with the prediction that business ethics in Iceland is good compared to the other Nordic countries. Most of the Nordic countries (Norway, Sweden, and Finland, but not Iceland), went through a financial crisis some 20 years ago. These countries did suffer a severe financial crisis, one of the big four of last century, it has been claimed,[25] but crony capitalism was not a part of the reason for failure as was the case in Iceland.[26]

Earlier in this chapter nepotism was blamed for decades of poor business practices in Iceland, though it became most devastating in the years leading up to the 2008 crisis. Managers were asked to judge how true this is and an absolute majority of 81% claim that favoritism is common in Iceland, with only 5% disagreeing with it. It should be kept in mind that participants are asked about the situation two years after the crisis, but still managers believe business practices in Iceland are extremely sour. In order to gain more understanding on how nepotism makes an impact on Icelandic business life, an open question was provided asking about examples from the managers. High on the list was "clique-recruitments," when less capable people were hired because of friendship, family relations, or other nonprofessional reasons. Various examples of rules being broken were provided in relation to recruitments practices, both in private and public institutions. Another example that frequently came up was when board members of a firm or an institution used their power to push through deals founded not on best price or service, but rather where their own interests lie, such as through friendship or even bribery (they themselves get a share of the profit being made on the deal).

Keeping these findings in mind, it does not come as a surprise that Icelandic firms do not emphasize business ethics in their strategy. Only 16% of the respondents believe that business ethics is a part of a company's strategy, and only 30% support the proposition that Icelandic firms actually practice good ethics. This indicates that Icelandic managers do not believe that ethics is viewed as an important part of the economy's restructuring plan, or that good ethics are being practiced.

The results change somewhat when respondents answer questions regarding their own firms. When the managers are asked whether being mindful of good business ethics is a priority, 70% of them claim that it is the case. Nonetheless, just 36% of them answer positively to having a formal guideline regarding business practices and ethical behavior. That might coincide with their view that, in general, firms do not include business ethics in their strategy. In less than half (46%) of the cases, managers are made responsible if they break their firms' code of ethics (these are the managers themselves responding). That might explain why they believe that only 64% of their employees take the firm's ethical standards seriously. In only 62% of cases it is believed that there are consequences for poor ethics practiced in their firms. Less than one-third believe there is a clear path to follow if employees notice unethical behavior.

When the respondents were asked to evaluate how business ethics might be different between industries, financial services/banking received the worst grading, and accounting the second worst. IT and manufacturing, on the other hand, received the highest grading. An interesting point is that all industries agree on the ranking, except the accounting industry. The accountants rank their own profession as having the best business ethics. Managers from the financial industry, however, grade their own industry second lowest, putting retail in a worse position.

When asked to find ways around the various ethical dilemmas, a solution mentioned was either to establish new, or make use of an existing, institution or a group outside of the core business community that can serve as a critic of business practices. Universities were often mentioned as an example of such an institution. This institution would function much as an arbitration board does, and would serve to present an assessment in a clear manner and identify unethical components as such. The design of such a "board of business behavioral translators" forms a potential part of future research. While there is still an incomplete picture of what this board would look like, the community would need to choose members before a crisis occurs. Such members would have to be trusted by different segments of the community, and the threat of "capture" by particular groups within the community would need to be addressed. Hence, universities might be ideal sources of participants. To support that, managers argue for stronger business schools' participation in the society's discourse on business ethics, and that they perhaps should be in the forefront of these discussions.

Final Thoughts

In this chapter, the authors attempted to demonstrate that one of the major causes of the Icelandic financial crisis of 2008 was the lack of good ethical practices in Icelandic business culture.

As we have mentioned before, the unethical business practices described in this chapter were not only exclusive to Iceland. What makes the Icelandic case exceptional, however, is the extraordinary involvement of the country's political elite in the way business was conducted. Both nepotism and weak business culture are to blame for the downfall of the Icelandic financial system, and most noteworthy in the case of Iceland is that these two factors are quite strongly interrelated.

Many experts agree that nepotism is one of the most significant reasons for the weak business culture in Iceland.[27] Of course in a relatively small, monocultural, and geographically isolated society like Iceland, nepotism is to a degree an inevitable factor. Yet, in modern times it was strongly underpinned by significant state intervention in the economy. This sort of a "new and improved" nepotism contributed to the ineffectiveness of the civil service by making regulation and supervision nearly impossible. Subsequently, the lack of supervision and regulation led to an unjustifiable expansion of the Icelandic banks, which precipitated the full-blown crisis in the country.

As to the Icelandic business culture itself, it has been sustained by business people, and particularly, by those who lack ethical standards. By being quite successful while demonstrating unethical behavior, they inadvertently encouraged unethical behavior in other business people in the country. Their actions maintained the weak business culture, thereby creating a vicious circle. In order to break this vicious circle and strive for a more ethical business environment, it is necessary to change the predominantly ignorant attitude toward ethics in everyday business activities. This is, however, going to be a long and painful process.

Key Terms

Business ethics—written and unwritten codes of principles and values that govern decisions and actions within a company.

Financial crisis—a situation in which the value of financial institutions or assets drops rapidly.

Rebuilding trust—regaining assured reliance on the character, ability, strength, or truth of someone or something.

Study Questions

1. How would you define the concept of "nepotism" in close knit communities?
2. What ideas do managers come up with as potential solutions to bad business ethics?
3. Which role could universities take on in order to improve business ethics?

Further Reading

Englund, P. (1999). The Swedish banking crisis: Roots and consequences. *Oxford Review of Economic Policy 15*(3), 80–97.
Honkapohja, S. (2009). The 1990's financial crises in Nordic countries. *Bank of Finland Research Discussion Papers 5*, 7–26.
Jonsson, A. (2009). *Why Iceland?* New York, NY: McGraw-Hill.
Jonung, L. (2008). Lessons from financial liberalisation in Scandinavia. *Comparative Economic Studies 50*, 564–598.

CHAPTER 12

Improving Organizational Integrity Through Humanistic Diversity Management

The Case of Minority–Majority Relations in Healthcare Organizations and Academic Institutions

Helena Desivilya Syna
Amit Rottman
Michal Raz

Introduction

In light of globalization processes, diversity of workforce and organizational membership constitutes a reality in most parts of the world.[1] Notwithstanding the pervasiveness of this phenomenon, its ramifications on humanistic organizational practices, particularly on workplace integrity, have hardly been examined.

Constructive engagement of diversity constitutes a vital component of humanistic management in the current organizational reality, embedded in a complex sociopolitical and cultural context.[2] Employers, employees, and members of organizations hardly grasp the potential impact of diversity on work climate and on relationship dynamics. Moreover, they experience difficulty in controlling their own prejudice and stereotypical judgments, thus impeding organizational integrity, as reflected in actual and perceived social and economic justice (equality and equity), inclusion, and an opportunity to express authentic voices.[3] Maintaining integrity within nationally and ethnically diverse organizations constitutes a particular challenge in divided societies, such as those ridden by protracted intergroup conflicts.[4]

This chapter aims to close some of the knowledge gaps and contribute to the understanding of the consequences of diversity on integrity in organizations, especially in a divided society ridden with protracted conflicts. We endeavor to illuminate best practices in this domain by exploring mechanisms whereby constructive relations among diverse groups in organizations can be fostered. Constructive bonds among diverse organizational members and groups denote respect and tolerance of differences, openness, inclusion, intergroup equality, equitable treatment, and opportunities for expressing unique and authentic voices.[5] We consider such benevolent relations as the primary markers of organizational integrity in the context of divided societies.

The chapter is based on the authors' research and praxis in the area of minority–majority relations in organizations, shadowed by protracted Israeli–Palestinian conflict.[6] This work has involved two cases: diverse nurses' teams (Jews, Arabs, and immigrants from former Soviet Union) in medical centers and diverse college students' population (Jews and Arabs).

The paper commences with framing of the diversity construct and modes of diversity management in organizations. It is followed by a brief introduction concerning the effects of protracted conflict on relations among adversarial and diverse groups in organizations. Then the two cases are presented and analyzed. The concluding section of the chapter integrates the insights from the two cases and delineates best practices model (a theory of practice) aimed at developing and implementing humanistic diversity management, thereby promoting integrity in diverse work teams and academic institutions, especially applicable to the context of divided societies. Critical evaluation of the proposed framework, pinpointing its strengths and pitfalls culminates the paper.

Diversity Management in Organizations

Diversity denotes variation in a wide range of group members' characteristics, including professional background and expertise, and salient demographic features such as age, gender, race, nationality, and ethnicity.[7] These scholars distinguished between surface-level and deep-level diversity. Surface-level diversity refers to the extent of demographic variation in a work unit, whereas deep-level diversity purports to disparities in personality, attitudes, values, and capabilities. We embrace the construal of diversity as a group characteristic, focusing mainly on the surface level, namely, differences in demographic characteristics such as race, nationality, ethnicity, religion, gender, social class, and other markers of social identity which have generated intergroup stereotypes, prejudice, acts of oppression, or discrimination.[8] Scholars of organizational behavior attempted to explain the mechanisms whereby diversity exerts an impact on intraorganizational relations. Nationality and ethnicity constitute a significant component of diversity in contemporary organizations, affecting the capacity to manage internal relations and consequently organizational integrity and effectiveness.[9]

Harrison and Klein distinguished among three different elements of diversity: (a) variety (differences in information, knowledge, and expertise), (b) separation (differences in position or opinion among unit members, which reflect disagreement on a horizontal continuum), and (c) disparity (differences in control of valued social resources such as pay and status among unit members which are distributed on a vertical continuum). The *variety* aspect of diversity accounts for the benevolent influence on organizational group functioning. Variety in members' characteristics (such as nationality or ethnicity) brings to the group a potential to view issues from different perspectives and consider greater array of options to solve organizational problems. In contrast with the positive effects of *variety*, *separation*, and *disparity* elements of diversity tend to perturb group functioning and impede its outcomes.[10]

The disruptive effects of diversity were explained by the theories of *social categorization* and *social identity*[11] and the notion of *faultline*.[12] According to the *social categorization* and *social identity* model people tend to define and distinguish themselves from others based on their group membership. Encountering individuals from different groups sets up the categorization process and gives rise to a tendency to form a more favorable image of one's own group in comparison to the attitudes toward individuals from dissimilar groups (*in-group favoritism*). In the context of nationally diverse organizational groups, *in-group favoritism* may affect the internal climate and dynamics, making it more difficult for "out-group" members to express their voices and exert influence.

The *faultline* model (hypothetical dividing lines splitting a group into subgroups and giving rise to polarization between in-group and out-group identities) refined the underlying mechanism accounting for the negative impact of separation and disparity in groups with diverse membership. Van Knippenberg, Dawson, West, and Homan explained the contingencies underlying the negative effects of diversity in contrast with its positive impact, maintaining that the actual adverse influence of social categorization depends on its salience, rather than on the mere presence of differences.[13] Thus, the negative effects of diversity tend to prevail when categorization salience is high, whereas its positive influence takes the lead when the work group embraces cooperative motivational orientation, team identity, and shared objectives, which in turn facilitate constructive interactions such as coordination and collaboration. As we argue later, the legacies of protracted national conflict tend to obscure the development of such benevolent group climate, instead accentuating faultlines—encouraging in-group favoritism by the majority members, in turn, impeding the advantages of diversity.

To counteract the potential adverse effects of diversity, organizations engage it by means of various management practices on the macro as well as on the micro (group) level.

What are the effects of diversity management in organizations? Which management patterns maximize the benevolent effects of diversity and promote integrity while minimizing the adverse influence of separation and disparity?

An extensive literature review on diversity in organizations by Ramarajan and Thomas revealed positive effects of diversity management in terms of intergroup equality, intergroup relations, and performance of diverse groups, and indicated the organizational level and individual level conditions fostering such outcomes.[14]

Based on their findings, these scholars maintain that increasing representation of diverse groups (minorities, women, and other excluded groups) in organizations, especially in positions of power and improving their career trajectories, appears to enhance intergroup equality. Moreover, Ramarajan's and Thomas' review has indicated that positive interactions among diverse group members and mutual perceptions concerning desirability of such intergroup contact tended to mitigate prejudice, negative attitudes, and enhance intergroup liking (termed *allophilia* by Pittinsky and Montoya[15]). Other organizational scholars showed relational benefits of diversity as reflected in intergroup respect, openness, inclusion, minority members' sense of integration in organization, and majority members' perception of uniqueness with regard to minority members.[16]

Ramarajan and Thomas qualify the positive findings concerning organizational diversity, stating that the effects in each of the three domains are independent, so that intergroup equality is not necessarily related to positive intergroup relations or enhanced group performance.[17] Research has yet not provided clear findings with respect to the links among the three domains. The other limitation of extant research pertains to differences in measurement levels: intergroup equality has been typically assessed at the macro level whereas intergroup relations and group performance have been assessed at a micro level. Hence, it is not clear whether parallel positive findings can be identified across levels.

Notwithstanding the importance of the positive findings on organizational diversity, another query one might pose concerns the conditions or circumstances underlying such positive effects. Extant research evinced the contingent nature of the positive outcomes. Thus, diversity management at organizational policy level, such as affirmative action, diversity committees, and especially assigned diversity personnel, appear to precipitate intergroup equality.[18] Similarly, group-level aspects, such as beliefs concerning the importance of fairness, equal access, legitimacy, integration, and learning tend to foster positive intergroup relations and high group performance.[19] Triana, Garcia, and Colella's research shows that organizational efforts supporting diversity moderate the effects of perceived racial discrimination and thereby enhance employees' affective commitment.[20] However, their findings also indicated that the pattern of relationships may change for different ethnic or social groups. Ethnic or national minorities for whom discrimination experiences have been particularly prevalent, therefore salient, and who maintain strong ethnic or national identity, such as African-Americans, tend to interpret organizational efforts to support diversity as hypocritical. Such attitudes are conceivable in the case of Arab citizens in Israel, especially in situations where they work in joint teams, usually enhancing the salience of social categorization.[21]

How does diversity management relate to organizational integrity? As argued in the preceding section, constructive engagement with issues of diversity at the macro-policy level and at the micro (group) level in organizations may foster equality and positive intergroup relations. Such effects are tantamount to the expected outcomes within the realm of humanistic management, fostering organizational integrity. We extrapolate from the literature embracing gender perspective in business ethics to other characteristics of diversity and maintain accordingly that equality and equity for minorities and other frequently excluded and marginalized groups should be an explicit priority in organizational practices.[22] Thus, practices encouraging integrity entail counteracting the prevailing models of doing business, corporate culture, and organizational management which are fundamentally unjust due to their structural and systematic bias favoring white men and other majority groups. In other words, promoting integrity warrants special attention, reflected in clear policy and actions designed to provide social and economic justice to excluded or marginalized social groups.

The Israeli case with its internal divisions, particularly the Jewish–Arab schism in light of the protracted national conflict, directs the task of humanistic diversity management primarily to the national majority–minority relations. Enhancing integrity in this case entails improving social and economic justice for the minorities and the capacity of both groups—minority and majority—to express their authentic voices. In order to embed our work in the relevant context, the next section of the chapter delineates the anticipated effects of protracted conflict on relations among adversary and diverse groups in organizations.

The Effects of Protracted Israeli–Palestinian Conflict on Jewish–Arab Relations in Joint Organizations

Previous studies have indicated numerous adverse consequences of the protracted conflict on individual motivation and wellbeing, on interpersonal perceptions, and group relations.[23] Continuous intergroup discord poses a profound barrier to intergroup relations due to accumulative negative changes in attitudes, feelings, motivations, and behavior. Such protracted conflict tends to intensify, often erupting into violence, and leading to perceptions of intractability: persistence and pervasiveness of the disputes, irreconcilable goals, threatened existential needs, and escalation.[24]

At the motivational level, each side embraces a highly competitive, intransigent stance, viewing the conflict as a "zero-sum game." In the emotional arena, parties' feelings toward one another are progressively transformed from anger to overall antagonism, often turning to hatred inflamed by vengeance. In the cognitive modality, adversaries rely on stereotypes and selective perception, disproportionately weighing negative information while discounting positive data. Increasingly negative perceptions of the other side breeds mutual distrust. At the behavioral modality, adversaries encounter mounting difficulties in communication.[25]

Changes at the individual level unfold in the social and group context as mounting ethnocentrism and groupthink.[26] Each group tends to believe that its own goals are just, whereas the opponent group's goals are illegitimate.[27] Groupthink symptoms include extreme within-group conformity and suppressed dissent.[28] At the community level, there is a polarization effect in which individuals and groups tend to join one of the rival camps, strengthening mutual animosity experienced by both sides and sustaining a culture of conflict.[29] Although overtly peaceful everyday relationships among Jewish and Arab citizens seem to mitigate these deep divisions, there is a constant potential for conflict eruption, including violent outbursts.

Surprisingly, research on the consequences of this protracted discord on the actual functioning of Jews and Arabs in mixed organizations virtually does not exist. Thus, it is not clear how well members of these joint teams are able to counteract the adverse ramifications of the protracted conflict. In light of the complexity of relations among national majority and minority groups in organizations, the question is how such diversity can be managed in a humanistic manner so as to enhance organizational integrity, offsetting the adverse effects of salient faultlines.

Our work aims to shed light on the actual modes of diversity management—how does it fit with humanistic patterns to engage this phenomenon, in light of the complex reality of protracted national conflict?

We seek to elucidate perceptions of Jewish and Arab members in joint organizations concerning national majority–minority relations (micro-level markers of organizational integrity), in joint medical teams and academic institutions, underscoring their attitudes concerning diversity management in their organizations and teams and outcomes of such efforts on the macro level—perceived equality and equity for minorities. We also examine what organizational level (e.g., organizational policies and practices) and group level factors (e.g., team or organizational climate, common organizational identity) geared at constructive engagement with diversity foster equality and equity (mitigate perceptions of discrimination) and positive intergroup relations within mixed groups. Finally, we explore the influence of national status (minority versus majority) on perceptions with respect to diversity management and organizational integrity on both macro and micro level.

We move now to a description and analysis of the two cases in an attempt to respond to the queries presented above. The first one constitutes a "naturalistic" case, portraying naturally evolving dynamics between Jewish and Arab nurses in mixed medical teams, whereas the second case involves premeditated interventions geared at improvement of relations between Jewish and Arab students in academic institutions.

Case 1: Diversity Management in Nationally and Ethnically Mixed Nurses' Teams

Jewish and Arab citizens of Israel have worked in joint medical teams, delivering healthcare services to both Jewish and Arab patients, from the inception of the state of Israel in 1948 through the present. Medical workers from both sides have experienced all phases of the protracted Israeli–Palestinian conflict, including the most intense escalation stages (wars, terrorist acts, and the two *intifada* uprisings). Thus, this case demonstrates an exceptional social phenomenon of health professionals from two adversary groups working in joint teams, treating patients from both groups even at times of violent conflict episodes. Maintaining integrity while managing diversity of work teams and delivering healthcare services in the shadow of protracted national conflict, constitutes a significant challenge.

We sketch extant findings of research in progress, which examines the internal dynamics in Jewish–Arab work teams, while tracing the benevolent contribution of team incentives as well as the adverse consequences of the protracted conflict. It underscores the hidden aspects of such processes, such as construal of majority–minority power relations and its repercussions on the work climate and quality (professionally equal, respectful of human rights, and culturally sensitive) of health service delivery to mixed patient population. We explore team members' awareness concerning the linkage between diversity management and organizational integrity and their evaluation regarding the institutional attention, policy, and actions in this domain.

Specifically, the study explicates the nature of processes within these teams, as reflected in decision making, communication patterns, cooperation, scope, type and intensity of conflicts, patterns of conflict management, and the factors underlying these processes. Drawing on the literature concerning diversity in work teams,[30] among the potential factors which presumably account for the dynamics in bi-national work teams of special interest are individual level factors such as members' emotions toward teammates (notably empathy), mutual trust and joint professional identity. Group level elements are also significant; these include perceived intrateam support and intragroup cohesion especially in the face of adverse events related to the protracted national conflict. The research also examines the subjective outcomes of the dynamics within bi-national teams such as individual members' perceptions of organizational justice and mutual national images.

The findings presented below have been derived from a pilot study, which employed qualitative methodology. The participants were 12 Jewish and Arab nurses, members of mixed medical teams who work in public medical centers in the northern region of Israel.

The research tools included individual semistructured interviews with nurses, members of mixed medical teams. The findings reported in this chapter are based on interviews with two Muslim nurses and three Jewish nurses (one of them an immigrant from former Soviet Union). The nurses were asked general questions probing their views on the following issues: the climate in diverse work team, communication patterns and cooperation, the impact of diversity on the team functioning (medical care), sense of discrimination and social identity, strengths and weaknesses of nationally and ethnically diverse teams, diversity management at their work organization, and team functioning at times of violent incidents associated with the protracted conflict (terrorist acts of Palestinians or Israel Defense Forces, military acts against Palestinians). Data collection for this research is still in progress, including both individual interviews as well as focus groups with Arab and with Jewish nurses.

The major themes which emerged from the extant interviews refer to the climate in diverse work team, communication patterns and cooperation, the impact of diversity on the team functioning (medical care), sense of discrimination, strengths and weaknesses of nationally and ethnically diverse teams, diversity management at the work organization, and team functioning at times of violent incidents associated with the protracted conflict.

Team Climate

The participants' ethnic diversity within the work team affects its climate primarily on occasions manifesting differences of opinions between nurses from different social groups. The disparities are viewed as cultural in nature and tend to exacerbate intergroup tensions in the work team, which in turn impede the overall atmosphere and mitigate cooperation. As put by one of the Arab nurses: "*When there are cultural differences, such as between Christians and Muslims, they quarrel and the result is bad, they do not talk…do not want to work on the same side…there is an atmosphere of discomfort…you do not feel comfortable to work with someone you do not feel at ease…*"

One of the Jewish and one of the Muslim nurses noted tensions arising from the cultural differences between nurses born in Israel (both Jewish and Arab) and nurses who are immigrants from former Soviet Union, as demonstrated in the following quotations: "*…They are cold, as if they don't have feelings, both toward peer nurses and toward patients…not as the nurses from eastern countries, such as Tripoli, Morocco, Iraq and the Israeli born, or Arab nurses; It makes unpleasant work atmosphere*"; "*They feel superior, patronizing, they think they know everything, they are not nice, do not talk nicely, I had few unpleasant situations with them… and the staff do not like to work with them…*"

One interviewee relayed a strong tendency of the nursing staff to interact with peers from the same social group: "sub-groups, sub-groups within the team… let's say the Russians with the Russians, Yemenite with the Yemenite, Moroccan with Moroccan…it's very salient.…" Such pattern of subgroupings within a single team alludes to the phenomenon of in-group favoritism[31] and the salience of faultline phenomenon.[32]

Communication Patterns and Cooperation

Akin to the impact of diversity on team climate, internal communication processes and cooperation may be disturbed as a result of conflicts between team members belonging to diverse social groups. This is more likely to happen following extreme events, such as a terrorist act, and medical care of the victims (and sometimes the perpetrators). However, according to the interviewees, usually communication and cooperation among staff in diverse teams are quite effective. The common goal of providing high quality care to patients facilitates such constructive interactions. It creates a joint team identity, which serves as a framework for organizing and coordinating behavior.[33] Arab and Jewish nurses were quite unanimous in their views about communication and cooperation in their respective diverse work teams. As put by the pilot study participants: "*Each nurse comes from different culture and has different values, but our work is different, we need to be cohesive, have consensus… we work for the patient, it's not a private business, we are here to help others and work here in cooperation even though each nurse has different mentality…*"; "*There is cooperation all the time, morning and evening… For example if I work with a Druze male nurse, it's obvious he takes care of the men… I don't have to tell him anything…*"

The Impact of Diversity on Care (Performance)

The interview responses seem to suggest that social diversity is reflected in somewhat different functioning amidst various social groups, which can be attributed to culture-bound customs and norms. Such cultural disparities occasionally cause disrespect, anger, and mitigate cooperative orientation among team members from diverse social groups. One of the Arab respondents relayed an incident which in her view had adverse impact on the team performance:

"I worked with a Russian nurse… I do care not only for the patient but also for his or her family, it's 90% of a cure. The family members have to feel that their loved one is in good hands… There was an old woman dying and her daughter wanted to stay with her, but the Russian nurse would not let her… she had no empathy, things like that interfere with the team functioning, and assists in treatment when the family trusts you…"

Discrimination Due to National/Ethnic Membership

Both Jewish and Arab nurses indicated instances of patients' racist attitudes and discriminatory behavior as a result of membership in different social group (especially national minority), as manifested in the following quotation: *"…one day a patient approached an Arab male nurse in a clinic in a kibbutz and told him something …that he got a job in a clinic because only Arabs work there…I told him (the Arab nurse) as I tell each of the new nurses—Arabs or Russians that they have to 'swallow a frog' when they come to work in a kibbutz… later they became familiar with him, the fact that he is an Arab… but he is an extraordinary nurse…"*

The minority members also reported personal experiences of discrimination as medical personnel, reflected in their perceived inability to voice criticism, especially toward superiors, fearing sanctions, as put by an Arab participant: *"There is one nurse in my team, an Israeli born Jew…This is personality, this is a character, she has no fear, once she told the head nurse that she is a liar. I as an Arab, cannot tell such a thing, because I know that the next day I am out…"* Unsurprisingly, Jewish nurses viewed discrimination from a majority perspective: They felt pressure to refrain from criticism toward their minority counterparts, concede in conflict situations in order to avoid accusations of racism and discrimination, thus preserving intact work relations, as expressed by one of the Jewish nurses: *"[…]Concerning a Muslim employee, she because she is also Muslim, when she notices that he refrains from working she get angry at him, no reservations; I cannot let myself to get angry at him. I know that he will right away say it's discrimination… I need to be careful…"*

Regardless of their minority or majority status, both groups at times experience frustration and bitterness associated with perceived racism and discrimination. In line with Triana, Garcia, and Colella's[34] findings, minority members tend to be more sensitive concerning discrimination, thus suspecting the sincerity of majority members' efforts to engender equitable and mutually respectful relationships.

Strengths and Pitfalls of Diversity in Work Teams

Some of the interviewees maintained that diversity promotes high quality care, culture-sensitive care: It facilitates intercultural understanding and helps to match treatment and care with the culture-bound norms and needs of patients from various cultural backgrounds, as put by one of the interviewees: "*Because we have patients from different cultures if we have a nurse from the same culture as the patient, she understands the patient's behavior, why he behaves that way, for example is hysterical, shouts...*"

Diversity can also be instrumental in promoting tailor-made work schedules, such as matching shifts in accordance with national, ethnic, or religious holidays. Another notable advantage of diversity, mentioned by the pilot study participants, was widening horizons and perspectives on various issues. By contrast, the major pitfall of diversity, which emerged from the interviews, was greater odds of conflicts and tensions due to incongruent perceptions. This finding corroborates results of previous research on team diversity.[35]

Diversity Management at Organizational Level

All five interviewees unanimously claimed that their organization has not adequately addressed the issue of social diversity in work teams in general, and has hardly dealt with the resulting difficulties and predicaments in daily work practices. In most instances, department managers opt to avoid direct engagement with diversity related issues. Instead they prefer to maintain seemingly harmonious work relations ("*industrial peace*"). The following quotations demonstrate the passive stance of the management with respect to diversity issues: "*The organization, I am not sure the management is aware, knows anything. My superior knows, but he hardly deals with the problems… since I am an experienced nurse I am expected to manage these issues…"; "Here it is difficult, I am expected to solve these problems, to ignore the racist thing…for example we had this Moroccan Jew patient, we had to put a Druze patient in the same room, he refused, said he cannot be with a Druze in the same room…"*

Refraining from confronting these challenges, not only does not mitigate the tensions, but amplifies frustration and bitterness, which may precipitate escalation of intergroup conflicts, damaging work relations at the team level. In line with the recent findings of Ramarajan and Thomas,[36] lack of diversity management may have adverse consequences in terms of performance and work relations.

Team functioning at times of violent incidents associated with the protracted conflict. The pilot study participants maintained that such violent incidents exacerbate tensions, consequently impinging on the team functioning. It is worth noting that when the event constitutes a war which can adversely affect all social groups in Israel (majority and minority alike), it may breed temporary intergroup solidarity, nonetheless, traces of intergroup tensions remain. Most cases of either party's violence (Israeli or Palestinian) produces highly tense team atmosphere, lack of intergroup tolerance, and impedes motivation for cooperation. The following quotations demonstrate such harsh experiences of members in diverse teams: "*I feel tensions, I feel we refrain from talking, some employees boil inside and later burst on another issue, not the violent incident…"; "… we try not to look at each other, to hide these things, not to bring your personal feelings to work, there is no place for politics, you cannot be detached from your feelings, it's very difficult, you have difficulty to concentrate, but you do it, you do your work…"; "…These tensions between Jews and Arabs burst during violent events, like war, terrorist acts…*"

In sum, our initial findings with respect to the case of mixed Jewish–Arab nurses' teams appear to corroborate previous evidence showing the adverse legacies of protracted conflict on the emotional, cognitive, and motivational modalities at the individual level as well as at the group level.[37] Although demographic characteristics such as nationality and ethnicity denote surface level diversity,[38] the study suggests that these features also act as deep level diversity. Thus, the negative effects of the prolonged national discord are by and large hidden, somewhat mitigated by the positive impact of the variety aspect in diversity and masked by the apparent harmony in teamwork on the overt level. This dual effect of a surface and deep diversity reflects a difficulty experienced by both Jewish as well as Arab nurses in authentically expressing themselves.[39] Such a latent facet significantly impedes recognition of employees' predicament and consequently, development and implementation of humanistic management practices, especially at the micro (group) level. This, in turn, has a potentially adverse impact on organizational integrity in terms of social and economic justice (equality and equity) and the capacity of expressing an authentic voice.

Case 2: Diversity Management in an Academic College

The second case entails several endeavors of conflict education programs involving Jewish and Arab college students. The projects were designed to promote a transformation of the intergroup relations in the shadow of protracted Israeli–Palestinian conflict, by means of raising awareness with respect to repercussions of intergroup conflict, mitigating mutual negative images of the participants from the two groups, promoting mutual cross-cultural understanding and empathy, and fostering motivation for cooperation. Major findings obtained from a follow-up research on this praxis are explored, underscoring their potential contribution to models of practice fostering humanistic management of diversity and thereby promoting organizational integrity in academic institutions.

As indicated earlier, protracted national conflict affects the region's residents' (including young people's) perceptions and attitudes of conflict and intergroup relations.[40] A marked proportion of the young population constitutes students at academic institutions, who may become the future leaders, thus shaping policies concerning diversity management in organizations, while dealing with the repercussions of prolonged national discord. Following an underlying social–psychological principle, ascribing to perceptions a central role in molding attitudes, intentions, and actual behaviors, various academic institutions conduct programs aimed at conflict education and engagement with intergroup tensions.[41] This assumption concerning the centrality of perceptions as determinants of attitudes and behavior constituted our point of departure in launching the program at the college. It also addressed the characteristics of the specific sociopolitical context. The rationale for the project rested on the working assumption that while the college's campus has remained outwardly tranquil, before, during the period of the Al Aqsa uprising and after the second uprising, there were lingering tensions which needed to be addressed openly in a constructive discussion (lest they erupt in a negative, even violent, fashion during times of stress). Hence there was a need to create positive forums for such interaction.

The conflict education program was based on a systems approach designed to engender changes in five modalities, infected by protracted conflict: motivation, cognition, affect, behavior, and environment. It entailed an action science focus[42] reflected in two aspects: (a) it has evolved from a theoretical framework attempting to operationalize its tenets within the intervention; (b) the program incorporated a systematic follow-up research within the intervention process so that the effectiveness of its operation could be examined. Such monitoring fostered learning, allowed to adjust the program according to the participants' needs, to the changing circumstances and unexpected effects, and nourished the conceptual models.

The theoretical framework of the project pooled together three streams of knowledge:

- Social identity, its complexity and diverse subjective representations; its dynamics and implications on the relationships between individuals and groups; and the phenomena of prejudice (its dynamics and implications).
- Social conflict with an emphasis on intergroup tensions in organizations (the meaning of intergroup conflict, its perceived sources and dynamics).
- Power relations, underscoring majority–minority relations and their effects on the parties' relationships in joint organizations.

The program was designed to assist the students from both groups in becoming aware and gaining an understanding of their own multiple identities and grasping their dynamic nature, encouraging them to become familiar and recognize the identities of their counterparts in the context of protracted conflict. Thus, the project aimed at fostering legitimization and acceptance of the adversary group and moderate negative feelings. Moreover, it was intended to engender hope by means of breeding and nourishing a dialogue between the two groups of students, focusing on *active listening*, allowing them to agree to disagree on certain issues, while creating a joint agenda for other problems of common interest. The program also attempted to empower the participants, equipping them with relevant knowledge and skills so they could become potential leaders of Jewish–Arab dialogue in joint organizations, thereby fostering humanistic management and organizational integrity. In terms of diversity management, it endeavored to enhance the variety aspects of diversity while minimizing the negative elements of disparity and separation.[43]

The program described here was conducted in an academic college in northern Israel in 2005, incorporating insights from other projects conducted at the same college.[44] The methodological approach entailed interfacing theory and practice—combining acquisition of knowledge and skills by means of theoretical and experiential learning, using a workshop format. This design was implemented in small groups and plenum discussions associated with current episodes, simulations and exercises, and mini-lectures aimed at summarizing the major concepts and theoretical models. Formative evaluation and action research accompanied the planning and implementation of the program. Data collection comprised observation and documentation of all of the class-meetings, content-analysis of the participants' diaries, and individual interviews with the participants. The individual interviews were conducted with 18 of the 20 participants and focused on the participants' feelings, perceptions, and thoughts concerning the Jewish–Arab relations and regarding the effects of the workshop on these sentiments and attitudes. The next section presents the major findings relevant to diversity management in organizations. The following thematic categories emerged from the research data: construal of the national conflict, motivation for intergroup contact, intergroup communication capacities, and majority–minority relations.

Construal of the Israeli–Palestinian Conflict

The participants evinced two main significant inclinations. First, members of both groups grasped the conflict as an intractable discord, lacking a feasible and foreseeable solution.[45] This tendency is intriguing in light of most participants' relative readiness and openness for contact with members of the other group. Yet, they appeared skeptical with respect to the benevolent impact of intergroup contact on resolving the national conflict at the macro-political level.

The students conceived the encounters in the course of the workshop as effective at the interpersonal level, namely changing their relationships locally at the college, despite the national conflict. This tendency was demonstrated when the participants were asked to formulate and present their personal vision regarding the future relationship between the parties. The students attempted to offer potential solutions to the national conflict, but each proposal was subsequently confronted and contradicted by other students (Jews and Arabs). Overall, most of the participants experienced a great difficulty to conceive and devise possible solutions. As expressed by two of the Jewish students: *"my problem was that I tried to solve the global problem… and I understood that we need to focus on the local level"* (C.) and *"we need to focus on the steps and pathways we have at hand, and not to try to get to the mountaintop"*(R.)

The second tendency, which emerged in the participants' construal of the national conflict, purports to their perceptions with respect to the centrality of the conflict and its salience. In this regard we identified some differences between the participants from the two groups. All of the Arab students tended to attribute a high salience to the national conflict, whereas the Jewish participants' attitudes were mixed. Some of them, mostly students with a leftist orientation, perceived the conflict as very salient and central in the lives of Israelis, as put by one of the students: *"where I live, there is nothing else you can do (besides learning to live in peace with the Arab). Your life is intertwined with theirs, whether you like it or not"* (G.t). By contrast, others viewed the conflict as relatively insignificant. Moreover, some even argued that the actual relationships between the two groups are more harmonious than as they are presented in the media, as illustrated by the following quotation: *"it seems to me that we express perceptions that we see in the media, and that actually things aren't that bad."* (R.)

Interestingly, the Jewish students who described the relationships as relatively calm were those who exhibited a rather low tolerance for the members of the other group. Conceivably, this apparent dissonance reflects an attempt to deny or conceal the conflict ("to sweep it under the carpet") as was demonstrated in the individual interviews: *"people don't really think that way. They are just trying to look like they care" (I.); "if there was a majority of people with the same opinions as mine, I'm sure that I would be feeling more confident to say the things I really thought' (H.)" "as long as it's within the limits of talking, so I can spare myself and just be silent and everybody smiles" (R.)*

Notwithstanding the "deadlock," the workshop seemed to affect some changes on the Jewish side with regard to understanding the Arabs' perspective on the national conflict. Specifically, it made them more aware of the importance of the identity-related components. While exploring the identity issue from the perspective of the Arab citizens in Israel, the Arab students had an opportunity to explain the complexity and conflicting sentiments they experience regarding their social identity. The following quotations vividly illustrate their predicament:

"I was visiting in an Arab country, and they call us Jews, or even worse, dogs of Jews, no one accepts us, they don't want to understand… it's a hard feeling," (S.); "we don't have an identity… the Palestinians don't accepts us, the Lebanese don't accept us… we put our identity on the side and we are moving on" (N.). At this phase, the Jewish students listened very carefully, and then reacted: "here is the conflict we have with them… There is a misunderstanding" (M.); "we don't understand them… this is our mistake…" (N.)

Following the joint discussions, the Jewish students appeared to gain a better grasp of the Arabs' conflicting identities and their different perspective on the national conflict.

Motivation for Intergroup Contact

The prolonged national conflict has eroded the students' motivation for intergroup contact. Notwithstanding the general tendency, there were differences between the two groups in their motivation levels: overall, the Arab participants exhibited a higher motivation for contact in comparison to their Jewish counterparts.

The groups not only differed in their motivation levels, but also in the reasons underlying this inclination. The Arab participants indicated their wish that the members of the other group would get to know them better, presumably regarding the workshop as an opportunity to develop positive contacts with members of the Jewish group. When asked about the reasons for participation in the workshop and their expectations concerning the project, the responses were: *"to have an opportunity to state my opinion" (R.); "that they (the Jews) hear me, I really like those Jewish-Arab encounters… because in the workshop we can change things," (R.); "maybe we could change their (the Jews) opinions" (S.).* The quotations suggest that the Arab students regarded the workshop as an opportunity to tell their own story, to reduce the social distance between them and the Jewish majority and to change the Jews' attitudes toward them.[46]

In contrast, the Jewish participants, including those who expressed high motivation for contact, expressed their desire to hear the other side, get to know them and to enrich their knowledge in general, as illustrated by the following quotations: *"the contribution is in that I can hear what they (the Arabs) think… what they feel" (M.); "I wanted to broaden my knowledge… for my personal enrichment." (N.).*

Overall, the Jewish participants showed greater variance in their motives and expectations concerning their contact with members of the other group, underscoring the need for contact on an individual level. By contrast, the Arab participants revealed a collective need for contact with the Jewish party and were quite uniform in their motives and expectations regarding this contact.

Finally, regarding the workshop's impact on the participants' motivation for contact, it seems that the workshop can barely ignite such an inclination among those lacking such a motivation in the first place. The workshop fell short in elevating the willingness for contact while impeding the capacity for creating transformations on other dimensions, such as emotions and behavior. These findings bear important ramifications with regard to promoting humanistic management of diversity in organizations. Such practices need to take into account gaps between the members of majority and minority in their sense of inclusion, respect for their identity needs, and capacity to express unique and authentic voices. Consequently, humanistic diversity management actions should provide primarily the minority members with resources for enhancing these perceptions and feelings, thereby improving organizational integrity.[47]

Intergroup Communication Capacities

The long-lasting conflict has impaired communication capacities, so that even those with high motivation for contact experienced difficulties in maintaining a discourse. Another communication problem, evident among the Jewish participants, focused on their difficulty in listening to the Arab participants' conflict narrative. The overall atmosphere in the workshop was relatively positive, seemingly allowing the participants to communicate openly and on a relatively comfortable basis. However, when the Arab participants attempted to directly express their perspective on the national conflict, the good atmosphere abruptly changed: the Jewish students revealed much less tolerance in listening to them.

The Arab participants revealed a difficulty in expressing their concerns and, particularly, criticism of the Jewish side in plenary discussions, presumably due to their minority status.[48] Instead, they exposed their opposition and divergent views in the individual interviews, while having a captive audience (the interviewer), as indicated in the following quotations: *"what disturbs me is that the other side doesn't like to broaden their perspective... they don't want to hear positive things. Always from the negative side"* (N.); *"no, not everyone were o.k. some of them are racist"* (R.)

Majority–Minority Relations

The Arab participants revealed tendencies which could be attributed to their minority status: the conflict appeared highly salient in their perception, they attributed a central weight to their national identity, exhibited a higher motivation for contact in comparison to their Jewish counterparts, their impetus for contact revolved around the need to voice their narrative so that the Jews get to know them, and they experienced a great difficulty in openly expressing their concerns and criticism toward the Jewish party.

By contrast, the Jewish participants showed prototypical inclinations of the majority: They appeared much more diverse in their construal of the conflict, referred to the national conflict by and large using concrete terms (the problem of land and environmental resources), exhibiting lower motivation for contact, with their major motives resting on broadening their knowledge and getting to know the other, and they experienced a considerable difficulty in listening to their Arab counterparts.

In addition to the above tendencies, the imbalanced power relations affected the workshop dynamics and the participants' behaviors in other areas:

- The Jewish participants, who expressed high motivation for contact, embraced an orientation of patronage, tended to express willingness to help their Arab counterparts due to this sense of superiority rather than as a consequence of developing mutual goals.
- In discussions concerning the national conflict, the Jewish students appeared to control the situation—they posed the questions, the Arab students responded and provided information, which the Jewish students, in turn, interpreted and analyzed.

In sum, the findings with regard to case 2 clearly indicate the negative residues of the protracted Israeli–Palestinian conflict, with some differences in its impact between the Jewish and Arab participants as members of the majority and minority groups, respectively. However, they also reveal some transformations, particularly in the awareness of the majority concerning the minority and in the perceptions of both groups with respect to the consequences of the conflict on diversity management in joint organizations, such as academic institutions and workplaces. Humanistic diversity management practices in the context of a divided society need to address the hidden residues of the protracted intergroup conflict, particularly its impact on a sense of inclusion and the capacity to express a unique and authentic voice, especially by the national minority. The results also validated the assumption with respect to the centrality of perceptions in shaping attitudes, intentions and actual behaviors, and corroborated the hidden facets of diversity effects in the context of protracted national conflict.[49]

Enhancing Organizational Integrity: A Proposed Model of Practice in the Context of Divided Societies

This section of the paper integrates the insights which have emerged from the two cases, subsequently delineating the proposed action model

designed to improve humanistic diversity management and thereby promote organizational integrity. Notwithstanding the differences between
the two cases, both substantiate our argument that cooperation, teamwork, and joint interactions constitute a particular challenge in divided
societies, such as those ridden by protracted national or ethnic conflicts.[50]
Both medical staff and students in demographically diverse institutions
do indeed grapple with such complex reality. The narratives sounded by
the participants in both projects point to intergroup biases and tensions
due to the salience of social categorization and faultline phenomenon.[51]

Perceptions of discrimination appear prominent among both national
minority and majority groups, but each one of these social groups constructs
and interprets this phenomenon from a different perspective. Members of
minority embrace a victim identity, presumably due to past experiences of
racist attitudes and discrimination, whereas majority members attempt to
behave in a politically correct fashion to avoid accusations and leave work
relations or dealings among Jewish and Arab students, at least superficially
intact. It is worth noting that both groups tend to experience predicament
as a result of alleged racism and discrimination, although the intensity of
these difficulties appears to be higher for the national minority.[52] Differential construal of discrimination and racism by minority in comparison to
majority and the emotional burden associated with this experience warrant
group-sensitive approach while managing diversity at a work place or academic institution. Such approach is compatible with humanistic diversity
management and tenets of social responsibility.[53]

Despite the clear need to address diversity issues at the workplace
and academic institutions, no organizational policy or practices directed
explicitly at diversity management enhancing organizational integrity
exist in the respondents' organizations. Our intervention in the college
was a unique initiative, undertaken occasionally in this and other academic institutions. Thus, medical employees and students are generally
left to their own devices, personal resources, informal coalitions, or assistance of informal third parties.[54]

Traces of protracted conflict become visible when asking directly
about expected outcomes of diversity, such as perceived organizational
justice—equality and equity versus discrimination due to national or
ethnic category. The adverse legacies of the ongoing national conflict

are accentuated with the occurrence of violent external incidents, associated with the protracted discord.[55] Both nurses and students expect effective engagement of diversity issues, including the unique features resulting from the context of protracted national conflict. They consider organizational integrity an important facet, however, barely identify any organizational level efforts to materialize relevant practices at the overall organizational or group level.

The parties in both cases experience difficulty in directly engaging in diversity issues related to the national conflict, such as subjectively perceived lack of equal opportunity, disrespectful treatment, and actual acts of discrimination. Thus, the nurses' and students' predicament remains by and large hidden, masked by the seemingly harmonic relations on the overt level.[56] This manifestation of the dual effect of surface and deep level diversity in everyday work life and student life hinders Jewish and Arab nurses' and students' opportunity to present authentic self or sound genuine voice.[57] Such a latent facet significantly limits recognition of employees' and students' predicament and consequently impedes organizational integrity, especially at the micro (group) level.

What can be done to alleviate the quandary of employees' and students' in diverse organizations in the context of divided societies so as to foster genuine organizational integrity?

Based on the insights drawn from our research and praxis associated with the two cases, we propose a model of practice, focusing on minority–majority relations. It underscores the role of subjective perceptions and the need to move them from the hidden sphere to the overt level—to the "center of the stage." Such a transformation would not only increase the odds of authentic expression of voices and identities, but would also prepare the ground for positive interaction and genuine dialogue by increasing awareness with regard to each side's needs and difficulties.[58] The model also ascribes a central role to negotiation, construed broadly as processes designed to define cultural identities and intergroup positions, or in general terms—negotiating relationships.[59] In addition, the proposed framework embeds the intervention in the specific organizational context. Finally, the model stresses the need to interface and coordinate diversity management at the micro (group) level and the macro (national policy) level.

The main components of the action framework:

1. Micro (group) level
   Relationship building actions
   - Negotiating reality and terms of engagement in joint small groups
   - Power-balancing (empowerment)—special attention directed to the national minority (work done separately with each national group)
   - Reflection and learning in joint small groups and periodical organizational plenum, and revising the activities accordingly
   - Contextual conditions in organizations
   - Positive Diversity Climate
   - Common minority–majority organizational identities
   - Professional and Academic Norms Supporting Equality and Cooperation
2. Macro (national policy) level
   - Legislation—legal safeguards
   - Implementation, monitoring, and follow-up of humanistic diversity management actions in organizations, by governmental institutions and authorities, such as the Equal Employment Opportunities Commission.
   - Coordination between macro and micro level actions
   - Partnership building between work organizations, academic institutions, and government.

The format of the micro-level actions of humanistic diversity management can be based on the approach undertaken in academic institutions. To prepare for the interface with the macro-level components, we propose establishing a steering committee in organizations, composed of senior representatives from human resources division (in work organizations) and from the students' dean office, representatives of employees (including representatives of senior management), and students from both groups and academic department chairs. This joint forum needs to build a genuine partnership.[60] Research has demonstrated that engagement with diversity issues, particularly those emanating from prolonged national discord, necessitates a collaborative alliance, reflecting upon power relations.[61]

It is worth noting that implementation of the micro-level component in academic institutions calls for special attention and sensitivity with regard to the needs of the minority due to differential motivational inclinations for contact and cooperation. In joint work places, especially based on teamwork (such as nurses' teams), superordinate goals, task and outcome interdependence tend to equalize the motivation for cooperation.[62]

Concluding Thoughts

Diversity has always been a component of organizational life in divided, conflict ridden societies such as in Israel, yet its ramifications on human relations in organizations have not been explored.[63] Consequently, there were no policies designed to manage diversity in a humanistic fashion so as to promote organizational integrity, reflected in actual and perceived economic and social justice, a sense of inclusion and the capacity to express a unique and authentic voice. Nowadays, corporate social responsibility and humanistic management constitute a bon ton of organizational practices. As our research and praxis demonstrate, such practices deem particularly important in organizations operating in the context of divided societies, saturated with protracted intergroup conflicts.

The proposed model of action constitutes a first step in this direction. Its strength resides primarily in the micro-level intervention, particularly the emphasis on the hidden facets of protracted conflict legacies and implementation of the negotiation component, both resting on the scholars' and practitioners' experiences in similar actions, particularly in academic institutions (albeit sporadic). Yet, this potential advantage needs to be qualified. Sustainability of the micro-level element of the proposed model of practice depends to a large extent on a continuous and active involvement of a committed expert third party.[64] The latter needs to facilitate the recurrent highly challenging, negotiation of relations between the majority and minority parties, monitor reflection and learning, activities of the steering committee and constantly muster support of the internal management. Those are extremely demanding tasks, which can hardly rely on voluntary actions. Providing such human resource by organizations for extended periods remains questionable, undoubtedly calling for difficult negotiation between the initiators/entrepreneurs and the organizational management, even in cases of organizational commitment to humanistic diversity management and promotion of integrity.

The major weaknesses lie in the implementation of the macro-level elements, including monitoring these processes. The Equal Employment Opportunities Commission is still in infancy in Israel, charged with ample missions however equipped with limited authority and resources to both implement as well as enforce its actions. This leads to another potential pitfall in our framework—coordination between the micro- and macro-level humanistic management of diversity. Finally, the need to deal with the adverse influence of the sociopolitical context on implementation of the micro-level intervention constitutes a significant challenge, thus a potential limitation of the proposed model of practice. Despite the reservations, we would like to end on a positive note, drawing on Mary Parker Follett's quote with regard to peace, as we consider organizational integrity an essential component of building peace and constructive minority–majority relations in nationally diverse organizations:

"We have thought of peace as passive and war as the active way of living. The opposite is true. War is not the most strenuous life. It is a kind of rest cure compared to the task of reconciling our differences. From war to peace is from the futile to the effective, from the strategic to the active, from the destructive to the creative way of life…. The world will be regenerated by the people who rise above these passive ways and heroically seek, by whatever hardship, by whatever toil, the methods by which people can agree."[65]

Key Terms

Diversity—variation in a wide range of group members' characteristics, including professional background and expertise, and salient demographic features such as age, gender, race, nationality, and ethnicity.

Surface level diversity—the extent of demographic variation in a work unit.

Deep level diversity—disparities in personality, attitudes, values, and capabilities

Elements of diversity:

Variety—differences in information, knowledge, and expertise.

Separation—differences in position or opinion among unit members, which reflect disagreement on a horizontal continuum.

Disparity—differences in control of valued social resources such as pay and status among unit members which are distributed on a vertical continuum.

Divided Society—a society split by deep schisms among its social groups, each having distinct cultural, religious, and political identities.

Faultline—hypothetical dividing lines splitting a group into subgroups and giving rise to polarization between in-group and out-group identities.

Markers of Integrity—respect and tolerance of differences, openness, inclusion, intergroup equality, equitable treatment, and opportunities for expressing unique and authentic voices.

Negotiation—processes designed to define cultural identities and intergroup positions, or in general terms, negotiating relationships.

Protracted Conflict—a lengthy, intense, identity-based dispute, coupled with uncompromising parties' goals.

Study Questions

1. What are the similarities and differences between the two cases in the difficulties encountered by the minority and majority group members in diverse organizations in the context of Israel's divided society?
2. How can the proposed model of practice mitigate the difficulties faced by each of the two groups (in particular by the minority members) and enhance organizational integrity? What specific practices should have the highest priority? Why?
3. How could you implement the proposed model of practice in your organization? Please show what adaptations need to be made in the model in order to tailor-make it to your organization and its sociopolitical context.

Further Reading

Kolb, D. M. (2004). Staying in the game or changing it: An analysis of moves and turns in negotiation. *Negotiation Journal 20*(2), 253–268.

Kolb, D. M., & Williams, J. (2000). *The shadow negotiation: How women can master the hidden agendas that determine bargaining success.* New York, NY: Simon & Schuster.

Li, M., & Sadler, J. (2011). Power and influence in negotiation. In M. Benoliel (Ed.), *Negotiation excellence: Successful deal making* (pp. 139–161). Tuck Link, Singapore: World Scientific Publishing.

Stephan, W. G. (2011). Improving relations between residents and immigrants. *Analyses of Social Issues and Public Policy 11*(1), 1–16.

Tjosvold, D. (2006). Defining conflict and making choices about its management: Lighting the dark side of organizational life. *International Journal of Conflict Management, 17*(2), 87–95.

Notes

Chapter 1

1. Co-operatives UK (2012).
2. Goffman (1959).
3. Barnhart and Steinmetz (1988).
4. Collins Concise Dictionary & Thesaurus (2002).
5. Kulik (2005); Mostovicz, Kakabadse, and Kakabadse (2011).
6. Kulik (2005), p. 357.
7. Niven (2012).
8. Suma Wholefoods (2012).
9. Suma Wholefoods (2012).
10. *Guardian* newspaper (2011, February 18).
11. Suma Wholefoods (2012).
12. FCU (2011).
13. Co-operative Bank (2011).
14. Co-operative Bank (2011).
15. Hogan, Hogan, and Kaiser (2010).
16. Lawrence (2008).
17. Co-op Bank website (2012).
18. Myllila and Takala (2011).
19. Gratton and Truss (2003).
20. Jahdi and Cockburn (2007, 2008).
21. Furstenberg, cited in Dülfer and Hamm (1985).
22. Cockburn (2007).

Chapter 2

1. Paine (1994); Treviño and Youngblood (1990); Turnipseed (1988); Victor and Cullen (1988).
2. Peterson (2002); Treviño (1986).
3. Deshpande, George, and Joseph (2000); Fritzsche (2000); Treviño (1986); Treviño, Butterfield, and McCabe (1998).
4. Gellerman (1986).
5. Aydemir and Eğilmez (2010); Dunlop and Lee (2004).

6. Peterson (2002).
7. Dunlop and Lee (2004).
8. Andrews (1989); Stead, Worrell, and Stead (1990); Treviño and Brown (2004).
9. Andrews (1989); Stead et al. (1990); Treviño and Brown (2004).
10. Andrews (1989); Stead et al. (1990); Treviño and Brown (2004).
11. Treviño et al. (1998).
12. Eisenhardt (1989); Yin (2003).
13. Caza, Barker, and Cameron (2004).
14. Ashkanasy, Windsor, and Treviño (2006); Aydemir and Eğilmez (2010); Treviño and Youngblood (1990).
15. Ashkanasy et al. (2006); Treviño and Youngblood (1990).
16. Treviño and Brown (2004).
17. Gintis, Bowles, Boyd, and Fehr (2002).
18. Schmincke (2010).
19. Treviño and Brown (2004).
20. Treviño and Brown (2004), p. 73.
21. Ashkanasy et al. (2006).
22. Caza et al. (2004).
23. Treviño and Brown (2004).
24. Treviño and Youngblood (1990).
25. Brass, Butterfield, and Skaggs (1998).
26. Peterson (2002).
27. Paine (1994).
28. Treviño and Brown (2004).
29. Brass et al. (1998).
30. Ashkanasy et al. (2006).
31. Brass et al. (1998).
32. Peterson (2002).
33. Caza et al. (2004); Dunlop and Lee (2004).

Chapter 3

1. Near and Miceli (2008).
2. Source: http://whistleblowing.blog.onet.pl/Raport-ACFE-do-narodow-edycja-,2,ID470029130,n (Retrieved on May 13, 2012).
3. Source: http://whistleblowing.blog.onet.pl/Raport-ACFE-do-narodow-edycja-,2,ID470029130,n (Retrieved on May 13, 2012).
4. Able and Frank (2006), p. 24.
5. See Rogowski (2007a).
6. Stachowicz-Stanusch and Wankel (2011).

7. Kaplan and Schultz (2007).
8. http://whistleblowing.blog.onet.pl/
9. Keenan (2002); King (1997); Miceli and Near (1994); Miceli, Rehg, Near, and Ryan (1999).
10. Near and Miceli (1985), p. 4.
11. Transparency International (2009a).
12. Dąbrowski (2011); Robbins (2004).
13. Wojciechowska-Nowak (2008), p. 51.
14. See Rogowski (2007b).
15. Dąbrowski (2011).
16. Source: http://www.batory.org.pl/programy_operacyjne/przeciw_korupcji/wsparcie_i_ochrona_sygnalistow
17. Dąbrowski (2011).
18. Dąbrowski (2011).
19. Hensel (1995), p. 196.
20. Kaplan, Rittenberg, and Schultz (2006).
21. Rogowski (2007a).
22. Martens and Kelleher (2004), p. 3.
23. Dąbrowski (2011).
24. Lacayo and Ripley (2002).
25. PwC (2011).
26. PwC (2011), p. 4.
27. Source: Based on PwC (2011); http://whistleblowing.blog.onet.pl/
28. Source: Based on PwC (2011); http://whistleblowing.blog.onet.pl/
29. Source: (May 2012); http://whistleblowing.blog.onet.pl/
30. See: (May 2012); http://www.whistleblower.pl/
31. Wojciechowska-Nowak (2011).
32. Dąbrowski (2011), p. 39.
33. Martens and Kelleher (2004), p. 3.
34. Arszułowicz (2005).
35. Kacprzak (2011).
36. Kacprzak (2011).
37. Dąbrowski (2011).
38. Domaszewicz and Miączyński (2008).
39. Aristotle (2010).
40. Nielsen (2010).
41. Lennick and Kiel (2006), p. 11.
42. See: http://www.opendemocracy.org.za/wp-content/uploads/2011/05/Recommended-draft-principles-for-whistleblowing-legislation-Nov-09-doc.pdf
43. Stachowicz-Stanusch (2011), p. 43.
44. Wankel and Stachowicz-Stanusch (2011).

45. Wankel (2010).
46. Near and Miceli (1985).

Chapter 4

1. In the Merriam-Webster dictionary, 2012 edition (on-line). Retrieved by the author on April 30, 2012.
2. In Miller, B. A., 2011, retrieved on Nov. 27th, 2011, at http://www.articlesbase.com/leadership-articles/.
3. In Stachowicz-Stanusch, A., & Wankel, C., in *Management education for integrity, ethically educating tomorrow's business leaders,* Emerald, 2011, p. 119.
4. Ibidem.
5. Retrieved by the author on January 20th, 2012, from the website, *Anticorruption,* www.corp-integrity.com/wp-content/uploads/2011/09/Anti-Corruption.pdf
6. Ibidem.
7. Retrieved by the author on Feb.15th, 2012, at www.adb.org
8. In Stachowicz-Stanusch, A., & Wankel, C., 2011, *Handbook of research in teaching ethics in business and management education,* Information Science.
9. Retrieved by the author on Nov.11th, 2011, at http://unglobalcompact.org
10. In Stachowicz-Stanusch, A., 2011, in *Organizational immunity to corruption, building theoretical and research foundations,* Information Age Publishing.
11. In Griffith & Harvey, 2002, *Thunderbird International Business Review* (Jul./Aug. issue), vol. *44*(4), pp. 455–476.
12. In Gaikwad, M., 2010, *Ethical issues in the workplace; how to handle,* retrieved by the author on Aug.11th, 2010, at www.buzzle.com/articles/ethicalissues-intheworkplace.html.
13. In Dogra, 2010, *Ethical issues in the workplace; how to handle,* retrieved on Aug. 11th, 2010, at www.buzzle.com/articles/ethicalissuesintheworkplace.html
14. In Rudder, C.F., 1999, Ethics in education: are professional policies ethical? *Educational Theory, 41*(1), pp. 75–88.
15. In Rudder, C.F., 1999, Ethics in education: are professional policies ethical? *Educational Theory, 41*(1), pp. 75–88.
16. In Khera, 2010, Ethics perception of the U.S. and its large developing country trading partners, *Global Management Journal, 2*(1), pp. 32–33.
17. In Khera, 2010, Ethics perception of the U.S. and its large developing country trading partners, *Global Management Journal, 2*(1), pp. 32–33.
18. Ibidem.

19. In Newman, J., and Fuquab, D., 2006, 'What does it profit an organization if it gains the whole world and loses its soul?', *Consulting Psychology Journal, 58*(1), pp. 13–22.
20. In Gentile, M., 2010, 'Keeping your colleagues honest: how to challenge unethical behaviour at work and prevail', *Harvard Business Review*, March, pp. 114–117.
21. In Bognanno, M., Budd, J., & Kleiner, M., 2007, 'Symposium introduction: governing the global workplace', *Industrial Relations 46*(2), pp. 215–221.
22. In Davenport, K., Lewellin, P.G., Logsden, J.M., & Wood, D.J., 2006, *A transformative framework for ethics and sustainable capitalism,* Sharpe: New York, p. 4.
23. Ibidem.
24. Ibidem.
25. In Tobias, L., 2004, 'The thriving person and the thriving organization: parallels and linkages', *Consulting Psychology Journal*, Practice and Research, *56*(3), p. 9.

Chapter 5

1. Farias and Sands (2012).
2. Zahra, Gedajlovic, Neubaum, and Schulman (2009).
3. Austin, Stevenson, and Wei-Skillern (2006).
4. Alvarez and Barney (2007).
5. Peterson and Seligman (2004).
6. Sosik, Gentry, and Chun (2011).
7. Sosik, et al. (2011), p. 11.
8. Becker (1998); Parry and Procter-Thomson (2002).
9. Becker (1998), pp. 157–158.
10. Palanski and Yammorino (2007).
11. Becker (1998).
12. Parameshwar (2005).
13. Peterson and Seligman (2004).
14. For example, Ruch et al. (2010).
15. Sosik et al. (2011).
16. Drucker (1992), p. 115.
17. Palanski and Yammarino (2007).
18. Paine (1994), p. 248.
19. Jacobs (2004), p. 216.
20. Palanski and Yammarino (2007).
21. Peterson and Seligman (2004).
22. Klein (2008).

23. Alvarez and Barney (2007).
24. Hall and Chandler (2005).
25. Dik and Duffy (2009), p. 427.
26. Dik and Duffy (2009).
27. Elangovan, Pinder, and McClean (2010).
28. Elangovan et al. (2010), p. 430.
29. Parameshwar (2005).
30. Buechner (1973) , p. 95 cited in Elangovan et al. (2010).
31. http://freesetglobal.com/
32. http://rainafrica.com/ethics/
33. www.rosecircles.com
34. For example, Hall and Chandler (2005).
35. Elangovan et al. (2010).
36. Hall and Chandler (2005).
37. Paine (1994).
38. Palanski and Yammorino (2007).
39. Zahra et al. (2009).
40. GlobeScan (2011).
41. Austin et al. (2006).
42. Frost et al. (2005).
43. Paine (1994).
44. Becker (1998).
45. Dik and Duffy (2009).
46. Sosik et al. (2011).
47. Becker (1998).
48. Peterson and Seligman (2004).

Chapter 6

1. Ardichvili, Mitchell, and Jondle (2009); Davis and Rothstein (2006); Kaptein (2010).
2. Grant (2011).
3. Becker (1998); Dudzinski (2004).
4. Kogut and Zander (1995).
5. O'Connell, Hickerson, and Pillutla (2011).
6. Collins and Porras (1996).
7. Drucker (1990).
8. Polanyi (1974).
9. Simmons (2002).
10. Paine (1994).
11. Dudzinski (2004); Paine (1994); Treviño (1990).

12. Becker (2009); Dudzinski (2004).

13. Chun (2005).

14. MacIntyre (1984), pp. 186–193.

15. Rego, Ribeiro, and Cunha (2010).

16. Fowers and Tjeltveit (2003).

17. Bright, Cameron, and Caza (2006).

18. Treviño (1990).

19. Dutton, Dukerich, and Harquail (1994).

20. Kurzynski (2009); MacIntyre (1984).

21. Kogut and Zander (1995).

22. Dudzinski (2004).

23. Pirson and Lawrence (2010).

24. Pirson and Lawrence (2010), p. 555.

25. Lewis (1944).

26. Kogut and Zander (1995).

27. Augustine (2003).

28. Reason and Bradbury (2001).

29. Schein (2001).

30. Ludema, Cooperrider, and Barrett (2001).

31. Collins and Porras (1996).

32. Ludema et al. (2001).

33. Ludema et al. (2001).

34. Jonsen and Jehn (2009).

35. Trevinyo-Rodriquez (2007).

36. Weick (1995).

37. Dutton et al. (1994); Weick (1995).

38. Rego et al. (2010); Simmons (2002).

39. Chun (2005).

40. Weick (1995).

41. Dudzinski (2004); MacIntyre (1984).

42. Weick (1995).

43. Dudzinski (2004).

44. Dutton et al. (1994).

45. Weick (1995).

46. Simmons (2002); Talwar (2009).

47. Collins and Porras (1995).

48. Weick (1995).

49. Rossouw (2008).

50. Verbos, Gerard, Forshey, Harding, and Miller (2007).

51. Berger and Luckmann (1966); Kogut and Zander (1995); Mesa (2010); Orlikowski (2002).

52. Weick (1995).
53. Ardichvili et al. (2009); Schein (1992).
54. Porter (1985).
55. MacIntyre (1984).
56. Caza, Barker, and Cameron (2004).
57. Ardichvili et al. (2009); Schein (1992).
58. Pålshaugen (2001).
59. Watts (2010).
60. Senge and Scharmer (2011).
61. Grant (2011).
62. Becker (1998); Bright et al. (2004); Caza et al. (2004).

Chapter 7

1. Zauderer (1992), p. 13.
2. Petrick (2008b), p. 1141.
3. Petrick (2008a), p. 110; Petrick (2008b), p. 1141.
4. Gosling and Huang (2010), p. 414.
5. Becker (1998), p. 159.
6. Koehn (2005), p. 132.
7. Yu and Miller (2003).
8. Cheung and King (2004); Waldmann (2000).
9. Wei (1996).
10. Hsu (2007); Koehn (2005); Petrick and Quinn (1997).
11. Wright, Szeto, and Cheng (2002).
12. Wright et al. (2002).
13. Waldmann (2000).
14. Hofstede, Hofstede, and Minkov (2010).
15. Jacobs, Guopei, and Herbig (1995).
16. Lee (1996).
17. Chang (1998).
18. White and Lean (2008).
19. Chang (2001).
20. TSMC (2012).
21. Pedersen (2006).

Chapter 8

1. For example, Knack and Keefer (1995); Mauro (1995); Shleifer and Vishny (1993).
2. Globerman and Shapiro (2003); Wei (2000).

3. Getz and Volkema (2001).
4. Fogel (2006).
5. Campos, Lien, and Pradhan (1999); Fisman and Svensson (2007); Shleifer and Vishny (1993).
6. Knack (1996).
7. For example, Coronel and Balgos (1998); De Dios and Ferrer (2001); Kang (2002); MacIntyre (2001).
8. Galang (2012).
9. Hutchcroft (1998).
10. Lange (2008).
11. Fisman and Miguel (2007).
12. Dyball and Valcarcel (1999).
13. TIRI (2012).
14. Deegan (2002).
15. Higgins (1957).
16. Denny (2004).
17. Hill and Shiraishi (2007).
18. Wagner and Jacobs (2008).
19. Wagner and Jacobs (2008).
20. Banyan (2010).
21. Batalla (2000).
22. Quah (2011).
23. Klitgaard (2011).
24. Gera (2011).
25. Aceron (2009).
26. Pimentel (2005).
27. ANSA (2010).
28. Diaz (2012).
29. TIRI (2012).
30. TIRI (2012).

Chapter 9

1. Andriof and McIntosh (2001); Snider, Hill, and Martin (2003).
2. Carroll (1999); Garriga and Melè (2004); Votaw (1972).
3. Lindgreen, Córdoba, Maon, and Mendoza (2010), p. 230.
4. Lindgreen, Swaen, and Campbell (2009), p. 429.
5. Lindgreen et al. (2009).
6. Schmidheiny (2006), p. 22.
7. Jenkins (2005), p. 528.

8. Although there are yearly cohorts since 2000 when the course was offered for the first time, it was only starting with the 2009 cohort that a special evaluation is carried out at the end of each course.

9. The Universidad de los Andes School of Management has been accredited by three international accreditation agencies: AACSB, EQUIS, and AMBA (Commonly known as the "Triple crown").

10. Arjoon (2000), p. 159.

11. Arjoon (2000), p. 159.

12. Student, Cohort 2011.

13. Student, Cohort 2011.

14. These learning objectives are assessed periodically by the committees of the following accrediting bodies to which UASM belongs: AACSB, EQUIS, AMBA, and the CAN (The Colombian Accrediting Committee).

15. Student, Cohort 2009.

16. Student, Cohort 2009.

17. Student, Cohort 2009.

18. Student, Cohort 2011.

19. Student, Cohort 2009.

20. Student, Cohort 2009.

21. Student, Cohort 2009.

22. Aristotle (1995); Fontrodona, Guillén, and Rodríguez (2011); MacIntyre (1993); Melè (2009); Polo (1997).

23. Aristotle (1995), p. 1729, 1094a1–8.

24. Melè (2009), p. 72.

25. Polo (1997).

26. Aranzadi (2011), p. 95.

27. Melè (2009), p. 72.

28. Melè (2009), p. 72.

29. Arjoon (2000), p. 159.

30. Letter to the Romans 7: 4–23

31. Polo (1997).

32. Aranzadi (2011).

33. Aranzadi (2011), p. 94.

34. Polo (1997), p. 123.

35. Aranzadi (2011), p. 96.

36. Koehn (1995), p. 536.

37. Melè (2009), p. 72.

38. Aristotle (1995), p. 1743, 1103a33–1103b2.

39. Arjoon (2000).

40. Arjoon (2000), p. 162.

41. Woodward and Miller (1994).

42. Arjoon (2000), p. 166.
43. According to Collins (2001, p. 70) "Level 5 leaders are a study in duality: modest and willful, shy and fearless." They build enduring greatness through a paradoxical combination of personal humility and professional will.
44. Collins (2009).
45. Collins (2011).
46. Polo (1997), p. 123.
47. Melè (2009), p. 71.
48. Melè (2009), p. 72.
49. Polo (1997), p. 128.
50. Polo (1997).
51. Melè (2009), p. 74.
52. Melè (2009), p. 74.
53. Yin (2009).
54. Eisenhardt (1989), p. 536.
55. Three of the researchers analyzed the essays while the head instructor stepped aside for this stage of the research process in order not to bias the classification.
56. Glaser and Strauss (1967).
57. Student, Cohort 2011.
58. Student, Cohort 2010.
59. Student, Cohort 2010.
60. Student, Cohort 2010.
61. Student, Cohort 2011.
62. Banaji, Bazerman, and Chugh (2003), pp. 56–64.
63. Student, Cohort 2009.
64. Student, Cohort 2011.
65. Student, Cohort 2010.
66. Student, Cohort 2009.
67. Student, Cohort 2011.
68. Student, Cohort 2011.
69. Student, Cohort 2009.
70. Student, Cohort 2009.
71. Martín López (1999).
72. Student, Cohort 2010.
73. Student, Cohort 2011.
74. Student, Cohort 2011.
75. Student, Cohort 2011.
76. Student, Cohort 2009.
77. Student, Cohort 2010.
78. Student, Cohort 2011.

79. Student, Cohort 2010.
80. Student, Cohort 2011.
81. Student, Cohort 2011.
82. Student, Cohort 2010.
83. Student, Cohort 2009.
84. Student, Cohort 2009.
85. Student, Cohort 2011.
86. Student, Cohort 2010.
87. Selznick (1957), p. 138.

Chapter 10

1. Akdag (2003).
2. Bostan (2009).
3. Ministry of Health (2008).
4. Ministry of Health (2008).
5. Ministry of Health (2003).
6. Ministry of Health (2003).
7. Ministry of Health (2008).
8. Diler (2009).
9. Diler (2009).
10. Celikay and Gümüs (2011).
11. Görgün (2009).
12. Görgün (2009).
13. Görgün (2009).
14. Tatar (2007).
15. Akdag (2003).
16. Tatar (2007).
17. Calhoun (1995).
18. Ministry of Health (2008).
19. Ministry of Health (2008).

Chapter 11

1. Special Investigation Committee (2010); Vaiman, Sigurjonsson, and Davidsson (2011).
2. Transparency International (2009b).
3. Vaiman, Davidsson, and Sigurjonsson (2010).
4. Vaiman and Sigurjonsson (2012).
5. Cole (2007).

6. Cole (2007).
7. Sigurjonsson (2010).
8. Jonsson (2009).
9. Sigurjonsson (2010).
10. Vaiman et al., (2010).
11. Wade (2009a), pp. 5–33.
12. Iceland National Audit Office (2009).
13. European Commission (2010); Sibert (2009); Wade (2009b).
14. Vidskiptabladid (2011).
15. Visir (2012).
16. Special Investigation Commission (2010).
17. Wade (2009b).
18. Wade (2009a), pp. 5–33.
19. Special Investigation Commission (2010).
20. Schwarzkopf and Sigurjonsson (2010).
21. Haralz (2007).
22. Brynjarsson (2009).
23. Jonsson (2009).
24. For example, see, Stachowicz-Stanuch, A. (Ed.) (2009).
25. Sigurjonsson and Mixa (2010).
26. Englund, (1999); Englund and Vihriälä (2003); Honkapohja (2009); Jannari (2009); Jonung (2008); Jonung, Kiander, and Vartia (2008).
27. Brynjarsson (2009); Vaiman et al. (2009, 2011).

Chapter 12

1. Desivilya and Palgi (2011a); Mor Barak (2010).
2. Friedman and Desivilya (2010).
3. Clair, Beatty, and Maclean (2005); Desivilya (2011); Mor Barak (2010).
4. Desivilya-Syna and Yassour-Borochowitz (2010); Friedman and Desivilya (2010); Hargie, Dickson, and Nelson (2003).
5. Clair et al. (2005); Triana, Garcia, and Colella (2010).
6. Desivilya and Rottman (2008); Desivilya-Syna, Raz, and Maoz (2011).
7. Mohammed and Angell (2004).
8. Ely and Roberts (2008); Ramarajan and Thomas (2010).
9. Desivilya and Palgi (2011b); Friedman and Desivilya (2010).
10. Harrison and Klein (2007).
11. Tajfel and Turner (1986).
12. Lau and Murnighan (1998).
13. van Knippenberg, Dawson, West, and Homan (2011).
14. Ramarajan and Thomas (2010).

15. Pittinsky and Montoya, 2009.
16. Brickson (2000); Carmeli and Gittell (2009); Dutton and Ragins (2009).
17. Ramarajan and Thomas (2010).
18. Kalev, Dobbin, and Kelly (2006).
19. Ely and Thomas (2001).
20. Triana et al. (2010).
21. van Knippenberg et al. (2011).
22. Thompson (2008).
23. Coleman (2004); Desivilya and Yassour-Borochowitz (2010); Syna-Desivilya (2004); Friedman and Desivilya (2010).
24. Bar-Tal (2011).
25. Syna-Desivilya (2004); Bar-Tal (2007, 2011).
26. Syna-Desivilya (2004).
27. Bar-Tal (2011).
28. Coleman (2000).
29. Desivilya-Syna and Yassour-Borochowitz (2010); Bar-Tal (2011).
30. van Knippenberg et al. (2011).
31. Byrne (1997); Tajfel and Turner (1986).
32. van Knippenberg et al. (2011).
33. Hinds and Mortenson (2005).
34. Triana et al. (2010).
35. Desivilya and Palgi (2011b); Desivilya (2008).
36. Ramarajan and Thomas (2010).
37. Syna-Desivilya (2004); Bar-Tal (2011).
38. Mohammed and Angell (2004).
39. Clair et al. (2005).
40. Bar-Tal (2011); Desivilya-Syna and Yassour-Borochowitz (2010).
41. Kuppermintz and Salomon, 2005; Stephan, Hertz-Lazarowitz, Zelniker, and Stephan (2004); Van Laar, Sidanius, and Levin (2008).
42. Dewey (1938); Schön (1983, 1987).
43. Harrison and Klein (2007); van Knippenberg et al. (2011).
44. Syna-Desivilya and Abu-Bakkar (2005).
45. Bar-Tal (2011); Syna-Desivilya (2004).
46. Clair et al. (2005); Desivilya and Rottman (2008); Friedman and Desivilya (2010).
47. Clair et al. (2005); Friedman and Desivilya (2010).
48. Clair et al. (2005); Desivilya (2011).
49. Clair et al. (2005); Desivilya-Syna and Yassour-Borochowitz (2010).
50. Desivilya and Rottman (2008); Desivilya-Syna et al. (2011); Hargie et al. (2003).
51. Tajfel and Turner (1986); van Knippenberg et al. (2011).

52. Mor Barak (2010); Triana et al. (2010).
53. Thompson (2008).
54. Mor Barak (2010).
55. Desivilya-Syna et al. (2011); Syna-Desivilya (2004).
56. Desivilya (2011).
57. Clair et al. (2005); Mohammed and Angell (2004).
58. Clair et al. (2005); Desivilya (2011).
59. Collier (2009); Kolb and McGinn (2009).
60. Desivilya and Palgi (2011a,b).
61. Bovaird (2006); Friedman and Desivilya (2010); Vangen and Huxham (2003).
62. Desivilya-Syna et al. (2011).
63. Desivilya and Rottman (2008); Desivilya-Syna et al. (2011).
64. Collier (2009).
65. Follett (1965), pp. 357–358.

References

Able, J. L., & Frank, J. (2006 Oct/Nov). How private companies stop fraud. *Chief Executive* 221, ABI/INFORM Global. Accessed on 20.01.2012.

Aceron, J. (2009). *G-watch's textbook count story.* Retrieved February 21, 2012, from http://www.oecd.org/dataoecd/27/51/42877391.pdf

Akdag, R. (2003). *Transformation in health.* Ankara, Turkey: Ministry of Health of the Republic of Turkey.

Akdag, R. (2008). *Development report: Transformation program of Turkey in health.* Ankara, Turkey: Ministry of Health of the Republic of Turkey.

Alvarez, S. A., & Barney, J. B. (2007). The entrepreneurial theory of the firm. *Journal of Management Studies 44*, 1057–1063.

Andersen, J. F., & Andersen, P. A. (1987). Never smile until Christmas? Casting doubt on an old myth. *Journal of Thought 22*(4), 57–61.

Andrews, K. R. (1989). *Ethics in practice: Managing the moral corporation.* Boston, MA: Harvard Business School Press.

Andriof, J., & McIntosh, M. (Eds.) (2001). *Perspectives on corporate citizenship.* Sheffield, UK: Greenleaf.

ANSA. (2010). The Bantay Lansangan (road watch) experience. Retrieved February 21, 2012, from http://www.ansa-eap.net/assets/200/59-1-4_Bantay_Lansangan_Road_Watch_Experience.pdf

Anti-Corruption (2011) http://www.corp-integrity.com/wp-content/uploads/2011/09/Anti-Corruption.pdf

Aranzadi, J. (2011). The possibilities of the acting person within an institutional framework: Goods, norms, and virtues. *Journal of Business Ethics 99*, 87–100.

Ardichvili, A., Mitchell, J.A., & Jondle, D. (2009). Characteristics of ethical business cultures. *Journal of Business Ethics 85*, 445–451.

Aristotle. (1995). The Nicomachean ethics. In J. Barnes (Ed.), *The complete works of Aristotle* (vol. 2). Princeton, NJ: Princeton University Press.

Aristotle. (2010). *Nicomachean ethics.* White Fish, MT: Kessinger. Cited after: Stachowicz-Stanusch and Wankel (2011).

Arjoon, S. (2000). Virtue theory as a dynamic theory of business. *Journal of Business Ethics 28*, 159–178.

Arszułowicz, M. (2005). Conference proceedings of 4th Annual Conference of European Academy of Business in Society (EABIS) *Odpowiedzialność biznesu i konkurencyjność: Rozwój kapitału ludzkiego dla zrównoważonego rozwoju.* Wyższa Szkoła Przedsiębiorczości i Zarządzania im. L. Koźmińskiego, Szkoła Główna Handlowa, Forum Odpowiedzialnego Biznesu.

Ashkanasy, N. M., Windsor, C. A., & Treviño, L. K. (2006). Bad apples in bad barrels revisited: Cognitive moral development, just world beliefs, rewards, and ethical decision making. *Business Ethics Quarterly 16*(1), 449–473.

Augustine. (2003). *City of god* (H. Bettenson Trans.). New York, NY: Penguin Classics.

Austin, J., Stevenson, H., & Wei-Skillern, J. (2006). Social and commercial entrepreneurship: Same, different or both? *Entrepreneurship, Theory and Practice 31*(1), 1–22.

Aydemir, M., & Eğilmez, Ö. (2010). An important antecedent of ethical/unethical behaviour: Religiosity. *Eurasian Journal of Business and Economics 4*(6), 71–84.

Banaji, M., Bazerman, M., & Chugh, D. (2003, December). How (un)ethical are you. *Harvard Business Review* 56–64.

Banyan. (2010, October 21). SBY's feet of clay. *The Economist*.

Barnhart, R. K., & Steinmetz, S. (Eds.) (1988). *Chambers dictionary of etymology.* Edinburgh, UK: Chambers Harrap.

Bar-Tal, D. (2007). *Living with the conflict: Socio-psychological analysis of the Jewish society in Israel.* Jerusalem, Isreal: Carmel Ltd.

Bar-Tal, D. (2011). Introduction: Conflict and social psychology. In D. Bar-Tal, (Ed.) *Intergroup conflicts and their resolution* (pp. 1–39). New York, NY: Psychology Press, Taylor & Francis Group.

Batalla, E. C. (2000). *De-institutionalizing corruption in the Philippines*. Paper presented at the Institutionalizing Strategies to Combat Corruption: Lessons from East Asia Conference, Makati, Philippines.

Bauman, Z. (1996). *Socjologia.* Poznań: Zysk.

Becker, G. K. (2009). Integrity as moral ideal and business benchmark. *Journal of International Business Ethics 2*, 70–87.

Becker, T. (1998). Integrity in organisations: Beyond honesty and conscientiousness. *Academy of Management Review 23*(1), 154–161.

Berger P. L., & Luckmann, T. (1966). *The social construction of reality: A treatise in the sociology of knowledge.* New York, NY: Doubleday.

Biuro Analiz i Dokumentacji Kancelarii Senatu, "Opinie i ekspertyzy", OE-172, czerwiec 2011. Cited after: Dąbrowski R. (2011). Demaskacja jako narzędzie do walki z korupcją. Kwartalnik policyjny, 3(17), 38–43.

Bognanno, M., Budd, J., & Kleiner, M. (2007). Symposium introduction: Governing the global workplace. *Industrial Relations 46*(2), 215–221.

Bostan, S. (2009). *Sağlıkta dönüşüm programının hastane işletmeleri üzerindeki değişim etkisi: yönetici perspektifi*, Ph.D Thesis. Karadeniz Teknik Universitesi.

Bovaird, T. (2006). Developing new forms of partnership with the 'Market' in the procurement of public services. *Public Administration 84*(1), 81–102.

Brass, D. J., Butterfield, K. D., & Skaggs, B. C. (1998). Relationships and unethical behaviour: A social network perspective. *Academy of Management Review 23*(1), 14–31.

Brickson, S. (2000). The impact of identity orientation on individual and organizational outcomes in demographically diverse settings. *The Academy of Management Review 25*(1), 82–101.

Bright, D. S., Cameron, K. S., & Caza, A. (2006). Amplifying and buffering effects of virtuousness in downsized organizations. *Journal of Business Ethics 64*, 249–269.

Brynjarsson, G. (2009). *Origins of the current economic downturn in Iceland.* Retrieved March 1, 2010, from IceNews: http://www.icenews.is/index.php/2009/01/09/origins-of-the-current-economic-downturn-in-iceland/#more-5209

Byrne, D. (1997). An overview (and underview) of research and theory within the attraction paradigm. *Journal of Social and Personal Relationships 14*(3), 417–431.

Calhoun, C. (1995). Standing for something. *Journal of Philosophy 92*(5), 235–260.

Campos, E. J., Lien, D., & Pradhan, S. (1999). The impact of corruption on investment: Predictability matters. *World Development 27*(6), 1059–1067.

Cao, G. (2007). The pattern-matching role of systems thinking in improving research trustworthiness. *Systemic Practice and Action Research 20*, 441–453.

Carmeli, A., & Gittell, J. H. (2009). High-quality relations, psychological safety, and learning from failures in work organizations. *Journal of Organizational Behavior 30*(6), 709–729.

Carnegie Forum on Education and the Economy. (1986). *A nation prepared: Teachers for the 21st century.* Washington: Carnegie Forum on Education and the Economy.

Carroll, A. B. (1999). Corporate social responsibility: Evolution of definitional construct. *Business and Society 38*(3), 268–295.

Caza, A., Barker B. A., & Cameron K. S. (2004). Ethics and ethos: the buffering and amplifying effects of ethical behavior and virtuousness. *Journal of Business Ethics 52*, 169–179.

Celikay, F., & Gümüş, E. (2011). Sağlıkta dönüşümün ampirik analizi. *SBF Dergisi 66*(3), 55–92.

Chang, J. (1998). The guanxi factor: Accounting ethics in China. *Australian CPA 68*, 44–46.

Chang, M. C. M. (2001). *The autobiography of Morris C. M. Chang* (Vol. 1, pp. 1931–1964). Taipei: Commonwealth Publishing. (In Chinese).

Cheung, T. S., & King, A. Y. (2004). Righteousness and profitableness: The moral choices of contemporary Confucian entrepreneurs. *Journal of Business Ethics 54*, 245–260.

Chun, R. (2005). Ethical character and virtue of organizations: An empirical assessment and strategic implications. *Journal of Business Ethics 57*, 269–284.

Clair, J. A., Beatty, J. E., & Maclean, T. L. (2005). Out of sight but not out of mind: Managing invisible social identities in the workplace. *Academy of Management Review 30*(1), 78–95.

Cockburn, T. (2007). Emotionally sustainable business and communities of commitment. *Social Responsibility 3*(4), 61–73.

Cole, D. (2007). *As go the geysers, So goes government*. Retrieved May 12, 2009, from US News & World Report: http://www.usnews.com/usnews/news/articles/070318/26corrupt.htm

Coleman, P. T. (2000). Intractable conflict. In M. Deutsch and P. T. Coleman (Eds.), *The handbook of conflict resolution: Theory and practice* (pp. 1–39). San Francisco, NJ: Jossey-Bass Publishers.

Coleman, P. T. (2004). Paradigmatic framing of protracted, intractable conflict: Toward the development of a meta-framework—II. *Peace and Conflict: Journal of Peace Psychology 10*(3), 197–235.

Collier, M. J. (2009). Negotiating intercommunity and community group identity positions: Summary discourses from two Northern Ireland intercommunity groups. *Negotiation and Conflict Management Research 2*(3), 285–306.

Collins Concise Dictionary & Thesaurus. (2002). Glasgow, UK: Harper Collins.

Collins, J. (2001, January). Level 5 leadership: The triumph of humility and fierce resolve. *Harvard Business Review, 79*(1), 66–76.

Collins, J. (2009). *Empresas que sobresalen. Por qué unas sí pueden mejorar la rentabilidad y otras no*. Bogotá, Colombia: Editorial Norma S.A.

Collins, J. (2011*). Empresas que caen y por qué otras sobreviven*. Deusto Ediciones S.A.

Collins, J., & Porras J. I. (1996). Building your company's vision. *Harvard Business Review 74*(5), 65–77.

Co-operative Bank. (2011). Retrieved on January 3, 2012 from http://www.co-operativebankinggroup.co.uk/corp/pdf/CBG_Results_2011.pdf

Co-op Bank Webpage, retrieved 18/02/2012

Co-operatives UK. (2012). *The UK co-operative economy 2011—Britain's return to co-operation*. Manchester, UK: Co-operatives UK.

Coronel, S. S., & Balgos, C. C. A. (1998). Pork and other perks: Corruption and governance in the Philippines. Pasig, Philippines: Philippine Center for Investigative Journalism.

Cresswell, J.W. (1998). *Qualitative inquiry and research design: choosing among five traditions*. Thousand Oaks, CA: SAGE Publications.

Dąbrowski R. (2011). Demaskacja jako narzędzie do walki z korupcją. *Kwartalnik policyjny 3*(17), 38–43.

Davis, A., & Rothstein, H. R. (2006). The effects of the perceived behavioral integrity of managers on employee attitudes: A meta-analysis. *Journal of Business Ethics 67*, 407–419.

De Dios, E. S., & Ferrer, R. D. (2001). Corruption in the Philippines: Framework and context. *Public Policy 5*(1), 1–42.

Deegan, C. (2002). The legitimizing effect of social and environmental disclosures: A theoretical foundation. *Accounting, Auditing, and Accountability Journal 15*(3), 282–312.

Deloitte, Polski Instytut Dyrektorów, Rzeczpospolita. (2007). Współczesna rada nadzorcza 2007, raport z badań, s. 16. Available at: http://www.deloitte. com/assets/Dcom-Poland/Local%20Assets/Documents/Raporty,%20 badania,%20rankingi/pl_WspolczesnaRadaNadzorcza_2007.pdf.

Denny, C. (2004, March 26). Suharto, Marcos and Mobutu head corruption table with $50bn scams. *The Guardian.*

Deshpande, S. P., George, E., & Joseph, J. (2000). Ethical climates and managerial success in Russian organizations. *Journal of Business Ethics 23*, 211–217.

Desivilya, H. (2008). Conflict in work teams. In C. Wankel (Ed.), *Handbook of 21st century management* (Vol. 2, pp. 44–56). Los Angeles, CA: SAGE Publications.

Desivilya, H. (2011). The role of negotiation in building intra-team and inter-team cooperation. In M. Benoliel (Ed.), *Negotiation excellence: Successful deal making* (pp. 361–381). Tuck Link, Singapore: World Scientific Publishing (WSP).

Desivilya, H., & Palgi, M. (2011a). Introduction. The nature of partnerships and the processes of their formation: Juxtaposing conflict and cooperation. In H. Desivilya& M. Palgi (Eds.), *The paradox in partnership: The role of conflict in partnership building* (pp. 1–18). Bentham Science e-Books. http://www. benthamdirect.org/pages/content.php?9781608052110

Desivilya, H., & Palgi, M. (2011b). Engaging the paradox in partnership: Balancing conflict and cooperation. In H. Desivilya and M. Palgi (Eds.) *The paradox in partnership: The role of conflict in partnership building* (pp. 197–211). City Of Dubai, U.A.E.: Bentham Science e-Books.

Desivilya, H., & Rottman, A. (2008). *Negotiating reality about Jewish-Arab citizens relations in Israel: The case of conflict education in a northern college— A praxis report.* International Conference on "Understanding Conflict: Cross Cultural Perspectives,"University of Aarhus, Denmark, August 2008.

Desivilya-Syna, H., Raz, M., & Maoz, I. (2011). *Managing diversity in medical teams: The challenge of social responsibility in the context of protracted national conflict.* CR3 Conference: The Power of Responsibility. Hanken School of Economics. Helsinki, Finland. April, 2011.

Desivilya-Syna, H., & Yassour-Borochowitz, D. (2010). Israelis' moral judgments of government aggression and violations of human rights: Is democracy under siege of protracted conflict? *Beliefs and Values 2*(1), 38–48.

Dewey, J. (1938). *Logic: The theory of inquiry.* New York, NY: Holt, Rhinehart and Winston.

Diaz, E. (2012, January 30). Private sector-led initiative gets backing of over 1,000. *BusinessWorld.* Retrieved from http://www.bworldonline.com

Dik, B., & Duffy, R. (2009). Calling and vocation at work: Definitions and prospects for research and practice. *The Counselling Psychologist 37*, 424–450.

Diler, M. (2009). *The impacts of health sector reform on the efficiency and productivity of public and private hospitals in turkey*, Master Thesis. Bilkent Universitesi.

Dogra, A. (2010). Ethical issues in the workplace: How to handle. Retrieved from http://www.buzzle.com/articles/ethical-issues-in-the-workplace.html Accessed on August 11, 2010.

Domaszewicz, Z., & Miączyński, P. (2008). Obywatel kapuś, czyli samotność demaskatora. "Gazeta Wyborcza", 30.09.2008.

Drucker, P. F. (1990). *Managing the nonprofit organization: Principles and practices.* New York, NY: Collins Business.

Drucker, P. F. (1992). *Managing for the future.* New York, NY: Penguin Group.

Dudzinski, D. M. (2004). Integrity: Principled coherence, virtue, or both? *The Journal of Value Inquiry 38*, 299–313.

Dülfer, E., & Hamm, W. (Eds.) (1985) *Co-operatives: In the clash between member participation and bureaucratic tendencies.* (A complete guide to the creation, promotion and supervision of co-operative societies resulting from an international symposium in Marburg.) London, UK: Quiller Press.

Dunlop, P. D., & Lee, K. (2004). Workplace deviance, organizational citizenship behavior, and business unit performance: The bad apples do spoil the whole barrel. *Journal of Organizational Behavior 25*, 67–80.

Dutton, J. E., Dukerich, J. M., & Harquail, C. V. (1994). Organizational images and member identification. *Administrative Science Quarterly 39*, 239–264.

Dutton, J. E., & Ragins, B. R. (2009). *Exploring positive relationships at work: Building a theoretical and research foundation.* Mahwah, NJ: Lawrence Erlbaum.

Dyball, M. C., & Valcarcel, L. J. (1999). The "rational" and "traditional": The regulation of accounting in the Philippines. *Accounting, Auditing and Accountability Journal 12*(3), 303–328.

Eisenhardt, K. M. (1989). Building theories from case study research. *The Academy of Management Review 14*(4), 532–550.

Elangovan, A., Pinder, C., & McLean, M. (2010). Callings and organizational behaviour. *Journal of Vocational Behavior 76*, 428–440.

Ely, R., & Roberts, L. M. (2008). Shifting frames in team-diversity research: From difference to relationships. In A. P. Brief (Ed.), *Diversity at work* (pp. 175–201). New York, NY: Cambridge University Press.

Ely, R., & Thomas, D. (2001). Cultural diversity at work: The effects of diversity perspectives on work group processes and outcomes. *Administrative Science Quarterly 46*, 229–273.

Englund, P. (1999). The Swedish banking crisis: Roots and consequences. *Oxford Review of Economic Policy 15*(3), 80–97.

Englund P., & Vihriälä, V. (2003). *Financial crises in developed economies: The cases of Sweden and Finland.* Stockholm: Handelshogskolan.

European Commission (2010). *Opinion on Iceland's application for membership of the European Union, Analytical Report (153).* Brussels, Belgium: European Commission.

Farias, C., & Sands, M. (2012). A case study: Seeds of Africa. *ACRN Journal of Entrepreneurship Perspectives 1*(1), 149–160.

First Credit Union. (2011). *56th annual report* (p. iii). New Zealand: First Credit Union.

Fisman, R., & Miguel, E. (2007). Corruption, norms, and legal enforcement: Evidence from diplomatic parking tickets. *Journal of Political Economy 115*(6), 1020–1048.

Fisman, R., & Svensson, J. (2007). Are corruption and taxation really harmful to growth? Firm level evidence. *Journal of Development Economics 83*(1), 63–75.

Fogel, K. (2006). Oligarchic family control, social economic outcomes, and the quality of government. *Journal of International Business Studies 37*(5), 603–622.

Follett, P. M. (1965). *The new state, group organization the solution of popular government.* Glouster, MA: Peter Smith.

Fontrodona, J., Guillén, M., & Rodríguez, A. (2011). Virtue: A necessary component of ethical administration. *Educación y Educadores 14*(2), 413–423.

Fowers, B. J., & Tjeltveit, A. C. (2003). Virtue obscured and retrieved: Character, community, and practices in behavioral science. *American Behavioral Scientist 47*, 387–394.

Friedman, V., & Desivilya, H. (2010). Integrating social entrepreneurship and conflict engagement for regional development in divided societies. *Entrepreneurship & Regional Development 22*(6), 495–514.

Fritzsche, D. J. (2000). Ethical climates and the ethical dimension of decision-making. *Journal of Business Ethics 24*, 125–140.

Frost, P., Dutton, J., Maitlis, S., Lilius, J., Kanov, J., & Worline, M. (2005). *Seeing organizations differently: Three lenses on compassion.* Ann Arbor, MI: Michigan Ross School of Business.

Gaikwad, M. (2010). Ethics in the workplace. Retrieved from http://www.buzzle.com/articles/ethics-in-the-workplace.html on August 11, 2010.

Galang, R. M. N. (2012). Victim or victimizer: Firm responses to government corruption. *Journal of Management Studies 49*(2), 429–462.

Garriga, E., & Melè, D. (2004) Corporate social responsibility theories: Mapping the territory. *Journal of Business Ethics 53*, 51–71

Gellerman, S. W. (1986). Why 'good' managers make bad ethical choices. *Harvard Business Review on Corporate Ethics* © 2003 Harvard Business School Publishing Corporation, Boston.

Gentile M. C. (2010, March). Managing yourself: Keeping your colleagues honest. *Harvard Business Review 88*(3), 114–117.

Gera, W. (2011). The crux of the crisis: A governance analysis of Philippine underdevelopment. In H. Kimura, Suharko, A. B. Javier and A. Tan (Eds.), *Limits of good governance in developing countries* (pp. 39–70). Yogyakarta, Indonesia: Gadjah Mada University Press.

Getz, K. A., & Volkema, R. J. (2001). Culture, perceived corruption, and economics: A model of predictors and outcomes. *Business and Society 40*(1), 7–30.

Gintis, H., Bowles, S., Boyd, R., & Fehr, E. (2003). Explaining altruistic behaviour in humans. *Evolution and Human Behavior 24*, 153–172.

Glaser, B. G., & Strauss, A. L. (1967). *The discovery of grounded theory: Strategies for qualitative research.* New York, NY: Aldine.

Globerman, S., & Shapiro, D. (2003). Governance infrastructure and US foreign direct investment. *Journal of International Business Studies 34*(1), 19–39.

GlobeScan. (2011). High trust and global recognition levels make fairtrade an enabler of ethical consumer choice. Retrieved February 15, 2012 from http://www.globescan.com/news_archives/flo_business/

Goffman, E. (1959). *Presentation of self to others.* New York, NY: Doubleday Anchor books.

Goodlad, J. (1990) Teachers for our nation's schools. San Francisco: Jossey-Bass.

Görgün, H. (2009). *Sağlıkta dönüşüm programının* çanakkale *yerelleri* üzerine *etkisi*, Master Thesis. Çanakkale Üniversitesi.

Gosling, M., & Huang, H. J. (2010). The fit between integrity and integrative social contracts theory. *Journal of Business Ethics 90*, 407–417.

Grant, P. (2011). An Aristotelian approach to sustainable business. *Corporate Governance 11*, 4–14.

Gratton , L., & Truss, C. (2003). The three-dimensional people strategy: Putting human resources policies into action. *Academy of Management Executive 17*(3), 74–86.

Guardian newspaper. (2011, February 18).

Hall, D., & Chandler, D. (2005). Psychological success: When the career is a calling. *Journal of Organizational Behavior 26*(2), 155–176.

Haralz, J. H. (2007). *Hefðir og umbreyting. Landsbanki* Íslands *1969–1988 [Tradition and Transformations: Landsbanki Islands 1969–1988].* Tímarit um viðskipti og efnahagsmál.

Hargie, O., Dickson, D., & Nelson, S. (2003). Working together in a divided society: A study of intergroup communication in the Northern Ireland workplace. *Journal of Business and Technical Communication 17*, 285–318.

Harrison, D. A., & Klein, K. J. (2007). What's the difference? Diversity constructs as separation, variety, or disparity in organizations. *Academy of Management Review 32*(4), 1199–1228.

Harvey, M. G., & Griffith, D. A. (2002, July/August). Developing effective intercultural relationships: The important of communication strategies. *Thunderbird International Business Review 44*(4), 455–476. doi: 10.1002/tic.10029

Hensel, M. (Ed.) (1995). *W poszukiwaniu skutecznej Rady czyli o kontroli spółek akcyjnych w gospodarce rynkowej.* Kraków, Polska: Wyd. Profesjonalnej Szkoły Biznesu.

Higgins, B. (1957). Development problems in the Philippines: A comparison with Indonesia. *Far Eastern Survey 26*(11), 161–169.

Hill, H., & Shiraishi, T. (2007). Indonesia after the Asian crisis. *Asian Economic Policy Review 2*(1), 123–141.

Hinds, P. J., & Mortenson, M. (2005). Understanding conflict in geographically distributed teams: The moderating effects of shared identity, shared context, and spontaneous communication. *Organization Science 16*(3), 290–307.

Hofstede, G., Hofstede, G. J., & Minkov, M. (2010). Cultures and organizations: Software of the mind (3rd ed.). New York, NY: McGraw-Hill.

Hogan, J., Hogan, R., & Kaiser, R. B. (2010). Management derailment: Personality assessment and mitigation. In S. Zedeck (Ed.). *American Psychological Association handbook of industrial and organizational psychology* (Vol. 3, pp. 555–575). Washington, DC: American Psychological Association.

Holmes Group, (1986). *Tomorrow's teachers: A report of the Holmes Group*, East Lansing, MI: Author.

Honkapohja, S. (2009). The 1990's financial crises in Nordic countries. *Bank of Finland Research Discussion Papers, 5*, 7–26.

Hsu, S. (2007). A new business excellence model with business integrity from ancient Confucian thinking. *Total Quality Management 18*, 413–423.

http://www.acfe.com/uploadedFiles/ACFE_Website/Content/rttn/2012-report-to-nations.pdf;

http://unglobalcompact.org/accessed 12.11.2011.

http://www.adb.org/Documents/Policies/Anticorruption/anticorrupt300.asp?p=antipubs accessed 23.01.2012.

http://www.amazon.com/gp/product1613505108/ref accessed 20.01. 2012

http://www.benthamdirect.org/pages/content.php?9781608052110

http://www.oecd.org/dataoecd/26/31/45019804.pdf accessed 02.02.2012.

http://www.unglobalcompact.org/docs/issues_doc/AntiCorruption/Bali _Business_Declaration.pdf accessed 01.09.2012.

http://www.unglobalcompact.org/docs/issues_doc/AntiCorruption/UNGC _AntiCorruptionReporting.pdf accessed 28.12.2011.

http://www.unglobalcompact.org/docs/issues_doc/AntiCorruption/UNGC _AntiCorruptionReporting.pdf accessed 28.12.2011.

http://www.unodc.org/documents/commissions/WGGOVandFiN/Thematic _Programme_on_Corruption.pdf accessed Jan 20,2012.

Hutchcroft, P. D. (1998). *Booty capitalism: The politics of banking in the Philippines.* Ithaca, NY: Cornell University Press.

Iceland National Audit Office (2009). *Upplýsingar um fjárframlög fyrri* ára *til stjórnmálastarfsemi [Information regarding the financial support that political parties received during the last years].* Retrieved January 25, 2010 from Iceland National Audit Office: http://rikisendurskodun.is/index.php?mod ule=news&action=show&news_id=154&language=is

Jacobs, D. (2004). A pragmatist approach to integrity in business ethics. *Journal of Management Inquiry 13*(3), 215–223.

Jacobs, L., Guopei, G., & Herbig, P. (1995). Confucian roots in China: A force for today's business. *Management Decision 33*, 29–34.

Jahdi, K. S., & Cockburn, T. (2007, November 29). *Good with money: Ethics at the Co-op bank.* 9th International Forum on the Sciences, Techniques and Art Applied to Marketing Academy and Profession. Madrid, Spain: Complutense University.

Jahdi, K. S., & Cockburn, T. (2008) Learning to co-operate: A case study in ethical banking. *Interface* [online journal] *8*(5) http://bcis.pacificu.edu /journal/

Jannari, K. (2009). *Report on banking regulation and supervision in Iceland: Past, present and future.* Retrieved July 15, 2009, from the Prime Ministry: http:// eng.forsaetisraduneyti.is/media/frettir/KaarloJannari__2009.pdf

Jenkins, R. (2005). Globalization, corporate social responsibility and poverty. *International Affairs 81*(3), 525–540.

Jonsen, K., & Jehn, K. (2009). Using triangulation to validate themes in qualitative studies. *Qualitative Research in Organizations and Management: An International Journal 4*, 123–150.

Jonsson, A. (2009). *Why Iceland?* New York, NY: McGraw-Hill.

Jonung, L. (2008). Lessons from financial liberalisation in Scandinavia. *Comparative Economic Studies 50*, 564–598.

Jonung, L., Kiander J., & Vartia, P. (2008). *The great financial crisis in Finland and Sweden: The dynamics of boom, bust and recovery, 1985–2000.*

European Economy, Economic Papers 367. Brussels, Belgium: European Commission.

Kacprzak, I. (2011). Ujawnili aferę, stracili pracę. „Rzeczpospilita", 14.04.2011. Retrieved from http://www.rp.pl/artykul/642747.html

Kalev, A., Dobbin, F., & Kelly, E. (2006). Best practices or best guesses? Assessing the efficacy of corporate affirmative action and diversity policies. *American Sociological Review 71*(4), 589–617.

Kang, D. C. (2002). *Crony capitalism: Corruption and development in South Korea and the Philippines.* Cambridge, UK: Cambridge University Press.

Kaplan, S. E., Rittenberg, L. E., & Schultz, J. J. Jr. (2006). Communicating wrongdoing. *Internal Auditor* Dec. *66*(6), 89–91. ABI/INFORM Global.

Kaplan, S. E., & Schultz, J. J. (2007). Intentions to report questionable acts: An examination of the influence of anonymous reporting channel, internal audit quality, and setting. *Journal of Business Ethics 71*(2), 109–124. Cited after: Ahmad, S. A., Smith, M., & Ismail, Z. (2010). Internal whistleblowing intentions in Malaysia: Factors that influence internal auditors' decision-making process. Retrieved on from http://www.internationalconference.com.my/proceeding/icber2010_proceeding/PAPER_104_InternalWhistleblowing.pdf

Kaptein, M. (2010). The ethics of organizations: A longitudinal study of the U.S. working population. *Journal of Business Ethics 92*, 601–618.

Keenan, J.P. (2002). Whistleblowing: A study of managerial differences. *Employee Responsibilities and Rights Journal 14*, 17–32.

Kell, G. (2006) *Business Against Corruption, Case Studies and Examples,* UN Global Contact Office,

Khera, I. P. (2010). Ethics perception of the U.S. and its large developing-country trading partners, *Global Management Journal 2*(1), 32–33.

King, G. III. (1997). The effects of interpersonal closeness and issue seriousness on blowing the whistle. *Journal of Business Communication 34*, 419–436.

Klein, P. (2008). Opportunity discovery, entrepreneurial action, and economic organization. *Strategic Entrepreneurship Journal 2*(3), 175–190.

Klitgaard, R. (2011). Fighting corruption. *CESifo DICE Report 9*(2), 31–35.

Knack, S. (1996). Institutions and the convergence hypothesis: The cross-national evidence. *Public Choice 87*(3), 207–228.

Knack, S., & Keefer, P. (1995). Institutions and economic performance: Cross-country tests using alternative institutional measures. *Economics and Politics 7*, 207–227.

Koehn, D. (1995). A role for virtue ethics in the analysis of business practice. *Business Ethics Quarterly 5*(3), 533–539.

Koehn, D. (2005). Integrity as a business asset. *Journal of Business Ethics 58*, 125–136.

Kogut, B., & Zander, U. (1995). What firms do? Coordination, identity, and learning. *Organizational Science 6*, 502–518.

Kolb, D., & McGinn, K. (2009). Beyond gender and negotiation to gendered negotiations. *Negotiation and Conflict Management Research 2*(1), 1–16.

Kulik, B. W. (2005). Agency theory, reasoning and culture at Enron: In search of a solution. *Journal of Business Ethics 59*, 347–360.

Kuppermintz, H., & Salomon, G. (2005). Lessons to be learned from research on peace education in the context of intractable conflict. *Theory into practice 44*(4), 293–302.

Kurzynski, M. (2009). Peter Drucker: Modern day Aristotle for the business community. *Journal of Management History 15*, 357–374.

Lacayo, R.,& Ripley, A. (2002, December 22). Persons of the year 2002: Cynthia Cooper, Coleen Rowley and Sherron Watkins. *Time magazine.*.

Lange, D. (2008). A multidimensional conceptualization of organizational corruption control. *Academy of Management Review 33*(3), 710–729.

Lau, D. C., & Murnighan, J. K. (1998). Demographic diversity and faultlines: The compositional dynamics of organizational groups. *Academy of Management Review 23*(3), 325–340.

Lawrence, F. (2008). *Eat your heart out: Why the food business is bad for the planet and your health*. London, UK: Penguin Books.

Lee, K. H. (1996). Moral consideration and strategic management moves: The Chinese case. *Management Decision 34*, 65–70.

Lennick, D., & Kiel, F. (2005). *Moral intelligence: Enhancing business performance & leadership success*. Upper Saddle River, NJ: Wharton School Publishing. Cited after: Stachowicz-Stanusch, A. (2010). Corruption immunity based on positive organizational scholarship towards theoretical framework. In: A. Stachowicz-Stanusch (Ed.), *Organizational immunity to corruption building theoretical and research foundations* (p. 44). Scottsdale, AZ: Information Age Publishing.

Lewis, C. S. (1944). *The abolition of man*. New York, NY: Harper One.

Lindgreen, A., Córdoba, J., Maon, F., & Mendoza, J. (2010). Corporate social responsibility in Colombia: Making sense of social strategies. *Journal of Business Ethics 91*, 229–242.

Lindgreen, A., Swaen, V., & Campbell, T. (2009). Corporate social responsibility practices in developing and ransitional countries: Botswana and Malawi. *Journal of Business Ethics 90*, 429–440.

Ludema, J. D., Cooperrider, D. L., & Barrett, F. J. (2001). Appreciative inquiry: The power of the unconditional positive question. In P. Reason, & H. Bradbury (Eds.), *Handbook of action research: Participative inquiry and practice* (pp. 189–199). Thousand Oaks, CA: SAGE Publications.

MacIntyre, A. (1984). *After virtue*. Notre Dame, IN: University of Notre Dame Press.

MacIntyre, A. (1993). Persona corriente y filosofía moral: reglas, virtudes y bienes. *Convivium 4*, 63–80.

MacIntyre, A. (2001). Investment, property rights, and corruption in Indonesia. In J. E. Campos (Ed.), *Corruption: The boom and bust of East Asia* (pp. 25–44). Quezon City, Philippines: Ateneo de Manila University Press.

Martens, L. T., & Kelleher, A. (2004). A global perspective on whistleblowing. *International Business Ethics Review 7*(2), 3–7.

Martín López, E. (1999). La responsabilidad de los ciudadanos en la construcción de la sociedad civil. En A. Rafael, G. Nicolás, & H. Monserrat, *Sociedad Civil, la democracia y su destino* (pp. 43–59). Pamplona, Spain: EUNSA.

Mauro, P. (1995). Corruption and growth. *The Quarterly Journal of Economics August 1995, 110*(3), 681–712.

Melè, D. (2009). *Business ethics in action: Seeking human excellence in organizations*. Palgrave Macmillan.

Merriam-Webster collegiate dictionary (11th ed.). (2007). Springfield, MA: Merriam-Webster.

Mesa, W. (2010). The composition of intellectual capital in non-profit orchestras. *Journal of Intellectual Capital 11*, 208–226.

Miceli, M. P., & Near, J. P. (1994). Relationships among value congruence, perceived victimization, and retaliation against whistle-blowers: The case of internal auditors. *Journal of Management 20*, 773–794.

Miceli, M. P., Rehg, M. T., Near, J. P., & Ryan, K. (1999). Can law protect whistle-blowers? Results of the naturally occurring field experiment. *Work and Occupations 26*, 129–151.

Miller B.A.(2011) http://www.articlesbase.com/leadership-articles/leadership-how-important-is-integrity-in-todays-business-world-is-integrity-an-afterthought-1063750.html, accessed 27.11.2011.

Mohammed, S., & Angell, L. C. (2004). Surface- and deep-level diversity in workgroups: Examining the moderating effects of team orientation and team process on relationship conflict. *Journal of Organizational Behavior 25*, 1015–1039.

Mor Barak, M. (2010). *Managing diversity: Toward a globally inclusive workplace* (2nd ed.). Thousand Oaks, CA: Sage Publications.

Mostovicz, E. I., Kakabadse, N. K., & Kakabadse, A. (2011). Corporate governance: Quo vadis? *Corporate Governance 11*(5), 613–626.

Myllila, S., & Takala, T. (2011). Leaking legitimacies: The Finnish forest sector's entanglement in the land conflicts of Atlantic coastal Brazil. *Social Responsibility 7*(1), 42–60.

Near, J. P., & Miceli, M. P. (1985). Organizational dissidence: The case of whistle-blowing. *Journal of Business Ethics 4*, 1–16.

Near, J.P., & Miceli, M. P. (2008). Wrongdoing, whistle-blowing, and retaliation in the U.S. government: What have researchers learned from the Merit Systems Protection Board (MSPB) survey results? *Review of Public Personnel Administration 28*(3), 263–281.

Near, J.P., Rehg, M.T., Scotter, J.R., Miceli, M.P. (2004). Does type of wrongdoing affect the whistleblowing process? *Business Ethics Quarterly, 14*(2), 219–242.

New York, http://www.unglobalcompact.org/docs/issues_doc/7.7/BACbook FINAL.pdf, accessed 22.01.2012.

Newman, J. L., & Fuqua, D. R. (2006). Practice and research, what does it profit an organization if it gains the whole world and loses its own soul? *Consulting Psychology Journal 58*(1), 13–22.

Nielsen, R. P. (2010). High-leverage finance capitalism, the economic crisis, structurally related ethics issues, and potential reforms. *Business Ethics Quarterly 20*(2), 299–330. Cited after: Stachowicz-Stanusch and Wankel (2011).

Niven, R. (2012). How local groups can benefit from community buying. *The Guardian online*, (Cockburn, 2007) Retrieved on March 30, 2012 at http://www.guardian.co.uk/voluntary-sector-network/community-action-blog/2012/mar/30/local-groups-benefit-community-buying

O'Connell, D., Hickerson, K., & Pillutla, A. (2011). Organizational visioning: An integrative review. *Group & Organizational Management 36*, 103–125.

Orlikowski, W. (2002). Knowing in practice: Enacting a collective capability in distributed organizing. *Organization Science 13*, 249–273.

O'Rourke, D., &Brown, G. D. (2003). Experiments in transforming the global workplace: Incentives for and impediments to improving workplace conditions in China. *International Journal of Occupational and Environmental Health 9*(4), 378–385.

Paine, L. S. (1994). Managing for organizational integrity. *Harvard Business Review* (March–April) 106–117.

Palanski, M., & Yammarino, F. (2007). Integrity and leadership: Clearing the conceptual confusion. *European Management Journal 25*(93), 171–184.

Pålshaugen, Ø. (2001). The use of words: Improving enterprises by improving their conversations. In P. Reason, & H. Bradbury, (Eds.), *Handbook of action research: Participative inquiry and practice* (pp. 209–218). Thousand Oaks, CA: SAGE Publications.

Parameshwar, S. (2005). Spiritual leadership through ego-transcendence: Exceptional responses to challenging circumstances. *The Leadership Quarterly 16*, 689–722.

Parry, K., & Proctor-Thomson, S. (2002). Perceived integrity of transformational leaders in organisational settings. *Journal of Business Ethics 35*, 75–96.

Pedersen, M. H. (*Jan–Feb*, 2006). Business integrity in China. *The China Business Review*, 32–36.

Peterson, C., & Seligman, M. (2004). *Character strengths and virtues: A handbook and classification*. New York, NY: Oxford/American Psychological Association.

Peterson, D. K. (2002). Deviant workplace behavior and the organization's ethical climate. *Journal of Business and Psychology 17*(1), 47–61.

Petrick, J. A. (2008a). Using the business integrity capacity model to advance business ethics education. In D. Swanson & D. Fisher (Eds), *Advancing business ethics education* (pp.103–124). Charlotte, NC: Information Age Publishing.

Petrick, J. A. (2008b). Integrity. In R. Kolb (Ed), *Encyclopedia of business ethics and society* (pp. 1141–1144). Thousand Oaks, CA: SAGE.

Petrick, J. A., & Quinn, J. F. (1997). *Management ethics: Integrity at work*. Newbury Park, CA: SAGE.

Pimentel, M. K. (2005). Procurement Watch Inc: The role of civil society in public procurement reforms in the Philippines. Retrieved February 21, 2012, from http://www.ippa.ws/IPPC1/BOOK/Chapter_3.pdf

Pirson, M. A., & Lawrence, P. R. (2010). Humanism in business—Towards a paradigm shift? *Journal of Business Ethics 93*, 553–565.

Pittinsky, T. L., & Montoya, M. R. (2009). Is valuing equality enough? Equality values, allophilia, and social policy support for multiracial individuals. *Journal of Social Issues 65*, 151–163.

Polanyi, M. (1974). *Personal knowledge: Towards a post-critical philosophy*. Chicago, IL: The University of Chicago.

Polo, L. (1997). Ética: *hacia una versión moderna de los temas clásicos*. Madrid, Spain: Unión Editorial.

Porter, M. E. (1985). *Competitive advantage: Creating and sustaining superior performance*. New York, NY: The Free Press.

PwC. (2011). Cybercrime: Protecting against the growing threat: Global Economic Crime Survey. November 2011. Retrieved from http://www.pwc.com/en_GX/gx/economic-crime-survey/assets/GECS_GLOBAL_REPORT.pdf

Quah, J. S. T. (2011). *Curbing corruption in Asian countries: An impossible dream?* (Vol. 20). Singapore: Emerald Group Publishing.

Ramarajan, L., & Thomas, D. (2010). *A positive approach to studying diversity in organizations. Working Paper, 11-024*. Harvard Business School.

Reason, P., & Bradbury, H. (2001). Introduction: Inquiry and participation in search of a world worthy of human aspiration. In P. Reason, &

H. Bradbury, (Eds.), *Handbook of action research: Participative inquiry and practice.* Thousand Oaks, CA: SAGE Publications.

Rego, A., Ribeiro, N., & Cunha, M. P. (2010). Perceptions of organizational virtuousness and happiness as predictors of organizational citizenship behaviors. *Journal of Business Ethics 93*, 215–235.

Richmond, V. P., Gorham, J., & McCroskey, J. C. (1987). *The relationship between immediacy behaviors and cognitive learning*, in M. McLaughlin (Ed.), Communication Yearbook 10 (pp. 574–590). Beverly Hills, CA: SAGE.

Robbins, S. P. (2004). *Zachowania w organizacji.* Warszawa, Polska: PWE.

Rogowski, W. (2007a). Whistleblowing: Bohaterstwo, zdrada czy interes? *Przegląd Corporate Governance 1*(9), 23–41.

Rogowski, W. (2007b). Whistleblowing, czyli czego się nie robi dla pozyskania zaufania inwestorów. *Przegląd Corporate Governance 2*(10), 1–18.

Rossouw, D. (2008). Practicing applied ethics with philosophical integrity: the case of business ethics. *Business Ethics: A European Review 17*, 161–172.

Ruch, W., Proyer, R., Harzer, C., Park, N., Peterson, C., Seligman, M. (2010). Values in action inventory of strengths (VIA-IS). *Journal of Individual Differences 31*, 138–149.

Rudder, C. F. (1999). Ethics in education: Are professional policies ethical? *Educational Theory 41*(1), 1991, 75–88.

Schein, E. H. (1992). *Organizational culture and leadership* (2nd ed.). San Francisco, CA: Jossey-Bass.

Schein, E. H. (2001). Clinical inquiry/research. In P. Reason, & H. Bradbury (Eds.), *Handbook of action research: Participative inquiry and practice* (pp. 228–237). Thousand Oaks, CA: SAGE Publications.

Schmidheiny, S. (2006, Spring). A view of corporate citizenship in Latin America. *The Journal of Corporate Citizenship* (21).

Schmincke, D. (2010). How selfishness eats profits. Retrieved from http://www.myarticlearchive.com/articles/8/209.htm

Schön, D. A. (1983). *The reflective practitioner.* New York, NY: Basic Books.

Schön, D. A. (1987). *Educating the reflective practitioner.* San Francisco, NJ: Jossey-Bass.

Schwarzkopf, D., & Sigurjonsson, T. O. (2011). *The structure of community networks defending the concept of "financial stability".* Working paper, Bentley University and Reykjavik University.

Selznick, P. (1957). *Leadership in administration.* Berkeley, CA: University of California Press.

Senge, P., & Scharmer, O. (2001). Community action research: Learning as a community of practitioners, consultants and researchers. In P. Reason, & H. Bradbury (Eds.), *Handbook of action research: Participative inquiry and practice* (pp. 238–249). Thousand Oaks, CA: SAGE Publications.

Shleifer, A., & Vishny, R. W. (1993). Corruption. *The Quarterly Journal of Economics 108*(3), 599–617.

Sibert, A. (2009). *Could Greenland be the new Iceland?* Retrieved January 22, 2010, from VOXEU: http://www.voxeu.org/index.php?q=node/3857

Sigurjonsson, T. O. (2010). Privatization and deregulation: A chronology of events. In R. Aliber (Ed.), *Documents on the asset price bubble in Iceland.* UK: Palgrave.

Sigurjonsson, T. O., & Mixa, M. W. (2011). Learning from the "worst behaved": Iceland's financial crisis and the Nordic comparison. *Thunderbird International Business Review 53*(2), 209–224.

Simons, T. (2002). Behavioral integrity: The perceived alignment between managers' words and deeds as a research focus. *Organization Science 13*, 18–37.

Snider, J., Hill, R., & Martin, D. (2003). Corporate social responsibility in the 21st century: A view from the world's most successful firms. *Journal of Business Ethics 48*(2), 175–187.

Sosik, J., Gentry, W., & Chun, J. (2011). The value of virtue in the upper echelons: A multisource examination of executive character strengths and performance. *The Leadership Quarterly 23*(3), 367–382. doi:10.1016/j .leaqua.2011.08.010

Special Investigation Commission. (2010). *The Report of the Special Investigation Commission.* Retrieved June 12, 2010 from the Special Investigation Commissions: http://www.rannsoknarnefnd.is/category.aspx?catID=27

Stachowicz-Stanuch, A. (Ed.) (2009). *Organizational immunity to corruption: Building theoretical and research foundations.* Scottsdale, AZ: Information Age Publishing.

Stachowicz-Stanusch, A. (2011) *Organizational immunity to corruption: Building theoretical and research foundations.* Scottsdale, AZ: Information Age Publishing.

Stachowicz-Stanusch, A., & Wankel, C. (2011). Anti-corruption practices and implementation mechanisms of the Fortune Global 500 as an answer for an ethical values crisis—research results. *Organization and Management 5*(148), 139–155.

Stead, W. E., Worrell, D. L., & Stead, J. G. (1990). An integrative model for understanding and managing ethical behaviour in business organizations. *Journal of Business Ethics 9*, 233–242.

Stephan, C., Hertz-Lazarowitz, R., Zelniker, T., & Stephan, W. G. (2004). Introduction to improving Arab-Jewish relations in Israel: Theory and practice in coexistence educational programs. *Journal of Social Issues 60*(2), 237–252.

Suma Wholefoods. 2012. Official website of Suma Wholefoods. Accessed on August 29, 2012. http://www.suma.coop/about/cooperation/ and http://www.suma.coop/about/

Syna-Desivilya, H. (2004). Promoting coexistence by means of conflict education: The MACBE model. *Journal of Social Issues 60*(2), 339–357.

Syna-Desivilya, H., & Abu-Bakkar, K. (2005). *Rescuing dialogue between Jews and Arabs: What students can tell us about living in protracted conflict environment?* The 18th Annual Conference of the International Association for Conflict Management, Seville, Spain, June 2005.

Tajfel, H., & Turner, J. C. (1986). The social identity theory of intergroup behavior. In S. Worchel and W. G. Austin (Eds.), *The psychology of intergroup relations* (pp. 7–24). Chicago, IL: Nelson-Hall.

Talwar, B. (2009). Comparative study of core values of excellence models *vis-à-vis* human values. *Measuring Business Excellence 13*, 34–46.

Tatar, M. (2007). *Türkiye' de sağlık reformları ve hasta açısından yeni sistemin getirdikleri* (pp. 154–167). Tüketici Yazıları, Hacettepe Universitesi.

Thompson, L. J. (2008). Gender equity and corporate social responsibility in a post-feminist era. *Business Ethics: A European Review 17*(1), 87–106.

TIRI. (2012). The integrity challenge. Retrieved February 21, 2012, from http://www.tiri.org/index.php?option=com_contentandtask=viewand id=490and Itemid=

Tobias, L. L. (2004). The thriving person and the thriving organization: Parallels and linkages. *Consulting Psychology Journal: Practice and Research 56*, 3–9.

Transparency International. (2009a). Recommended draft principles for whistleblowing legislation. Retrieved from Right2INFO.org website: http://right2info.org/resources/publications/publications/09_12_02%20 ti-draft%20principles%20WB%20legislation.pdf

Transparency International (2009b). *Corruption Perception Index.* Retrieved May 11, 2009, from Transparency International: http://www.transparency.org /policy_research/surveys_indices/cpi

Treviño, L. K. (1986). Ethical decision making in organizations: A person-situation interactionist model. *Academy of Management Review 11*, 601–617.

Treviño, L. K. (1990). A cultural perspective on changing and developing organizational ethics. In R. Woodman, & W. Passmore (Eds.), *Research in organizational change and development.* Greenwich, CT: JAI Press.

Treviño, L. K., & Brown, M. E. (2004). Managing to be ethical: Debunking five business ethics myths. *Academy of Management Executive 18*(2), 69–81.

Treviño, L. K., Butterfield, K. D., & McCabe, D. I. (1998). The ethical context in organizations: Influences on employee attitudes and behaviours. *Business Ethics Quarterly 8*, 447–476.

Treviño, L. K., & Youngblood, S. (1990). Bad apples in bad barrels: A causal analysis of ethical decision-making behaviour. *Journal of Applied Psychology 75*, 378–338.

Trevinyo-Rodgriquez, R. N. (2007). Integrity: A systems theory classification. *Journal of Management History 13*, 74–93.

Triana, M., Garcia, M. F., & Colella, A. (2010). Managing diversity: How organizational efforts to support diversity moderate the effects of perceived racial discrimination on affective commitment. *Personnel Psychology 63*, 817–843.

TSMC. (2012). http://www.tsmc.com (Taiwan Semiconductor Manufacturing Company Limited)

Turnipseed, D. L. (1988). An integrated, interactive model of organizational climate, culture, and effectiveness. *Leadership & Organizational Development Journal 9*, 17–21.

United Nations (2006) http://unglobalcompact.org/ accessed 12.11.2011.

Vaiman, V., Davidsson, P. A., & Sigurjonsson, T. O. (2009). Revising a concept of corruption as a result of the global economic crisis—the case of Iceland. In A. Stachowicz-Stanusch (Ed.), *Organizational immunity to corruption— Building theoretical and research foundations* (pp. 363–372). Katowice, Poland :The Katowice Branch of the Polish Academy of Sciences.

Vaiman, V., & Sigurjonsson, T. O. (2012). Re-thinking ethics education in business schools in the post-financial crisis epoch: An Icelandic perspective. In A. Stachowicz-Stanusch, & C. Wankel (Eds.), *Handbook of research on teaching ethics in business and management education.* Hershey, PA: IGI-Global.

Vaiman, V., Sigurjonsson, T. O., & Davidsson, P. A. (2011). Weak business culture as antecedents of economic crisis: The case of Iceland. *Journal of Business Ethics 98*(2), 67–83.

van Knippenberg, D., Dawson, J. F., West, M. A., & Homan, A. C. (2011). Diversity, faultlines, shared objectives, and top management team performance. *Human Relations 64*(3), 307–336.

Van Laar, C., Sidanius, J., & Levin, S. (2008). Ethnic-related curricula and intergroup attitudes in college: Movement toward and away from the in-group. *Journal of Applied Social Psychology 38*(6), 1601–1638.

Vangen, S., & Huxham, C. (2003). Enacting leadership for collaborative advantage: Dilemmas of ideology and pragmatism in the activities of partnership. *British Journal of Management 14*, 61–76.

Verbos, A. K., Gerard, J. A., Forshey, P. R., Harding C. S., & Miller, J. S. (2007). The positive ethical organization: Enacting a living code of ethics and ethical organizational identity. *Journal of Business Ethics 76*, 17–33.

Victor, B., & Cullen, J. B. (1988). The organizational bases of ethical work climates. *Administrative Sciences Quarterly 33*, 101–125.

Vidskiptabladid. (2011). *Three hundred individuals that enjoy the rights of a suspect under criminal procedural law*. Retrieved February 27, 2012 from Vidskiptabladid: http://www.vb.is/frett/68245/

Visir. (2012). *Baldur's violation of law are major*. Retrieved February 27, 2012 from Visir: http://www.visir.is/brot-baldurs-eru-storfelld/article/2011110409255

Votaw, D. (1972). Genius became rare: A comment on the doctrine of social responsibility Pt 1. *California Management Review 15*(2), 25–31.

Vries, K., Manfred, F.R., & Miller, D. (1987). Interpreting organizational texts. *The Journal of Management Studies 24*, 233–247.

Wade, R. (2009a). Iceland as Icarus. *Challenge 52*(3).

Wade, R. (2009b). *A Speech in Reykjavik on January 13, 2009*. Retrieved September 30, 2009 from Economic Disaster Area: http://economicdisaster.wordpress.com/2009/01/13/robert-wades-speech-in-reykjavik/

Wagner, B. B., & Jacobs, L. G. (2008). Retooling law enforcement to investigate and prosecute entrenched corruption: Key criminal procedure reforms for Indonesia and other nations. *University of Pennsylvania Journal of International Law 30*, 183–265.

Waldmann, E. (2000). Teaching ethics in accounting: A discussion of cross-cultural factors with a focus on Confucian and Western philosophy. *Accounting Education 9*, 23–35.

Wankel, C. (2010). Orienting business students to navigate the shoals of corruption in practice. In A. Stachowicz-Stanusch (Ed.), *Organizational immunity to corruption building theoretical and research foundations* (pp. 53–68). Scottsdale, AZ: Information Age Publishing.

Wankel, C., & Stachowicz-Stanusch, A. (2011a). *Handbook of research on teaching ethics in business and management education*. Information Science Reference.

Wankel, C., & Stachowicz-Stanusch, A. (Eds.). (2011b). *Management education for integrity: Ethically educating tomorrow's business leaders*. Bingley, UK: Emerald Group Publishing Limited.

Wankel, C., & Stachowicz-Stanusch, A. (2012). *Effectively integrating ethical dimensions into business education*. Scottsdale, AZ: Information Age Publishing.

Watts, S. (2010). Identification and the cultural organization: How the concept of identification can impact the constituencies who work within cultural organizations. *The Journal of Arts Management, Law, and Society 40*, 200–216.

Wei, S. J. (2000). How taxing is corruption on international investors? *The Review of Economics and Statistics 82*(1), 1–11.

Wei, X. (1996). The characteristics of Confucian ethics. In B. Carr (Ed.), *Morals and society in Asian philosophy* (pp. 145–155). London, UK: Curzon Press.

Weick, K. E. (1995). *Sensemaking in organizations.* Thousand Oaks, CA: SAGE Publications.

White, D. W., & Lean, E. (2008). The impact of perceived leader integrity on subordinates in a work team environment. *Journal of Business Ethics 81*, 765–778.

Wojciechowska-Nowak, A. (2008). *Jak zdemaskować szwindel? Czyli krótki przewodnik po whistle-blowingu.* Warszawa, Polska: Fundacja im. Stefana Batorego.

Wojciechowska-Nowak, A. (2011). *Ochrona prawna sygnalistów w doświadczeniu sędziów sądów pracy. Raport z badań.* Warszawa, Polska: Fundacja im. Stefana Batorego. Retrieved from http://www.batory.org.pl/doc/Sygnalisci_raport_20110415.pdf

Wood, D. J., Logsdon, J. M., Lewellyn, P. G., & Davenport, K. (2006) *Global business citizenship: A transformative framework for ethics and sustainable capitalism.* Armonk, NY: M. E. Sharpe Co.

Woodward, K., & Miller, S. (1994). What is virtue? *Newsweek 123*(24), 38–39.

Wright, P., Szeto, W. F., & Cheng, L. T. W. (2002). Guanxi and professional conduct in China: A management development perspective. *The International Journal of Human Resource Management 13*, 156–182.

www.tnv.com.pl accessed on 28.02.2011.

www.tnv.com.pl/gpmi accessed on 13.03.2011.

Yin, R. K. (1994). *Case study research: design and methods* (2nd ed.). Thousand Oaks: SAGE Publications.

Yin, R. K. (2003). *Case study research: Design and methods.* Thousand Oaks, CA: SAGE.

Yin, R. K. (2009). *Case study research: Design and methods* (4th ed.). Thousand Oaks, CA: SAGE Publications, Inc.

Yu, H. C., & Miller, P. (2003). The generation gap and cultural influence: A Taiwan empirical investigation. *Cross Cultural Management 10*, 23–41.

Zahra, S., Gedajlovic, E., Neubaum, D., & Shulman, J. (2009). A typology of social entrepreneurs: Motives, search processes and ethical challenges. *Journal of Business Venturing 24*(5), 519–532.

Zauderer, D. G. (1992). Integrity: An essential executive quality. *Business Forum Fall*, 12–16.

Index

OTHER TITLES IN OUR PRINCIPLES OF RESPONSIBLE MANAGEMENT (PRME) COLLECTION

Oliver Laasch, Monterrey Institute of Technology, Collection Editor

- *Academic Ethos Management: Building the Foundation for Integrity in Management Education* by Agata Stachowicz-Stanusch, due out December 2012
- *Responsible Management: Understanding Human Nature, Ethics, and Sustainability* by Kemi Ogunyemi, due out February 2013
- *Marketing to the Low-Income Consumer* by Paulo Cesar Motta, due out June 2013
- *Educating for Values-Driven Leadership: Giving Voice to Values* by Mary Gentile, due out August 2013
- *Managing Corporate Responsibility in Emerging Markets: Issues, Cases, and Solutions* by Radon Jenik and Achuthan Mahima, due out September 2013

Announcing the Business Expert Press Digital Library

Concise E-books Business Students Need for Classroom and Research

This book can also be purchased in an e-book collection from your library as
- a one-time purchase,
- that is owned forever,
- allows for simultaneous readers,
- has no restrictions on printing, and
- can be downloaded as PDFs from within the library community.

Our digital library collections are a great solution to beat the rising cost of textbooks. e-books can be loaded into their course management systems or onto student's e-book readers.

The **Business Expert Press** digital libraries are very affordable, with no obligation to buy in future years. For more information, please visit **www.businessexpertpress.com/librarians**. To set up a trial in the United States, please contact **Adam Chesler** at *adam.chesler@businessexpertpress .com* for all other regions, contact **Nicole Lee** at *nicole.lee@igroupnet.com*.

www.ingramcontent.com/pod-product-compliance
Lightning Source LLC
Chambersburg PA
CBHW060327200326
41519CB00011BA/1858